W9-AYJ-846

The Erotics of Instruction

THE EROTICS
OF INSTRUCTION

Regina Barreca and

Deborah Denenholz Morse, *editors*

University Press of New England : Hanover and London

University Press of New England, Hanover, NH 03755
© 1997 by University Press of New England
All rights reserved
Printed in the United States of America   5   4   3   2   1
CIP data appear at the end of the book

Contents

Preface   vii

Acknowledgments   xix

REGINA BARRECA
Contraband Appetites: Wit, Rage, and Romance in the Classroom   1

JOHN GLAVIN
The Intimacies of Instruction   12

REBECCA A. POPE
Hayley, Roz, and Me   28

VANESSA D. DICKERSON
The Teachings of Small Smothered Lives: The Erotics of
Instruction in Henry James's *The Turn of the Screw*   52

MARY ANN CAWS
Instructive Energies   71

JAMES R. KINCAID
Eroticism Is a Two-Way Street, and I'm Working Both Sides   81

GERHARD JOSEPH
Bartleby and the Professor   94

DEBORAH DENENHOLZ MORSE
Educating Louis: Teaching the Victorian Father in Trollope's
He Knew He Was Right   98

ROBERT POLHEMUS
A Jamesian Sentimental Education: *What Maisie Knew:* French
Literature, Sacred History   116

ABBY H. P. WERLOCK
"With a Man There Is a Difference": The Rejection of Female
Mentoring in Hemingway's *For Whom the Bell Tolls*   127

DRANDA TRIMBLE
Making Love to the Gods: Four Women and Their Affairs
with Education   147

MONTANA KATZ
Truth or Consequences: Mamet's *Oleanna* in the Real World   156

MYRA GOLDBERG
But I Thought He Liked My Paper   166

List of Contributors   177

Preface

The goal of this volume is to provide a window to the world of teacher/student relationships, and to raise issues concerning eroticism and the very process and practice of instruction. Each of the essays in this collection confronts the most provocative—and often least discussed—aspects of the seductions of the classroom. Whether it is perceived as an instrument of dominance or a mode of revelation, the educational process involves an emotionally suffused link between human beings. Its intimacies form a tangled web of intellectual aspiration and erotic desire. In our culture, the idea of education is inextricably bound up with constructions of power, governance, and an erotically charged allegiance or submission to the father- (or, with increasingly frequency, mother-) teacher.

In response to a legitimate and necessary awakening to the potentially damaging gender dynamics of the places in which we work and study, we have perhaps denied a literary tradition that explores the fertile (so to speak) possibilities of the mentor-pupil relation. Erotic attraction in the classroom *can* lead to sexual harassment, but it does not *necessarily* or *inevitably* lead to it. The desire for knowledge, although it often includes erotic speculation about the mentor or student, is a much more complicated and enveloping impulse, an admirable and necessary longing. The passion for learning encompasses a range of feelings and experiences, central to which, quite often, is an extraordinary relationship between the possessor of seemingly arcane knowledge and the one who yearns to possess this seeming wisdom. And the intricacies of these relations are as complex and various as other significant human bonds.

All the writers in this volume have recognized and struggled with the intimate and at times erotic relationship between teacher and student, a connection that is charged with all the electricity of shared discovery of the mind embodied in a literary text, the union of the author's, the teacher's, and the student's intellects. Little wonder, then, that the ardor with which we explore the textual body might give rise to erotic fantasies. What needs to be recognized and acknowledged is, first, that acts of learning and teaching are acts of desire and passion. Second, the personal history that both student and teacher bring to the place of instruction informs the tenor of the relationship, as the following essays attest. It matters if one is, for instance, a black woman teaching at a small white college in the South, as the introduction to Vanessa Dickerson's thoughtful article makes clear. In a very different instance, Deborah Morse's essay explores the interpenetrations of the personal and the pedagogical as she tells how the death of her physician father impelled her search for the perfect father/mentor, both in life and in the fiction of Anthony Trollope.

The posture one takes in relation to the roles of student and teacher evolves over time and is rooted in early experiences of the pleasure of reading. Our growing awareness of our sexuality often coincides as well with our intellectual awakening. Regina Barreca's essay "Contraband Appetites" most directly addresses these issues, but these concerns are implicit in all the volume's articles.

"I grew up falling—falling down, falling in love, falling apart. I fell in love with every English teacher I had from junior high onward" begins Barreca's essay. Barreca argues that "instead of sex being sublimated as ambition, in these cases what we're dealing with is ambition sublimated as sex." Barreca's essay explains "those of us who fell for the professor," who

cast ourselves as Cinderella intellectuals, waiting for the phrase—rather than the slipper—that fit us perfectly. We waited, at fourteen, at nineteen, at twenty-five or even thirty-five, for the figure who would see what was hidden and special and glorious in us, who would love us for our smart selves alone and not our yellow hair—or so we thought—who would play out every fantasy of sibling rivalry we ever had and choose us from among all our peers for attention.

While Barreca links us in our common, often voracious desire for approval, she also reminds us of the intensity of our imaginations. Little wonder, Barreca muses, that "the difference between desire and imagination mirrors . . . the confusion between loving the profession and loving the professor." Barreca reminds us that heroines as different as Charlotte Brontë's repressed Lucy Snowe (*Villette*) and George Eliot's passionate Dorothea Brooke (*Middlemarch*) have loved the professor, and survived that love to create their own lives. In the end, Barreca tells us, "waking from a dream of seduction is not easy, but leaving behind the idea of love in order to embrace the love of an idea is a distinct pleasure."

John Glavin echoes Barreca in "The Intimacies of Instruction" when he states that the pupil responds—indeed, falls in love—with the professor because she is really falling in love with an idealized vision of herself. However, Glavin anatomizes teaching as seduction, forcefully arguing that pedagogical discourse is in desperate need of reform. Glavin's confrontation with teaching strategies is historicized, a consideration of sex, gender, and pedagogy in literature and life, from Sophocles, Madame de Renal, and Julien Sorel (*The Red and the Black*) through W. H. Auden, *The Prime of Miss Jean Brodie*, and *Dead Poets Society*, to a 1993 forum on gender and seduction in teaching published in *Harper's* magazine. Glavin identifies the current pedagogical arena as a place of seduction or abuse. The successful teacher begins "with glamorous self-presentation . . . goes on to inveigle the pupils as partners in a game . . . mentor and selected neophyte(s) may go on to derive an ever 'deeper instinctive satisfaction,' if and as that game succeeds. They arrive at a [here Glavin borrows from Lacan] 'final stage' in a relatively few prolonged cases (the Brodie set, the Dead Poets Society: each teacher's crème de la crème), in which the seducer 'frees himself entirely and does exactly what he pleases.'" Glavin explores the dangers of the imperious, "incandescent lecturer," the teacher as seducer; among the most potent of these dangers is the professor's self-authenticating refusal to allow difference, what Glavin terms "the teacher as Dracula, to be honest. Teaching as cloning, to be kind." The contemporary classroom rewards this seductive pedagogy, which, Glavin argues only half facetiously, may be "a genuine form of Narcissistic Personality Disorder."

"To my great relief, I don't fall in love with younger women," begins Rebecca Pope's essay "Hayley, Roz, and Me." Pope continues with her assertion that "Life as a semi-out feminist teacher in a conservative and Church-affiliated institution is challenging enough without having to worry about falling in love, or lust, with any of my students." However, in Pope's essay she examines the literary genre of girls' school fiction from the early twentieth century to the present day, a genre in which "raves"— homoerotic crushes on teachers or older students—abound. From the ambiguity of Elizabeth Bowen's "enigmatic" *Eva Trout*, in which the lesbian erotics are shrouded in mystery, to the more explicit accusations of Lillian Hellman's *The Children's Hour* (1934) (in which the accused lesbian Martha commits suicide) to Dorothy Strachey Bussy's *Olivia* (1949), in which the lesbian relationship ends murkily in a death that could be either suicide or murder, Pope uncovers the "regulatory agenda"

of the classic girls' school novel. *Olivia*, for example, "still figures lesbianism as doom, and implies that lesbian teachers recruit." In Josephine
Tey's *Miss Pym Disposes* (1947), Pope illuminates the plot dynamics that
allow a "crime of passion"—the murder of a schoolgirl by a rival girl's
homosexual lover—to be "recast as a crime of class arrogance." However, Pope identifies in Tey's novel a "departure from psychoanalytic
theory and, perhaps, its pathologizing of female homoeroticism." Tey's
near-normalizing of homoerotic relations is echoed in a more recent story,
Edna O'Brien's "Sister Imelda," in which the "intimacy between the
narrator and Sister Imelda is from the start an electrifying mix of pleasure, pain, longing, and dread." Few fictional heroines fare as well as the
headmistress of Winifred Holtby's *South Riding* (1936), who cites Tennyson on Arthur when she asserts that in loving her, her students follow
the dictum that "we needs must love the highest when we see it." In her
analysis of films from Leontine Sagan's groundbreaking *Madchen in
Uniform* (1931) to the 1960s' *The Trouble with Angels*, Pope finds film
versions of the girls' school story more subversive, more "politically
transgressive" than its fictional counterparts. Finally, Pope quotes Elaine
Marks's argument that "desire is the central force in teaching, a force that
can be dangerous if it is not recognized and controlled but without which
the language and literature classroom is a dry and boring place." Pope
concludes her essay with the wish for her own students' "guiltless revelry
in the pleasures—however they come by them—of texts, and pain, if pain
there must be, that can be named and assuaged."

"Teaching at a small, private, predominately white, conservative liberal arts college in the South, I have found without fail each year among
student evaluations of my courses some strong objections to the discussion of, allusions to, or references to sexuality in my classes." So begins
Vanessa Dickerson's essay "The Teachings of Small Smothered Lives: The
Erotics of Instruction in Henry James's *The Turn of the Screw*." Dickerson first explores the gender and race conflicts inherent in her Southern
classroom, a space in which she is often the only African-American. She
speculates about the reasons for her students' virulent attacks on her
openness about sexuality in literature: "Perhaps I had presented these
ideas with too great a satisfaction, thinking, like Strother Purdy, somewhere in the depths of my being, 'that sex does not go away for being
hidden,' that 'no one can be a master of the novel without including the
terrible power physical love exerts.'" Dickerson wonders if she should
have been more clinical, if she has been too irreverent and playful with

her sexual references in the classroom. Finally, she admits to wondering if "these students would have been so troubled or resistant to my connection of the sexual with the intellectual now and then had I not been a female and a black female at that?" From there Dickerson evokes Jane Gallop's questioning of the definition of sexual harassment, an analysis that, according to Dickerson's reading, "both touches on the difficulty and questions the desirability of separating the erotic from the intellectual." Finally, Dickerson moves to a consideration of teacher-pupil relations in Henry James's *The Turn of the Screw*. In her exegesis, Dickerson focuses on the "'teachings of . . . small smothered life' by representing the interactions of a governess . . . and children . . . This use of one silent or subdued figure to screw down others . . . " Dickerson rehistoricizes James's text, placing it within the discourse on the New Woman and within the larger Victorian "Woman Question." Her intricate explication of *The Turn of the Screw* discusses the governess's instruction and the tutelage of Quint and Jessel that is directed toward little Flora and Miles. Dickerson's exploration of James's text concludes with the recognition that she and James's governess have much in common, that "what my reading of *The Turn of the Screw* comes down to is an understanding that the governess who dared in her nineteenth-century milieu to broach issues of sexuality in her relations with her charges teetered on the edge of a precipice . . . and a black female professor in a Southern white conservative classroom may very well find that the phrase, 'turn of the screw' takes on yet another interesting dimension."

Mary Ann Caws's essay "Instructive Energies" reflects on the "energetics"—the energy and erotics—of the workplace, specifically the classroom. Energetics, Caws argues, "is about developing: the self, the mind, those of others, in the classroom and museum and library." Caws's own mode of energetics includes a good deal of intertextuality, in particular the kind of painting-with-poem visual-cum-aural analysis that the late Jean Hagstrum describes in his classic *The Sister Arts*—and that he actually taught in the classroom, as his former students can gratefully attest. Using Yeats's "Leda and the Swan" as an example, Caws outlines her teaching method. She examines the subtle interplay of Yeats's poem, Tintoretto's painting, "other Ledas and some other swans of literature and art," and finally "other kinds of swans, black and white: of Baudelaire and Mallarmé, of Ruben Dario and Neruda and Thomas Mann . . . " Caws expands her energetics to encompass the foreign: the visual with the verbal, the erotics of translation, the mentor as woman.

As Caws muses on the erotics of the classroom, she decides that "energy, just pure unadulterated *energy*, can be attractive. Even grown-up, aging energy. Even when it isn't male. Do I mean seductive, erotic, *winning?* Is it fun to manifest? To watch? It seems to be, sometimes, all of the above." However, Caws is nothing if not relentlessly and scrupulously honest; she carefully presents the many pitfalls for the energetic, nurturing woman professor. Despite her misgivings, though, Caws comes down on the side of energetics with a final cautionary note: "There is a responsibility attached to the erotics of instruction . . . and to the energetics of anything . . . [They] don't come without a price . . . and in that, they are like any other privilege, meaningful."

James Kincaid's essay "Eroticism is a Two-Way Street, and I'm Working Both Sides" anticipates criticisms of the subject of erotics and pedagogy—that is, the very idea informing this volume. Kincaid embarks on a simultaneous critique of and apologia for this book itself. Kincaid's piece is a tour de force, along the lines of his brilliant article on *Frankenstein* published in *Novel* in the Fall 1990 issue ("Words Cannot Express: *Frankenstein*'s Tripping on the Tongue"), in which Kincaid speculated about the incestuous underpinnings of Shelley's text. Here, on one hand, Kincaid argues that "Students and Teachers Burn for Truth, Not One Another," yet he leaves open the possibility that there might be either no eroticism at all in the classroom or smut everywhere. It depends on one's perspective, Kincaid surmises, and it's all a part of the subjective erotic universe in which each of us lives and has our being, so it's difficult to be empirical or scientific about the problem after all. "Eroticism is the air we breathe" he asserts; especially, to many people's way of thinking, in the cloistered, timeless air of the ideal imagined classroom, "this smudgy, sun-filtered atmosphere: warm and drowsy, protected and changing, vaguely Eastern in its exoticism and its serene indifference to anything but its own comforts." Along the way, Kincaid brings up the family romance, the teacher *in loco parentis,* and the incest taboo, all of which give rise to the mythos of the "dry, wizened, sterile" teacher, the Ichabod Cranes of the classroom. Kincaid comically demythicizes professor-student erotic fantasies, citing "academic folktales" in which the beautiful young student offers to do anything for a good grade and the professor replies, at long last, "Study!"

In "Bartleby and the Professor," Gerhard Joseph considers the politics of teaching—the influence of gender, class, and race on the erotics of instruction. Joseph opens with a scenario in which he is confronted by an angry, working-class, African-American female student who, deservedly, received a "D" in his class, and who immediately signed up for another tour of duty with him the next semester. He remembers the guilt and anger and confusion he felt at the time, and now decides that he is grateful to this student, who he remembers because she refused to back down from the issues that are truly implicit in the classroom:

What was unusual and disturbing and—yes, exhilarating—about Jane was the uncompromising tenacity with which she kept bringing to the surface what is usually kept implicit in the urban classroom within which I teach: the complex hegemonic interweave within the teacher-student economy of older and younger, of male and female, of white and African-American, of Anglo and Latino, of middle and working class . . . Without apparent fear of my greater power institutionalized in my control of grades and demonstrated by that earlier D, she just kept challenging, from the depths of her own psychic and cultural needs, my psychic and cultural authority as coherent Subject who is Supposed to Know.

Deborah Morse's "Educating Louis: Teaching the Victorian Father in Trollope's *He Knew He Was Right*" connects Morse's own physician father's death when she was fifteen to her search for the ideal father/mentor in literature and life. From her initial recognition of the passions that she herself experienced as a college student yearning for the perfect father, Morse proceeds to an explication of *He Knew He Was Right*, Trollope's prodigious novel of estrangement and madness. As Morse explains her central concern in her essay: "I am fascinated by the Victorian father/mentor. Perhaps I am ready, now that *I* am the mentor, to focus more centrally on the reeducation of the authority figure in Trollope." Morse focuses on Trollope's estranged upper-class gentleman Louis Trevelyan, whose will to be always right eventually drives him to madness. In *He Knew He Was Right,* Morse analyzes how

the locus of English political power is explored. *He Knew* dissects the obsessive will to power of a member of the Victorian elite. In successive vignettes, we see how Louis Trevelyan, Victorian gentleman par excellence, the perfect husband and father, refuses to learn what Trollope's thinking women and men have to teach about the possibilities for more liberated relationships between the sexes, between the generations—and perhaps, within the Empire.

Morse illuminates Trollope's narrative strategies linking racial and gender dominance, arguing that Trollope "makes us aware that Trevelyan has been instructed by his society to think that his privileged life is his birthright as an upper-class Victorian man." In discussions of what Morse terms "scenes of instruction," she demonstrates how Trollope manifests his understanding of the erotics and power dynamics of instruction.

Ultimately, as Morse concludes, "Trevelyan's resistance to his instructors in compassion, love—and feminism—leads to his own madness and death." However, in the figures of more reasonable, loving, egalitarian male characters in the novel, there is "hope that the authority of the new Victorian fathers . . . will be based upon a commitment to loving equality between men and women."

Robert Polhemus's article "A Jamesian Sentimental Education: What Maisie Knew: French Literature, Sacred History" links Henry James' nineteenth-century novel of manners both to biblical stories and to French literary traditions of erotic and sentimental education. The introduction to Polhemus's essay reminds us that

desires, images, and concepts joining together the roles of teacher, father, and lover have made their lasting marks on our Judeo-Christian heritage, as the Bible shows and tells. The Adam and Eve creation story, the sexual history of patriarchs such as Lot, David, and Solomon, the erotic Song of Solomon and its Christian allegorical interpretations, the theology of the Trinity and of the Virgin Mary all offer examples of the mysterious intertwinings of religion, erotics, kinship relations, and moral pedagogy that permeate our cultural and literary traditions.

Polhemus comments upon his choice of the nineteenth-century novel—and of James's *What Maisie Knew* in particular—in relation to this topic:

The nineteenth-century novel in English explored in depth relationships between teacher-father-lover figures and figures that—seizing on Dickens's resonant epithet "child-wife" in *David Copperfield*—we might call *child-wives*. My subject is pedagogy in James's great and infinitely suggestive novel *What Maisie Knew*, specifically some of the things that the narrator imagines Maisie Farange and her stepfather Sir Claude learn from and teach one another—and that James imagines they teach himself and his readers as well. Sir Claude is, in Maisie's mind, her favorite teacher of many in the novel and her desired father-lover.

Polhemus connects Maisie with other innocent, pure, redemptive figures of young girls in Victorian fiction: Little Nell in Dickens's *The Old Curiosity Shop*, Florence Dombey in *Dombey and Son*, little Eppie in *Silas Marner*; figures who, Polhemus argues, "concentrated, as did the traditional Virgin of Roman Catholicism, religious feeling and faith in nurturing idealism—*Notre Jeune Fille* instead of *Notre Dame*, but sacred nonetheless." Polhemus concludes:

Father-lover and child-wife are sublimated into a faith and art of pregnant renunciation, sired and tutored by an author, Henry James: the novelist, as teacher-father-lover, takes Maisie Farange for his child-wife. The child gives him, with his theme, moral dignity, as she does Sir Claude. And, like Sir Claude, James gives her dignity and importance. The moral seed of the artist James is preserved by the chaste intercourse of the child and the new Lot, and the child's seed of faith, hope and charity is preserved by the intoxication and rapture of art.

Abby Werlock's "'With a Man There Is a Difference': The Rejection of Female Mentoring in Hemingway's *For Whom the Bell Tolls*" posits the original and heterodox possibility that in his novel, Hemingway mourns the inability to hear the female mentor's voice—both his own and that of his hero, Robert Jordan. In her essay, Werlock focuses on the many scenes of instruction in which the Spanish women—Maria, the young victim of a gang rape, and her older comrade Pilar, the wise and brave soldier, the sage—try to teach Jordan a different way of thinking. Werlock uses Carol Gilligan's terminology, her identification of women's "different voice," as she argues that Maria and especially Pilar use speech that is informed with different, more compassionate values than is Jordan's. As Werlock notes, "the two women repeatedly attempt to educate the professor, but Jordan proves ultimately incapable of absorbing their lessons." Both in her stories and in her own enactment of Hemingway's "grace under pressure," Pilar seems to embody a feminist rebuke to Jordan's masculine teachings. Werlock argues that "significantly, neither Pilar nor Maria have ever killed anyone. Both her [Pilar's] stories reveal vividly the violence and death which she sorrowfully abhors. Within Pilar are contained the components of all life—love as well as brutality, human commitment as well as killing—and she gives voice to her memories and her intuitive wisdom." In Maria's dreams of rewriting history in the mother's voice, in her retelling of the rape episode to Jordan, and in Pilar's maternal protection of her "daughter" Maria, Werlock locates the effort to reeducate Hemingway's hero. Yet Jordan ultimately rejects his lover Maria's own heroism and her mentorship, and even Pilar's stern wisdom. Ultimately, Jordan listens only to his own grandfather's voice, the voice he hears in his head that tells him to adhere to the "male code of heroism, duty and bravery" and to ignore the feminine voices espousing "personal relationships and commitments to living." Robert Jordan dies at the novel's close, and his creator, Ernest Hemingway, commits "the suicide with whose dark attraction he had dwelt so long."

In her essay "Making Love to the Gods: Four Women and their Affairs with Education," Dranda Trimble comments on the experiences of four mature women graduate students, women raised in the South to boot, and so taught to be pliant and self-sacrificing. Trimble recalls the painful history of intelligent, hardworking women who were ready at the drop of a hat to fall into bed with even the dreariest male professor, even David, who "was balding and thin, and a shabby dresser," the professor/seducer of Trimble's best friend. Trimble's reminiscences are proof that the teacher has an enormous responsibility, as Mary Ann Caws has argued. In discussing another friend's crush on her flirtatious professor, Trimble suggests that they both "fail to take into account the vulnerability of a woman finding herself in love with her career, but uncertain of her ability to succeed." This relationship ended with the professor's departure for another university, but not before Trimble's friend had gotten a divorce, thinking she was irrevocably in love with her professor. Fortunately, this story—unlike many professor/student love affairs—has a happy ending, with the woman both reconciling with her husband and pursuing her academic career. Finally, Trimble offers us an account of her own early writing. Through all of her vicissitudes, all her erotic longings for her professors, there was a significant constant: Trimble refused to change her writing to please her male professors. Ultimately, she came into her own both as poet and teacher.

For Montana Katz, the possibility that "erotics" might enter the realm of instruction is distinctly dangerous. She confronts the issue of sexual harassment on college campuses through a reading of the David Mamet play *Oleanna*. Katz argues that *Oleanna* functions, in a disturbing way, to distract us from what is really at stake in the issue of sexual harassment. According to Katz, by eliciting audience sympathy for the unjustly accused male professor—whose job and property are jeopardized by the unfounded allegations—*Oleanna* "serves as a time-worn tool to turn the tables of attention and blame toward women, toward those who are the actual victims of sexual harassment." *Oleanna*, Katz argues, is a reactionary distortion of the true nature of sexual harassment on college campuses, reflecting male fears of female strength and sexuality.

Myra Goldberg's "But I Thought He Liked My Paper," begins with a remembrance of fiction she had written in the '70s, in which she traces a pattern of "affair with professor, guilt, renunciation, the inability to carry through on what's personally important, and confusion, that disease of young women." Although these stories were not based on actual incidents, Goldberg looks back at her own experiences as a student and explores the erotic dynamics underlying her own fiction. She revives memories of her college life—her attraction to male mentors and their fervent response, her subsequent disenchantment with their obsession with her face rather than her work—and she thinks about the place these real-life experiences had in shaping her art. In the stories she discusses in her essay, Goldberg discerns a thematics of displaced rage and renunciation. "I Paint What I See," for example, focuses on Emily, a young female artist, who sleeps with her painting teacher "on the floor of his office" when she is a student, but later, when she is herself a rising artist with a show of her own, refuses to sleep with her famous artist/mentor. Emily, however, worries about this latter decision, torn between her longing for success and fame and her allegiance to "some long line of women," both her own family—generations of battered women like herself, a daughter beaten by a brutal father—and the female artistic tradition, all the women who have struggled to have their paintings recognized for their merit, not because the artist had traded her body for a critic's favor. Finally, Goldberg compares her own work with the stories her students have written. In particular, she applauds her student Anita's story "Sometimes I Just Felt Sorry for Him," in which Anita dissects the sexual politics of her "slimy" teacher's classroom. Instead of sleeping with him, Anita responds to her teacher's intimidation by reporting him to higher authority figures and confronting him herself. As Goldberg reports, "Times have changed. Everyone, except the boys, now knows the story."

The story belongs to all of us, to everyone who has spent time dreaming of the text, the teacher, or the student; some know it, others work hard not to know it. The pleasures and proprieties of the classroom are not explained in any textbook—for which we should be grateful—and it is not the task of this volume to codify any notion of correct behavior or legislate the niceties of sexually nuanced teaching activity. These essays, however, offer a range of responses to the process of teaching as an act of creation and reinvention. They focus our attention on the breath and bodies and emotional textures of those who choose the dangers of daring to teach—and daring to learn.

September 1996   R. B. and D. D. M

Acknowledgments

We want to thank, from the heart, all those who have supported this collection from its first incarnation—as an MLA panel—to this final form. We are especially grateful to Margaret Mitchell, graduate student and research assistant at the University of Connecticut, for her extraordinary work with the manuscript; without Margaret this book would have been late, slow, and far less lively. We cannot thank her enough. In addition, we'd like to thank Julie Nash, Lee Jacobus, Michael Meyer, Brenda Murphy, and Jane Kim of the University of Connecticut. We also wish to acknowledge the excellent work at UPNE, especially that provided by Phil Pochoda and Ann Kraybill. The editors would also like to applaud the patience of our families, friends, and colleagues, and tell our husbands that we are particularly thankful for their perspectives and encouragement. We dedicate the book to our teachers, our students, and to all those signs saying "hidden drive."

REGINA BARRECA

Contraband Appetites
Wit, Rage, and Romance in the Classroom

I grew up falling—falling down, falling in love, falling apart. I fell in love with every English teacher I had from junior high onward. My seventh grade teacher, Mr. Frisco, had a handlebar mustache, wore pop-art ties the size of dinner plates, and looked like an illustration from a Peter Max poster. I wanted to be sure I learned his name right away, so I tried to figure out how to remember it. Not knowing there was a word for mnenomic devices, I nevertheless convinced myself that I could remember his name by thinking that it was like a food shortening—Crisco—but with an "F." At his next class I greeted him cheerfully, heart pounding beneath my black Danskin leotard—and he asked me what I said. I replied, horrified, "I just said hi." "But what did you call me?" he asked. "I called you Mr. Fazola, isn't that right?" I realized, of course, what I had done the moment I opened my mouth—substituted Mazola for Crisco, but I could hardly explain that to him—"your name is like a cooking oil, but different." I had sabotaged myself in my longing for his attention and approval, which were the best substitutes I could find for his true love, and so I pretty much shut up for the rest of the term. He was the first teacher I fell for, but not the last.

I would bet that many of the women, and maybe nearly as many of the men, who enter our profession have fallen in love with their teachers over the years. Sometimes we sublimate effectively, and become the beloved in our own classes, imitating, perhaps unconsciously, the mannerisms and habits of an influential professor. Sometimes we sleep with the teacher, sometimes we marry him or her, often we translate our desire into a love of the subject, or the text, or the way the light hits a four o'clock window in a November classroom.

I believe it's nearly everybody's plot, but maybe some will feel only disdain for those of us who fell prey to the nets cast by the particularly seductive atmosphere of the professor's office. But they would also find unsympathetic such diverse texts as *Villette, Small World, The Prime of Miss Jean Brodie,* and *Middlemarch,* not to mention the Mamet play *Oleanna.* Those of us who fell for the professor cast ourselves as Cinderella intellectuals, waiting for the *phrase*—rather than the slipper—that fit us perfectly. We waited, at fourteen, at nineteen, at twenty-five or even thirty-five, for the figure who would see what was hidden and special and glorious in us, who would love us for our smart selves alone and not our yellow hair—or so we thought—who would play out every fantasy of sibling rivalry we ever had and choose us from among all our peers for attention.

I want to argue that instead of sex sublimated as ambition, in these cases what we're dealing with is ambition sublimated as sex. Consider Virginia Woolf's line in *The Voyage Out,* when nineteen-year-old Rachel is both attracted to and repelled by Richard Dalloway's kiss. She's aroused, but she isn't certain why; mostly he fascinates her because she imagines the public and important life he leads in London. When Rachel tells her forty-year-old friend about the kiss, she ponders the split between being attracted to the man and being attracted to the profession, and declares that "there must be something wrong in this confusion between politics and kissing politicians" (83). Fay Weldon makes much the same sort of comment when, in *Down Among the Women,* one of her younger characters kisses a man nearly forty years her senior, tickled by the thought of how much of life he has seen. The narrator tells us in the usual wry, Weldonian way, "It isn't her desire that is stirred, it is her imagination, but how is she to know this?" The point about the difference between desire and imagination mirrors the one about the confusion between loving the profession and loving the professor.

At what point, I would like to ask, did the moment come for each of us when we realized that we wanted to be the teacher, and not sleep with the teacher? Was it the day we entered the first room with a woman at the head of the class? I know from both sides of the desk that female students have trouble, sometimes, dealing with female professors. As I have found to be the case with many of my colleagues at other institutions, I am often—very often—an associate advisor rather than a major advisor, even when the young woman's field of study falls under my aegis (which is the academic version of always a bridesmaid, never a bride).

Now I could make all kinds of characteristically feminine self-deprecating remarks, but to be fair to my other colleagues who are in the same situation, I can say without too much hesitation that the student in question will often choose a senior male. And if this sounds a little too much like "Wild Kingdom," then so be it. I did it myself as both an undergraduate and graduate student. Just in case it made a difference, I wanted that male protector; it wasn't that I didn't like and respect the women on the faculty, but I made my choices looking for a particular kind of validation that, it seemed to me at the time, a man could more easily provide than a woman. Looking at some of my very best students today, I'd say the same unspoken, almost unrealized need applies to them. Rereading John W. Kronik's 1990 article on men mentoring women, I see that men struggle with the right ways to deal with female students like the one I was, wanting to offer support without making a pass, being the best advisors they can be; and yet, maybe because of my own suspect past, I've spent some time considering the framework for this particular dyad. Obviously many others have considered it as well, without the sensitivity apparent in Kronik.

In John Updike's recent novel *Memories of the Ford Administration*, for example, we're told that "In the Sixties, indeed, gentle and knowing defloration had been understood by some of the younger, less married faculty gallants as an extracurricular service they were being salaried to perform." In *The Professor of Desire*, Philip Roth's hero imagines lecturing to the students in Literature 341, where he discloses "the undisclosable—the story of the professor's desire," where he makes clear that he finds "our classroom to be, in fact, the most suitable setting" for the "accounting of my erotic history."

Professors retain, for students, the magical quality of being both available and distant at the same time. The relationship resembles a courtly romance; desire is ritualized into a series of intellectual curtsies and bows which, while always flavored by the sexual, were never meant to be translated into the physical, despite Updike's chronicling of the '60s. Teachers were taboo—or should have been—since there was a sort of "intellectual" incest at work, a prohibition which meant that the student was free to love and want, while the teacher was required to remain disinterested, distinguished, and practically disembodied. (Shaw's Henry Higgins protests that a pupil is "sacred," declaring that "teaching would be impossible unless pupils were sacred"). A student felt—rightly or wrongly—that the teacher, like a parent, was a safe object of desire, since it was necessarily one-way: girls I knew in college fantasized about cute teachers the way we fantasized about Sting from the band The Police.

Now my professors looked like Sting about as much as I looked like Sinead O'Connor, but they still made us sigh and giggle. One of Sting's biggest hits was, of course, the classic "Don't Stand So Close to Me." "Young teacher, the subject of schoolgirl fantasy," Sting begins, wearing in his video the academic robes he earned getting his teaching degree. A line that made it as graffiti on London tube station walls goes as follows: "He sees her, he starts to shake and cough, just like the old man in that book by Nabokov." "Who the hell is Nabokov?" appeared scrawled over underground posters, but since it was inevitably spelled correctly, it always seemed that whoever wrote it knew damned well who Nabokov was.

The teacher as unattainable object of desire has a number of implications. I should admit that I did twice as well in the classes of teachers I adored as in any others because I jumped through every hoop to get their attention. Male and female teachers alike captured my imagination, but sexual desire was reserved for male teachers alone. Otherwise it was just love. Nothing inspires you like the desire for recognition from an authority figure who rarely pays attention to anyone. It provides a rush of excitement, of validation, and most importantly, a sense of power. Jessica Benjamin, among others, has told us about the attractively unattainable. She discusses the fantasy of erotic submission, in which a woman longs to be "released into abandon by another who remains in control." It seems to me to sum up the situation; in this case, the professor eroticizes the pursuit of learning while intellectualizing the pursuit of the love object, making the intellectual sexual and the sexual academic. The phrase "sexual academic" turns out to be an interesting one: one friend to whom I mentioned it said "sexual academic" was an oxymoron, like jumbo shrimp or greater Cleveland; another disagreed, declaring that, if anything, "sexual academic" was not oxymoronic but redundant, like, he said, the phrases "working mother" or "dysfunctional family."

There is something essentially paternalistic, nearly theological, about the traditional classroom. The instructor assumes naivete or ignorance, announcing a sort of intellectual damnation, and you spend all your time working toward, hoping for, the miracle of grace, the passing of redemption—the singling out of the self to announce that you, alone, have been saved. One of my first college instructors passed back our seminar papers while he said, charmingly, nastily, "Lucky for all of you that it is early in the term; there is still room in state universities." I hated him that minute, but I also told myself that I would show him. That "show him" impulse

turns for many people into a version of "show and tell" that is not exactly
fit for classroom discussion. But the "show him" impulse is also inherent
in the setup we choose to call academia; it's what Eliza, in the warped
musical version of *Pygmalion,* sings to Henry Higgins in "Just You Wait;"
it's what the real Eliza in Shaw's play holds out as her gravest threat: I
will become what you are. Shaw's Eliza's revenge is to *become* Higgins.
"I'll teach phonetics," she laughs, "You can't take away the knowledge
you gave me . . . Oh, when I think of myself crawling under your feet and
being trampled on and called names, when all the time I had only to lift
up my finger to be as good as you, I could just kick myself" (131–32).
This is the moment of her ultimate betrayal.

The representation of the professor/lover in works by women is
significantly different from the way it is presented in works by men.
One of the most apparent differences is the female writer's refusal to
allow for the high seriousness demanded by the gentleman scholar.
Dorothea Brooke, the heroine of George Eliot's *Middlemarch,* is a push-
over for the first half-learned man that she meets, but the narrator isn't.
The narrator's wit in the presentation of the romance between this
unlikely pair is infused with outrage at the inappropriateness of
Dorothea's desire for the old man. Dorothea imagines that "the really
delightful sort of marriage must be that where your husband was a sort
of father, and could teach you Hebrew if you wished it" (32). The reader
is made to feel, of course, that such a marriage could be described in
many ways, but *not* as "really delightful." The phrase exposes as folly
the heroine's matrimonial ambitions. Eliot takes the enthusiastic, attractive, and powerful young woman through the usual steps and presents
us with what has been regarded as the appropriately happy ending: the
heroine meets and marries a man some years her senior who will shape
her ambitions to fit acceptable conventions and teach her to harness her
energies for use as his helpmate. But there is a catch. As she becomes
progressively drawn to him, Dorothea's relationship with Casaubon
parodies the teacher/lover duet and shows the fissures and faults inherent
in such a plot.

Dorothea makes the mistake that colors all feminine affection for the
teacher/lover: confusing scholarship with kissing a scholar. If a man is
loved not for himself alone but for his access to knowledge that is
prohibited to women, he is in danger of becoming merely metonymic. He
will be discovered to be like the Wizard of Oz, yelling for Dorothy/ea to
ignore the man behind the curtain. If he is loved for any form of power—

and knowledge is the most seductive of all these—he is in danger of losing that love once the source of power is discovered. If she realizes that he is not as intelligent, as informed, or even as unique as he first appeared, he is lost. Everyone except Dorothea realizes that her dream of marrying the teacher/lover will fail because Casaubon can barely fulfill the first part of the definition, while being practically incapable of coming to grips with the second. Casaubon, for example, concludes that "the poets had much exaggerated the force of masculine passion" since he feels so little of it; the narrator points out that it "had once or twice crossed his mind that possibly there was some deficiency in Dorothea to account for the moderation of his abandonment" (87). Casaubon's lack of passion is, in fact, the subject of his neighbors' broadly comic commentary. "He has got no good red blood in his body," says one, and another replies "No. Somebody put a drop under a magnifying-glass, and it was all semicolons and parentheses" (96). Dorothea's guardian is concerned about her husband's ability to keep things stable at Lowick, Casaubon's suitably named estate: "There may be a young gardener, you know—why not? . . . I told Casaubon he should change his gardener" (102). The subtext to his remark is as unsubtle as a D. H. Lawrence novel.

In Charlotte Brontë's *Villette,* we meet another version of Casaubon in the person of M. Emanuel, a colleague of our heroine Lucy Snowe, who insists on treating the younger woman as a student rather than a colleague. Attracted to her for her intellect, her nevertheless holds contempt for the intellectual capacities of women. That he has very definite ideas concerning "woman of intellect" is not surprising to Lucy, who has been in the academy long enough to expect such disparagement. Lucy sighs that "here he was at home." Lucy records his theories about intelligent women, and the transcription of such ideas by a woman, obviously both the object and subject of such a tirade, places them within a frame that renders them the object of her decision:

A "woman of intellect," it appeared, was a sort of *"lusus naturae,"* a luckless accident, a thing for which there was neither place nor use in creation, wanted neither as wife nor worker. Beauty anticipated her in the first office. He believed in his soul that lovely, placid, and passive feminine mediocrity was the only pillow on which manly thought and sense could find rest for its aching temples; and as to work, male mind alone could work to any good practical result—hein? (443)

The final "hein?" indicates both her exact transcription of his voice as well as M. Emanuel's anticipation of agreement from his audience. Lucy makes clear, however, that these remarks are more worthy of ridicule than respect.

M. Paul will not permit Lucy unmediated access to those materials he considers dangerous to her as a woman. Her gender defines what she may and may not read, for example. In a passage particularly satisfying because of its explicitly satiric treatment of the male-constructed curriculum, M. Emanuel will not give his younger colleague the gift of a book without first whipping out his penknife and editing the text:

After looking over the two volumes he had brought, and cutting away some pages with his penknife (he generally pruned before lending his books, especially if they were novels, and sometimes I was a little provoked at the severity of his censorship, the retrenchments interrupting the narrative), he rose . . . (434–35)

In his desire to control Lucy's reading, he resembles the male characters created by Lennox and Austen. But the most significant aspect of M. Emanuel's desire to control Lucy's reading is his well-articulated and unmistakable fear of what he defines as the "contraband appetite for unfeminine knowledge." Lucy is perplexed, like many female students before and after her, by her mentor's withdrawal of approval at the exact moment when she felt herself to be achieving her goals:

But, strange grief! . . . when I voluntarily doubled, trebled, quadrupled the tasks he set, to please him as I thought, his kindness became sternness; the light changed in his eyes from a beam to a spark; he fretted, he opposed, he curbed me imperiously; the more I did, the harder I worked, the less he seemed content. Sarcasms of which the severity amazed and puzzled me, harassed my ears; then flowed out the bitterest inuendoes against the "pride of intellect." I was vaguely threatened with, I know not what doom, if I ever trespassed the limits proper to my sex, and conceived a contraband appetite for unfeminine knowledge. (440)

M. Emanuel's unwillingness to allow Lucy free rein in her studies, his desire to control the process and progress of her learning, is reminiscent of those lover/teacher characters we have already encountered in earlier texts, and a forerunner of those who present themselves throughout women's writings until the present day. The teacher/lover is an attractive figure for many reasons, but it is interesting to note the ways in which these characters' pretensions are deflated by the humor of their female student/lovers. Only wit could effectively undercut the power of these figures. Eliot, of course, takes this figure to his most dangerous extreme in Casaubon, but M. Emanuel is certainly a version of this character. As such, he is open to Brontë's deft satire; his comments on the education of women sound more like a fool's than a hero's.

But M. Emanuel is the romantic center of the text; he does procure Lucy a schoolroom of her own, after all. She can and does speak intimately to him, refusing to censor herself, unwilling to cut passages from her own tale even if her words must sound "literal, ardent, bitter" (591). Finally, Lucy realizes that she prefers him "before all humanity" (592), and agrees to be his wife. They then immediately part: "he gave me his pledge, and then his farewell" (592). A narrative tangle, surely? Lovers can meet, pledge, and then be driven apart by outside forces working against their will, but it is disruptive to the traditional marriage plot to have them decide to go on to other things besides the cultivation of their relationship. Brontë, who has already presented the reader with several important passages undercutting the supremacy of both textual and social convention, must be understood to be demonstrating the same refusal to adhere to the "script" at the end of her novel.

Fay Weldon offers an excellent updated example of a relationship along these lines in her short story "Ind. Aff.," which stands for inordinate affection. When the twenty-five-year-old unnamed female narrator falls in love with her forty-six-year-old thesis director (who is already married and the father of three children), she falls in love with her idea of him rather than with him as a man. The narrator, who tells her story from the perspective of one who has learned her lesson and is now simply imparting it, has come to understand that she had confused "mere passing academic ambition with love," believing this man's assessment of the world and of herself ("He said I had a good mind but not a first class mind and somehow I didn't take it as an insult") when she should have been coming up with her own conclusions.

Peter Piper (the name itself should indicate a certain lack of respect on the part of Weldon for such characters), the Cambridge professor who has been married to a swimming coach for twenty-four years, likes to "luxuriate in guilt and indecision," and has taken his student/mistress with him on a holiday to see whether they are "really, truly suited," to make sure that it is "the Real Thing" before they "shack up, as he put it." The narrator is desperately drawn to her teacher because he represents much more than he actually offers. To maintain her affection for Peter, she overlooks his stinginess ("Peter felt it was less confusing if we each paid our own way"), his whining ("I noticed I had become used to his complaining. I supposed that when you had been married a little you simply wouldn't hear it"), the fact that often when she speaks "he wasn't listening," the fact that he might not want her to go topless at the beach ("this might be the area where age differences showed") as well as overlooking his "thinning hair" because he seems authoritative (speaking in "quasi-Serbo-Croatian") and powerful. He "liked to be asked questions," and obviously adores the adoration of his student. She loves him with "Inordinate Affection," she claims. "Your Ind Aff is my wife's sorrow" Peter moans, blaming this girl who was born in the first year of his marriage for his wife's unhappiness, and absolving himself from any blame.

The question of whether particular events happen because of the inevitable buildup of insurmountable forces or, instead, because of a series of particular moments that might have been avoided with care, caution, or consideration, is brought to bear not only on the narrator's relationship with Peter but on the question of World War I. With the background material effortlessly supplied by Weldon, even readers unfamiliar with the story of Princip's assassination of the archduke will be able to see the way Princip's tale parallels that of the narrator. Was the war inevitable? Was it, as Peter Piper claimed, bound to "start sooner or later," because of the "social and economic tensions" that had to find "some release"? Along the same lines of reasoning, was the twenty-four-year marriage between Peter and the woman who is known only as Mrs. Piper doomed to failure, or was it instead pressured into failure by the husband's infidelity? Was it, as the narrator's sister Clare says (herself married to a much older professor), a fact that "if you can unhinge a marriage, it's ripe for unhinging, it would happen sooner or later, it might as well be you"? Is it, in other words, the narrator who is assassinating the Piper marriage?

The climax of the story occurs when the narrator and Peter are waiting to be served wild boar in a private restaurant. She notices a waiter, whom she describes as being "about my age" (showing her keenly felt awareness of the difference in age between herself and Peter). She has felt desire for Peter in her mind, and has learned to feel "a pain in the heart" as an "erotic sensation," but in looking at the virile, handsome man her own age she feels "quite violently, an associated yet different pang which got my lower stomach." She describes this desire as the "true, the real pain of Ind Aff!" Her desire for the waiter has nothing to do with his position, his authority, or his power. It has to do with his "flashing eyes, hooked nose, luxuriant black hair, sensuous mouth." She thinks to herself in a moment of clear vision "what was I doing with this man with thinning hair?" She thinks to herself, when she automatically tells Peter that she loves him, "how much I lied." She has freed herself from the confines of his authority, and declares in opposition to his theory that "If Princip hadn't shot the archduke, something else, some undisclosed, unsuspected variable, might have come along and defused the whole political/military situation, and neither World War I nor II ever happened." She then gets up to go "home."

"This is how I fell out of love with my professor," declares the narrator, describing their affair as "a silly, sad episode, which I regret." She sees herself as silly for having confused her career ambitions with desire, and silly for trying to "outdo my sister Clare," who had married her professor (but has to live in Brussels as a sort of cosmic penance). Piper eventually proved spiteful and tried to refuse the narrator's thesis, but she won her appeal and, delightfully, can confirm for herself that she does indeed have a "first-class mind" after all. She feels, finally, a connection to poor Princip, who should have "hung on a bit, there in Sarajevo," because he might have "come to his senses. People do, sometimes quite quickly."

The destructive habit of falling in love with teachers, priests, bosses, or any one who seems both far above you and out of reach is dangerous if it ever plays itself out as more than a fantasy, because you are very likely to have fallen in love with the idea of an authority rather than the person—him or her self. Getting the professor is like getting Dad, but without anything overtly or consciously foul or disgusting; it's getting all the perks without meeting the prerequisites: you get a man of power, of authority, of the sexy kind of attraction that drew women to—say—Henry Kissinger, when he had as much innate sex appeal as Yoda. If you're drawn to someone on the podium or behind the big desk and are relying, metaphorically, on the furniture rather than the man, he's inevitably going be disappointing once you see him in his socks and shorts stepping into your bathroom to brush his teeth. He's going to lose the glamour that kept you enthralled the first time that status is undermined: when a waiter (handsome or not) raises an eyebrow at his mispronunciation of an item on the menu, or when you discover that his first book was very badly reviewed.

Those who live by the sword die by the sword; those who enter sexual relationships where seduction depends more on the size of a bibliography than anything else are almost inevitably doomed from the start. Waking from a dream of seduction is not easy, but leaving behind the idea of love in order to embrace the love of an idea is a distinct pleasure. Sometimes even when you grow up falling, in other words, you can end up landing safely, not in someone else's arms, but on your own two feet.

Works Cited

Benjamin, Jessica. *The Bonds of Love: Psychoanalysis, Feminism, and the Problem of Domination.* New York: Pantheon, 1988.
Brontë, Charlotte. *Villette.* London: Penguin, 1980.
Eliot, George. *Middlemarch.* New York: Penguin, 1965.
Kronik, John W. "On Men Mentoring Women: Then and Now." *Profession* 1990.
Lodge, David. *Small World.* New York: Macmillan, 1984.
Mamet, David. *Oleanna.* New York: Pantheon, 1992.
Roth, Philip. *The Professor of Desire.* New York: Farrar, Straus & Giroux, 1977.
Shaw, George Bernard. *Pygmalion.* New York: Penguin, 1941.
Spark, Muriel. *The Prime of Miss Jean Brodie.* New York: Penguin, 1984.
Updike, John. *Memories of the Ford Administration.* New York: Knopf, 1992.
Weldon, Fay. *Down Among the Women.* 1972. Chicago: Academy Chicago, 1984.
———. "Ind. Aff." In *Moon Over Minneapolis, or Why She Couldn't Stay.* London: HarperCollins, 1991.
Woolf, Virginia. *The Voyage Out.* New York and London: Harcourt Brace Jovanovich, 1920.

The Intimacies of Instruction

But who wants to admit, who can face admitting, what we do to teach well?

As I write this, PBS regularly runs an ad about teaching that sternly warns fledgling instructors in every field that it is not enough to make students learn, the teacher's obligation is to make them want to learn. When Big Bird alighted we lost a world in which by common consent the recalcitrant pupil was understood to be behaving stupidly. Hostility has now become the adolescent badge of authenticity; indifference, the cool response. Take me, try to take me, silently, and sometimes not so silently, challenge all but the nerds. Charm my resistance. Captivate my indifference. Please me, entertain me, divert me, fascinate me, thrill me—seduce! The students' code name for all this is enthusiasm.

This pedagogy pumps the classroom into a clash of narcissisms. Which will win: the resistant, adolescent or post-adolescent narcissism of the student, demanding to be wooed, or the exhibitionist-performative narcissism of the teacher, setting out to conquer? The "good" teacher need be no more than, and is never less than, the superior narcissist, whatever his or her mastery of a field, someone who can enthrall, overpower, subject the enormous force of culturally-enforced adolescent self-admiration. Without a counter self-adulation, honorable people tend pretty regularly to teach badly. The fact that they tend to be also somewhat dull honorable people should not matter as much as it does, but classrooms are no place for scruples. Of course, we can resist. Generously, we might reread bad teaching as a badge of integrity. But who wants to claim it: the puce badge of mediocrity?

But I have told you already, Diotima, that my ignorance is the reason why I come to you, for I am conscious that I want a teacher; tell me then the cause of this and of the other mysteries of love. (Sophokles to Diotima: *The Symposium*)

It doesn't require a Sophokles, still less the mysteriously sybilline Diotima, to connect wanting a teacher to the mysteries of love. As we in the teaching profession know, the headline-grabbing teacher who recently seduced her students into murdering her husband is scandalous only in the way that Baudrillard maintains Watergate was scandalous. We have to insist this one's different, and bad, to camouflage her, or his, and our, deep and continuous pedagogic connection to seduction as usual.

All teaching, all successful teaching, falls into one of two kinds: abusive or seductive. The rest is merely instruction: tedious, safe, unlikely to make a difference. Both abusive and seductive teaching are, of course, inevitably corrupting. Compared to teaching, even the Puritan caricature of acting seems honest. And journalism gets to look downright Delphic in its candor.

Walter Ong, S.J., calls the abusive sort "agonistic," the pattern that dominated classrooms from antiquity up to the early twentieth century (*Fighting for Life* 41–45). An agonistic teacher sets himself up as a student's opponent and by various forms of brutality, more or less playful, bullies him into learning. It's always he and him, because historically the models derive from all-male institutional environments. Ong tends to regret this older, nostalgia-fumed "alliance" between contestation, masculinity, and orality (140–41), when teaching meant, in a Latin etymology at least, testing the testicles to testify.

In contrast, seductive teaching—for most of us, our teaching—might be called feminized, so called at least by someone like Father Ong, who observes in passing: "A woman's scream can carry a great distance, but intelligibly articulated speech is another problem" (141). However, I'd prefer to call the counter-agonistic the *Romantic,* if only because it's the principal business of this chapter to show how seductive teaching is precisely what successful female teachers are refused. *Romantic* teaching can take its motto from Beethoven's supremely Romantic superscription to the *Missa Solemnis:* "From the heart—may it return—to the heart." Rather than, say, to the buttocks, the target—indeed the aspiration—of so many agonists. Romantic teaching is what Jarrell makes fun of, and gets just about right, when he describes a process in which "the faculty . . . reasoned with the students, 'appreciated their point of view,' used Socratic methods on them, made allowances for them . . . but there was one allowance they never under any circumstances made—that the students might be right about something, and they wrong" (*Pictures From An Institution* 75). It's the kind of education, he says, that makes the student want to cry out: "Whip me, whip me, Mother, just don't be Reasonable!" (76).

Tough agonistic pedagogy continues to be authenticated in some contemporary representations of teaching—in, for example, the movie *Stand*

and Deliver—but, beyond the ghetto, for most of this century at least, seduction's pretty much cornered the middle-class pedagogic market. In a surprisingly unabashed way, both elite and popular culture urge instructors to amalgamate father and lover into seductive mentor, to both male and female pupils alike.

Of course, groups like the MLA or the NCTE only irregularly encourage teachers, or their spouses, to seduce students into adultery or fornication, and even less regularly to homicide. But they do constantly, and centrally, champion perjury, the *lingua franca* for all forms of seduction. Emerson made exactly this point at the dawn of modern pedagogy. He insisted that, in affirming that of which the student has no actual experience, but must take on the basis of the teacher's word, the student's witness can only be false. After all, the student wouldn't need to have taught what his or her experience already witnesses as authentic. Indeed, we can frame this as a kind of geometric postulate: curious but inescapable. The more effective the teacher, the more likely he—or she—is to make the student bear false witness: the more engaging, the more memorable, the more lastingly impressive the teacher, the more profoundly perjured the student.

The fraud accelerates as the student-witness segues into the increasingly engaged, and freighted, roles of pupil and, finally, of disciple. And this formulation applies equally to the incandescent lecturer and the Socratic mentor who *leads, conducts, guides, directs, steers* a "good" discussion. With either style, the student is always being called on primarily to witness only the teacher, whatever the ostensible subject. In *Pictures From An Institution,* the prize pupil Constance, trailing clouds of false witness, says of Gottfried Rosenbaum's inspired teaching: "He seems to know what you would have done if you could have done it instead of what you did; . . . It takes the weight of your pieces right off your shoulders" (122). From the shoulders, it's no stretch to the neck. The teacher as Dracula, to be honest. Teaching as cloning, to be kind.

We can hear the political and institutional foundation for this pedagogic self-display emerging as early as 1921 in the U.K.'s Newbolt Report "on the teaching of English in England." The Report insists that a new kind of teaching displace, at least in English classes, the forms of instruction on which classrooms had previously been able to depend:

Literature, not being a knowledge subject, cannot and should not be *taught*. It is to be communicated to the students in such a way that they will experience it rightly, that right experience being the sole aim of literary work. Now this makes literature awkward material for class-room purposes. The teacher, being a teacher, has a standing, an almost overwhelming temptation—to teach. The very atmosphere of the class-room, with its paraphernalia of study, is one in which the wings of poesy cannot readily beat. But such obstacles will, we believe, be overcome if literature be experienced in the way that it ought to be, that is through the living voice and by actual impersonation. (*The Teaching of English in England* 150)

Teaching, English at least, becomes *lived experience communicated through impersonation:* seduction. The English teacher heralds teaching's affective-cognitive reform, a reform in which feeling and knowing become one and the same, or, perhaps more accurately, in which feeling becomes the only ground for knowing. Where English led, the other humanities (at least) surely and swiftly followed. Almost at once we are asking questions like: *Describe how you would feel, if you were Marie Antoinette in her cell at the Conciergerie? Would you be likely to offer Columbus gifts if you spotted him attempting to land on the shore of your island?* And, bobbing in the wake, science became merely boring, the cabbage patch of the nerds.

The path this new teaching followed went, and continues, something like this. Successful teaching starts with glamorous self-presentation ("S\he's so cool"). It goes on to inveigle the pupils as partners in a game (I admit to revising Lacan on analysis here). Mentor and selected neophyte(s) may go on to derive an ever "deeper instinctive satisfaction," if and as that game succeeds. They arrive at a "final stage" in a relatively few prolonged cases (the Brodie set, the Dead Poets Society: each teacher's crème de la crème), in which the seducer "frees himself entirely and does exactly what he pleases" (Lacan 50).

In this final stage, seductive pedagogy may become a genuine form of Narcissistic Personality Disorder—from which, thankfully, most of us and our students are saved by semester break. Unbroken, however, grandiose fantasy can entrap favorite student and favored teacher in a pattern of behavior that becomes not only ruthless but (as we'll see below) self-righteous exploitation, feeding in both parts of the pairing apparently insatiable appetites for admiration and attention (*Diagnostic And Statistical Manual of Mental Disorders* 351). This paradigm is not the quite distinct and very different dynamic of pedophilia, which obsesses over prepubescent children. Here we are tracing ephebophilia. The ephebophile fixes on adolescents or young adults. The older person does not select the object for primarily carnal reasons. Either he or she feels empowered by the subjugation of someone younger and weaker, or, paradoxically, experiences a release of frustrated narcissism, seeing in the younger person an idealized version of the self.

Quite apart from whatever need drives the teacher, this seduction ordinarily works because the enthralled pupil is at the same time and through the same dynamic falling in love. The student is falling not so much for the teacher as for the idealized vision of self that the teacher seems to make possible, seems to bring, as it were, into being—hence the inevitably Oedipal dimension to any teacher's success. The magnetic teacher tells a lifestory—whatever the ostensible subject, from accounting to zoology, and whatever the ultimate trajectory of the pupil-teacher bond. The teacher both models and describes that lifestory. And the students recognize it as (really, deeply) about themselves, often unexpectedly, but almost immediately, and with a joyous clarity that feels like truth, and that certainly works like romance. In Mamet's *Oleanna* the young female pupil directs a vendetta against the male teacher precisely because her narcissistic rage cannot find herself mirrored in his hermetic, self-referential discourse. But Mamet's teacher is almost indescribably incompetent. (I wanted to leave at the intermission but my companion suggested that it would help to think of the play as about chickens. And it did.) In the winning teacher's story, however, we joyously recognize our selves as having—perhaps for the first time—the chance of narrative, the possibility of history.

This summons works all the more enchantingly in adolescence and young adulthood, when we are being forced to shed the unchecked childish self in response to the spiraling demands of an increasingly indifferent world. Underprivileged children are so hard to teach in large part because they bring such an impoverished, battered narcissism into the classroom. They feel nothing but hostility toward themselves, and therefore even the most charming teacher is hard-pressed to locate psychic material that can be pedagogically inflated. But privilege-primed, middle-class children introject what the teacher mirrors, and sense with shock the awakened self. They are back affectively at the earliest stages of primary narcissism, when infant and parent appeared (to the infant) all-in-all. They feel the teacher speaking not simply to them but about them, even in the large lecture where the teacher cannot attach a face to a name.

It is thus the crucial capacity to feel and to communicate enjoyment of the self that separates the successful teacher from the bore. Society licenses the teacher to do what virtually no other adult in the real world can. He or she stands up several times a week for fifty, seventy-five, ninety minutes, to exhibit with unconditional authority the self. This is not the self enveloped in a role or in a part, not wearing a uniform or enclosed by a vestment, and certainly not playing by any sort of rules. The teacher is there simply and obviously to improvise the self, and to carry off that self-improvisation without inhibition until the class comes, by the teacher's consent, to an end. (Isn't that why so many of us prolong class just that extra minute after the period officially ends, to confirm exactly how much our narcissism controls this particular site of exhibition?) The successful teacher is rarely the smartest or the most knowledgeable member of a department, as less admired colleagues know from chagrined experience, merely the most self-confident. He or she enjoys—needs, also—more than anything else that sheer power to exhibit the self untrammeled that insists that everything s\he thinks and feels and knows ought to be interesting and relevant to everyone who listens. And that enjoyment guarantees in turn the student's enchantment.

Classes end. Semesters end. Students graduate. Before they leave, the average undergraduate encounters from twenty-four to forty different teachers; the average high school student, forty-eight to fifty. That limits the damage. Nevertheless, the harm is inevitable whenever teaching really *takes*. It would be a comfort to believe that only those "final-stage" seducers do harm, those who take carnal advantage of their pupil's surrender. But the truth is: the more powerfully the student introjects the teacher's story, the heavier the price the deluded student must later pay for that enchantment. This is not only a matter of personal or romantic involvement. We all know about famous graduate departments whose new Ph.Ds never write the books they once promised, so brilliantly have they been taught. The professor is always talking about, is exhibiting, his\herself. And the enthralled student's reading of that narrative is always misprision, a false witness not only to the teacher's grandiosity but to the student's own. Can *grandeur* ever be separated from *folie?*

To anyone who's been taught (let alone anyone who teaches) that connection should be, painfully, obvious. But what's surprising, and what occupies the remainder of this chapter, is the way in which culture conspires to cover up teaching's dark side, and particularly how it manages that cover-up through the construction of gender. Clearly, the one thing we cannot ever permit ourselves to teach is teaching itself.

Teaching and Gender

When W. H. Auden was a schoolmaster, he "threatened 'to cut my prick off' if the boys continued to fool about . . . next time a hullabaloo broke out in class, [he] opened his fly, brought out this [piece of butcher's] meat, and appeared to be actually carrying out the threat with a sharp knife" (Carpenter 112). Of course the immediately pliant, teachable boys cried out: "No, sir! Don't do it!" Auden, with his usual directness, had got clearly to the center, if not the heart, of the male pedagogic matter. The male teacher's sexuality is virtually the precondition of his success, germinating intellectual and emotional growth not only in the pupil but for the mentor himself. And our culture regularly celebrates his seductive story.

But teaching that is centered on a female instructor heads in exactly the opposite direction. Her teaching is also based in dynamic seduction. Nevertheless we demand, paradoxically, that the pupil resist her wiles. In fact, female-taught classes succeed in exact proportion to the intensity with which both male and female pupils frustrate or re-project the teacher's inevitably vitalizing, erotic allure. Leon Botstein, the president of Bard College (1993), is therefore only half right when he insists that "a sexual relationship between a teacher and a student is, in fact, at odds with the task of teaching" (*Harper's* 34). The odds are raised only when the teacher's a woman. Teaching's task *is* almost nothing but sexual, when the teacher's male.

Botstein formulates his rule in a *Harper's* magazine forum (September 1993) provoked by universities and colleges that have banned "student-professor romances" (33). In addition to President Botstein, the other faculty participants in the forum were: Joan Blythe, Associate Professor of English at the University of Kentucky; John Boswell, A. Whitney Griswold Professor of History at Yale; and William Kerrigan, Professor of English at the University of Massachusetts at Amherst. Kerrigan most enthusiastically (and controversially) framed the argument against the ban; that is, he argued *for* [male] professorial seduction:

There is a kind of student I've come across in my career who was working through something that only a professor could help her with. I'm talking about a female student who, for one reason or another, has unnaturally prolonged her virginity . . . there have been times when this virginity has been presented to me as something that I, not quite another man, half an authority figure, can handle—

a thing whose preciousness I realize . . . these relationships exist between adults and can be quite beautiful and genuinely transforming. It's very powerful sexually and psychologically, and because of that power, one can touch a student in a positive way. (36)

Here we have the self-righteous paradigm behind every form of professorial seduction, from the least to the most personal, even after we set aside the aging fantasies of archaic grandiosity, like "male and female students for twenty-five years . . . come to me right and left . . . take their clothes off in my office." We are left with a sexualized pedagogy that is essentially, and nobly, unself-interested, utilitarian, and therapeutic. Perhaps pleasurable too, but pleasure is by no means its justification.

This scenario our culture, at least, cannot retranscribe with the genders reversed. Of course, virginity is not supposed to be a problem for young men to offload. But should they be suffering from such burdens, and even if cheerleaders are far above their aspirations, it's unlikely they would need or want to rely on middle-aged female biologists and mathematicians to assist them. If they do, that dependence inevitably supplies a comic turn. Just recall the giggle-making conclusion to the '50s tearjerker *Tea and Sympathy*. It concludes with the housemaster's wife—played by that good and gracious *lady* Deborah Kerr—generously introducing the sexually uncertain schoolboy (John Kerr) to the fullness of his masculinity. But she has no illusions about how this action will be read. Unbuttoning her blouse, she implores: "When you think back on this—and you will—be kind." We snicker, but her anxiety is telling. She's making herself ridiculous; she knows it, and even the bland wimp that was John Kerr is highly unlikely in later years to think that what happened between them was "quite beautiful and genuinely transforming." We know how he tells that story. And it's not likely to be kind.

But what about the other, earlier tradition that presents the older, married woman as a young man's ideal erotic tutor: Madame de Renal to Julien Sorel, the Marshallin to Octavian? Obviously that scenario continues to resonate for us with considerable power; twenty-five years later everyone still recognizes jokes about Benjamin and Mrs. Robinson. But a mistress can seduce successfully only if she is not also the schoolmistress (though schoolmarms to cowboys are a very different matter in the deeply Oedipal Western). She can teach only if her only field is erotics. When she crosses disciplines, she becomes not merely dangerous but demonic: "rapacious and predatory" (Joan Blythe, *Harper's* 42).

This fundamental fear of and anger at academic women surfaces almost immediately; even in (but isn't it obvious one should say *especially* in) the self-congratulatorily seductive male professors of the forum:

KERRIGAN: " . . . A generation of academic feminists . . . push this legislation [banning student-professor romances] because in an era when a leer constitutes rape, they believe they are powerful enough to punish womanizing male colleagues."

BOSWELL: "Why are they so disturbed? Is this simply one of the few areas they can regulate?" (38)

Unsurprisingly, the only female professor in the group does not protest this sudden eruption of academic male contempt for academic women. Professor Blythe does mention her anger at being "cast . . . as a potential raptor" and thus *stripped* of her ability to teach (42). But she seems to know that her place in this forum depends on acting like one of the other good old academic boys, bellyaching about the "castration of the humanities" (38). Talking like a man is the only way our culture legitimates seducing like a teacher.

In fact, if he avoids sexuality, the teacher is likely to replace mastery with Masters and Johnson, the gloomier pages. We see this brilliantly explored in Randall Jarrell's coruscating, mordant, but inexplicably unread 1952 academic novel, *Pictures From An Institution*. At the end his nameless narrator, a poet-in-residence loosely modeled on Jarrell, has nothing left but to "throw away and throw away and throw away" (237). In his own words, he has "misjudged somehow" everything: Benton, the college at which he's been teaching, his students there, and his colleagues. As the passage continues, that "somehow" geminates. It becomes a *willed confusion* that preserves the narrator's opacity. But it also develops into an extended metaphor that seems to spot an unused or lapsed or—perhaps best—refused sexuality as the source of his failure: "There was no need for us [he and Benton] to judge each other, we said, we knew each other too well; we knew each other by heart. Then we yawned, and turned sleepily from each other, and sank back into sleep" (237). He's left only with his wife, whose "hello" is "small and far-off in the silence" (238).

What he hasn't got is the prize pupil, Constance, who has been carried off to Cape Cod by his best friend, the college's composer-in-residence, Gottfried Rosenbaum. Gottfried is both a paragon and a paradigm of seductive teaching. The naive Constance remarks of his composition class, with no sense of double entendre: "He goes over your piece as if he were you, and the next girl's piece as if he were her—she." Gottfried receives Constance as a sort of present from his elderly wife, Irene, because "Gottfried has no one . . . but you are . . . you are *really and truly*, Constance, all that a daughter would be for us if we had a daughter" (225). Jarrell packs a lot into that "really and truly"—not to mention that "all." Irene, we come to understand, has more or less purchased a "faux-daughter" in order to be replaced by her. She casts Constance as an Abishag to the musical Gottfried's David, a coupling to which the book explicitly refers earlier, the maiden enrolled to rekindle the dying fires of an aging authority (184).

In contrast, however, the narrator has refused all along not only his own sexuality but also any admission of the semi-incestuous triolism being happily soldered by the obliging wife for the pupil-child and her father-mentor. Instead, the narrator insistently stations Constance as "always, an almost unmixed blessing," a child who cannot, must not be seduced. "I could have said to her what, in *The Tales of Hoffman*, the old man says of his daughter: that she is *sage, modeste, et belle*" (133). He immediately observes parenthetically, in this novel of perpetually deconstructive parentheses: "(I suppose this should have made me distrust my feeling: the daughter that he says this about is, after all, an automaton of his own making.)" But then he goes on to elaborate only on the public, not the parenthetical statement. He preserves Constance's modesty, her "dreaming composure," her "essential absence or removedness"; that is, he fervently constructs an artificial incest taboo and then fiercely maintains its integrity. As a result, the narrator finds himself self-stationed permanently, frigidly, impotently, outside the sexual transactions that generate, in the novel and in the culture on which it draws, not only erotic fulfillment but pedagogic satisfaction. For men.

The reverse story plays itself out in tales like Emlyn Williams's prodigiously successful *The Corn Is Green*: adapted for Bette Davis in 1941 from a long-running play that had given Ethel Barrymore one of her greatest triumphs in New York, and a little earlier had starred Sybil Thorndike in London, the same Sybil Thorndike of whom Miss Jean Brodie observes, "*She* is the great actress and the rest of the cast have got the team spirit" (*Brodie* 116). The plot of *The Corn Is Green* follows a relentlessly virginal spinster teacher, Miss Moffat, to Edwardian Wales, where she uses a small inheritance to set up a free school for the children of the mines. There she discovers an enfant sauvage, Morgan Evans (John Dall), an illiterate young miner of striking potential. She works herself and her pupil exhaustively, finally even perjuring herself and her helpers to train him to win an Oxford scholarship.

Morgan Evans is clearly the romantic lead in this scenario, especially as played in the film by the handsome John Dall, already a man but easily twenty years younger than Davis. Just to underscore that point, we're even given an entirely gratuitous scene of Evans-Dall in the bath soaping away coalpit grime. (Take that, Laura Mulvey!) The spark between young laborer and older teacher clearly drives both plot and education. She excites him to learn, and precisely because she succeeds, he gains a brilliant future, while she must be discarded and punished. To make this separation happen, the story redirects the hero's sexuality from Miss Moffat to her young and vulgar maid, whom Evans impregnates during a drunken rage at being "the schoolmistress's little dog." When the pregnancy is discovered, the schoolmistress decides to adopt the child as her own, convinced that her pupil can never fulfill his promise if he marries young. She even insists that her prodigy see neither child nor teacher again. And so in the film's final moments, as the singing miners ("Men of Harlech," of course) bear a triumphant Evans through the snow toward the train, Oxford, and hegemony, Miss Moffat is framed against a window, chilled, isolated, and, even in her own judgment, guilty. It is a guilt she even seems to embrace. In the final moment her cook, the infant's real grandmother, gleefully orders the teacher to come down into the kitchen to nurse the child, a comedown she'd better get used to. And the teacher responds: "Moffat, my girl, you mustn't be clumsy this time."

Even Miss Moffat's dreary prospect seems inviting when we contrast it to the teacher-student situation in Muriel Spark's enormously popular and successful *The Prime of Miss Jean Brodie* (1961): novel, play, film, and television series. Here both teacher and pupil are female, and, therefore, if the pupil is to survive, she must not only resist and abandon but actually destroy the teacher. Paradoxically, nowhere does the patriarchal suspicion of female sexuality police more vigilantly than in this feminist text, with its extraordinary proto-feminist heroine.

British literature, that treasure trove of false consciousness, provides few more winning or winsome displays of false witness than the novel's early, enchantingly duplicitous scenes of instruction. They leave us all yearning to be so lusciously deluded. The little girls sit under the mellow shade of a Keatsian autumn. They prop schoolbooks in their laps to deceive their headmistress, something at which, like the Dead Poets' boys, they become only more skilled in their years as the crème de la crème. And they listen, day after dazzling day, dazed and seduced by Miss Brodie's hazily sexual confabulations. "If anyone comes along," said Miss Brodie, "in the course of the following lesson, remember that it is the hour for English grammar. Meantime I will tell you a little of my life when I was younger than I am now, though six years older than the man himself" (*Brodie* 19). By the tale's end, "Tears had already started to drop from Sandy's little pig-like eyes and Sandy's tears now affected her friend Jenny, later famous in the school for her beauty, who gave a sob and groped up the leg of her knickers for her handkerchief" (21). As Miss Brodie promises, and the plot proves, girls gotten at such "an impression-able age" are the teacher's "for life" (164).

At the novel's crisis, Miss Brodie, in a fascinating form of transference, becomes "obsessed by the need for Rose [Stanley, one of the set] to sleep with the man she herself was in love with," the Art teacher, Mr. Lloyd (175). Her plans are foiled when Sandy Stranger—she of the "pig's eyes" in the earlier quote—sleeps with Lloyd herself, and then "betrays" Miss Brodie to the headmistress, who has long been seeking a way to rid herself of that "advanced and seditious" (39) instructor. Though Rose Stanley escapes unharmed, the novel seems to insist that Miss Brodie, though technically innocent, is nevertheless culpable. We see the novel's parallel between the older woman's early and constant erotic display of herself and the exhibitionist who exposes himself to Sandy's friend Jenny, "the terrible beast . . . by the water of Leith" (100–101). All the final disgrace in some way rightly redounds to Jean Brodie. But we also feel little of the admiration for Sandy the betrayer that we are instructed to feel for the hapless, would-be-heroic miner, Morgan Evans. We can see Sandy as traumatized by her premature induction into the older woman's erotic history and imagination. But she also becomes mean-spiritedly revengeful and, finally, paranoid, as she turns from adoring acolyte to moral police-man, obsessed with fabricating "incriminating documents" against her mentor. Sandy finishes the novel as a cloistered nun clutching the bars of her grill whenever anyone, friend or foe, comes to her enclosure. Fiction offers us no more gripping image of the price everyone pays, teacher and pupils, for the instructor's seductive grandeur.

The first and last lines of the novel pay a kind of forced tribute to the great teacher: "There was a Miss Jean Brodie in her prime." Sandy's accomplishments root in the teacher's extraordinary powers of inspiration, for good as well as evil. But when one turns to director Peter Weir's enormously popular and appalling film *Dead Poets Society*, we find no comparable balance being struck. Here the teacher John Keating is only the, and the only, hero.

Weir, of course, came to international fame by loathing school. His film *Picnic at Hanging Rock* made it seem as though disappearing in a desert outcrop was infinitely preferable to continuing to live on in a girls' boarding school (at least in Australia). With *Dead Poets,* he generates a comparable indictment of American boys' boarding schools. On the first day of classes, the boys go through a series of numbing, humbling vignettes of traditional instruction in science, mathematics, Latin. Eventually they arrive at English. A pause. And then the new, clearly non-agonistic English teacher, Mr. Keating (Robin Williams), makes his entrance, humming the Russian Imperial Anthem "God Save the Tsar," insisting that the better sort of student will address him as "my Captain." He refuses to teach in a "class-room, with its paraphernalia of study, . . . in which the wings of poesy cannot readily beat" (Newbolt). Instead, he leads the boys to a kind of trophy room filled with glass cases of Edwardian team pictures.

Poignantly, the film cuts from the young faces pressed against the glass, improbably peachy faces—this is the fifties, well before tetracycline—to the spectacularly spotless faces that stare back from the tarnished frames. Keating tells the boys to listen to their predecessors, who are, he insists, "now fertilizing daffodils," to hear them saying what he has just told the boys himself: Carpe Diem. A paradigmatic moment of the new teaching, everything the Newbolt reporters could desire: poetry "communicated to the students in such a way that they will experience it rightly" (Newbolt). But that rightly is, of course, Keating's own "living voice," in Williams's sepulchral whisper, his "actual impersonation." He croons the phrase behind them, initiating their leaders into a long seduction in which they seize not their day but his. Ultimately, they reject their parents and their own lives to recreate his past, his friends, his dead society, warped into the delusion that by reliving his life they will begin to live their own. Quoting Thoreau, Keating promises to teach his followers how to suck the marrow out of life. He winds up sucking the marrow from the boys.

Like Jean Brodie, Keating also creates a homosocial microcosm within and against the larger world of the school, the boys orbiting around him under, as he says, "the picture of Uncle Walt" Whitman. But in contrast to the early chapters of Spark's delicate novel, Keating's seduction seems coarse and heavy-handed, like most things issuing from the mind of Mork. When his prize pupil, Neill (Robert Sean Leonard), finally tries to stand up to his father, he insists "I've got to tell you what I feel." But the boy can only follow up that claim by saying "Nothing," a sort of voided Cordelia. He is only Keating's shadow, and when Keating's light is blocked—"Keating, you stay away from my son," the father barks, surfacing the erotic menace that plays peek-a-boo throughout the film— the boy finds himself with no alternative but suicide. His more fortunate friends are merely beaten, disgraced, or expelled. Certainly, no one is led into a promised land.

But *Dead Poets Society*, and the enormous audiences that made it popular, cannot acknowledge that Keating is its villain. They—to save appearances, I won't say we—persist in seeing the teacher solely as the hero and his seduction as stimulus rather than manipulation. He leaves the film acclaimed, as the last stalwarts defy the headmaster, climbing up on their desks and calling out "O Captain, My Captain." We literally see the final frame, the adoring face of the ultimate ephebe, through his eyes. Of course, the film's success derived from its ability to pander to the adolescent and post-adolescent narcissism with which this chapter began. But to accomplish that seduction, it required, ready to hand and handle, the culture's nostalgic myth of the innocently seductive teacher. We might then want to claim that Spark's distant and dispassionate narrator tells the counter-tale to scenarios like that of *Dead Poets Society*. Urging us to resist the dangerously lovable teacher, Spark emerges as counter-peda-gogue, a social and intellectual critic alert to the institutionalized nature of school- and classroom erotics, and to the questionable models of power incorporated within even the highest ideals of education. (Among many other things, the novel is an incisive reading of the connection between the Depression and Fascism, and between Fascism and "high" culture.) But her novel also seems to buy heavily into the polarized and sexually politicized structures at the core of the teaching institution. After all, no one considers punishing, let alone betraying, Mr. Lloyd, the girls' actual seducer.

This dark fear about a novel and a novelist I love becomes even grimmer after Mrs. Spark's discussion of the original of Jean Brodie in her recent autobiography, *Curriculum Vitae*. Miss Christina Kay was Muriel Camberg's own beloved teacher at James Gillespie's school. "Miss Kay was nothing like Miss Brodie," Spark insists, "she was far above and beyond her Brodie counterpart. If she could have met Miss Brodie, Miss

Kay would have put the fictional character firmly in her place" (*Curriculum* 57). But why, one is then forced to ask, did *you* put Miss Brodie in Miss Kay's place in the first place! Why not pay this powerful mentor the compliment of an accurate portrait? Why lose the opportunity to paint for once a powerful female teacher who leads without seduction? There is a sense throughout this section of the memoir that Spark is using it to apologize to Miss Kay. But the autobiography nevertheless ensures our unhappy sense that, like Sandy Stranger within the novel, Muriel Spark, in writing the novel, betrayed the beloved teacher—and without at least Sandy's apparent cause. That betrayal roots, in part, in a dynamic driven by Muriel Spark's own formation, a process that has everything to do with a formidable and ultimately successful struggle against masochism. But for all of the importance, courage, and style of that particular history, her novel and her memoir also return us to the encompassing cultural problem generated by the oddly torqued narrative of the pedagogue. Returns us, that is, to the problem that surrounds us and is us.

The deaths of children that conclude *Dead Poets* and *Jean Brodie* make seductive/destructive teachers seem exceptional. But it's arguable that these extreme fictions are generated to some degree precisely to cover the less traumatic—but not for that reason undamaging—seductions that, as *Harper's* forum insists, every campus hosts. The (perhaps) majority of us merely fail our students, even, or perhaps especially, those whom we pass. But from the official Newbolt Report through elite fiction to popular film, our entire contemporary discourse of teaching percolates through un-self-supervised and underregulated, even institutionally supported, seduction. Thinly disguised, seduction shapes the official rhetoric of course critiques and teaching evaluations, which in turn impact decisions of remuneration, evaluation, promotion, and even retention. At every level, students expect from, and demand of, themselves and their instructors performances that match those reified either heroically in films like *Dead Poets,* or demonically by moronic incompetents who teach in films like the unspeakable *Ferris Bueller's Day Off.* And not least insidiously, instructors represent themselves, their success, their failure, their capacity or incapacity to teach, through internalized models of education generated by the valorization of false witness.

Until we reform this discourse, we continue to reel and stumble under the rogue star that dogs all our courses, fall, spring and summer, with no alternative, perhaps, but a self-diminishing sense that we should really not try too hard to succeed at teaching, this odd and intimate business.

Works Cited

American Psychiatric Association. *Diagnostic and Statistical Manual of Mental Disorders DSM-III-R.* Washington, D.C.: American Psychiatric Association, 1987.

Carpenter, Humphrey. *W. H. Auden: A Biography.* Boston: Houghton Mifflin, 1981.

"*Harper's* Forum: The New Rules About Sex on Campus." *Harper's,* September 1993, 32–42.

Jarrell, Randall. *Pictures From An Institution.* 1952. New York: Avon, 1980.

Miller, Jacques-Alain, ed. *The Seminar of Jacques Lacan, Book I: Freud's Papers on Technique 1953–1954.* Trans. with notes by John Forrester. New York: Norton, 1991.

Newbolt Report: The Teaching of English in England. London: H.M.S.O., 1926.

Ong, Walter, S.J. *Fighting For Life: Contest, Sexuality, and Consciousness.* Ithaca: Cornell University Press, 1981.

Spark, Muriel. *Curriculum Vitae.* Boston: Houghton Mifflin, 1993.

———. *The Prime of Miss Jean Brodie.* 1961. New York: New American Library, 1984.

REBECCA A. POPE

Hayley, Roz, and Me

Well, let me ask you this, do you believe that teachers who for years, for decades, for centuries, explained to children that homosexuality is intolerable; do you believe that textbooks that purged literature and falsified history in order to exclude various types of sexual behavior, have not caused ravages at least as serious as a homosexual teacher who speaks about homosexuality and who can do no more harm than explain a given reality, a lived experience?

The fact that a teacher is a homosexual can only have electrifying and intense effects on students to the extent that the rest of society refuses to admit the existence of homosexuality. (*Foucault Live* 215–26)

To my great relief, I don't fall in love with younger women. Life as a semi-out lesbian feminist teacher[1] in a conservative and Church-affiliated institution is challenging enough without having to worry about falling in love, or lust, with any of my students. My relief is many-layered, and both personal and professional; I'm happy with my partner of ten years and wouldn't want to jeopardize my life with her; I'm not eager to put my job at risk; I'm not the sort who thrives on emotional confusion. And then there are the practicalities—in Elizabeth Bowen's enigmatic novel *Eva Trout,* a clergyman asks Eva about her relationship with a teacher named Mrs. Arble. "What—exactly—took place?" asks Father Clavering-Haight. "She abandoned me. She betrayed me," Eva responds. He continues, "Had you a sapphic relationship?" "What?" she asks. Undaunted, he presses on, "Did you exchange embraces of any kind?" "No," Eva answers, "She was always in a hurry" (203).

Some years ago, after Stonewall, but before being gay became, as *Cosmo* and *Newsweek* now assure me, fashionable, I was a student at a Catholic women's college. The intense and conflicted (nonsexual) relationship I had with a professor there has, I suspect, left me fairly well defended against the temptation of teacher-student intimacies. My tale is a familiar one. As the ambitious and favored senior of a professor famously in rebellion against the intellectual mediocrity of the institution,

I was eager to please and flattered by her attention. What a presence she had in the classroom. In her trademark black dress and pearls, her graying hair in a tight chignon, she was distant, demanding, sophisticated—like no woman I had ever met. Certainly not like the nuns, who were unfailingly nice and nurturing and thus simple, it seemed to me, and consequently uninteresting. Long Fridays at off-campus libraries—I was, of course, her research assistant—ended with restaurant meals and plenty of wine, sensory pleasures beyond my student's budget. During these times the boundaries and institutional roles I depended on to order our feelings and behavior seemed suspended. I tried hard to maintain them and was thrilled to transgress them. Now, as a teacher myself, and thus familiar with feeling ill-paid and unappreciated, I can make some deductions about what possible pleasures and pains my undergraduate adoration may have given to her. Then, as her student, I was in what I call my Victor Frankenstein stage of psychosexual development—ever eager to channel erotic energy into intellectual projects so as not to recognize its unconventional nature. Our relationship was to me a heady brew of intellectual stimulation and gratified longing, for contact, for approval, for intellectual respect and encouragement. I drank to intoxication; I'm not sure how I managed to finish my senior thesis.

The relationship ended, just before my graduation, with anger, confusion, and mutual recrimination. The hangover lasted a long time. I'm not much interested in assessing blame and complicity. Rather, what interests me is that this narrative and minor variations on it are so common. How many academics—and I count myself among these—would have become lawyers had they not fallen in love with a teacher and transformed desire for that teacher into the much safer desire to *be* a teacher? Many women can tell stories of extravagant crushes on a favorite female teacher or a particular teaching nun. Indeed, falling in love with a female student or teacher has been, for a number of lesbians I know, the way they figured out that they were lesbians. (Lesbians, by the way, tend to be very scrupulous about their power when they have it—a function, no doubt, of being so often on the wrong end of power; all of the women I know who have fallen in love with students waited until those students were graduates before they slept with them, if they slept with them at all.) And while the pain and confusion that closes my narrative may be a fairly common end for these sorts of stories, I want to argue that this close is not merely common but conventional, that our reading and film watching teach us that close relations between female teachers and students generate not new teachers but pain, monstrosity, and, sometimes, even murder. To what extent, I wonder now, did these conventional representations create expectations of disaster that helped determine the outcome of my own story? And even though I now recognize the regulatory agenda of these narratives, do they still operate in my own avoidance of much out-of-office contact with my own female students?

In other words, where is the girls' school version of James Hilton's *Good-bye, Mr. Chips,* and why is Miss Brodie the female teacher we know best through literature and film? Cultural understanding of the homoerotic crushes or "raves" of schoolgirls for older students or teachers changed in England and America during the late nineteenth and early twentieth centuries. What had been understood as energies which, when "properly" harnessed, could be trained to public duty and compulsory heterosexuality became—under the gaze of the sexologists, and thanks to increasing public concern that middle-class women educated in single-sex boarding schools and colleges were rejecting the traditional roles of wife and mother—deviant and pathological desires.[2] Of course similar anxieties existed about male/male bonds. Indeed, Hilton's text, published in England in 1933 and in the United States a year later, carefully addresses these anxieties. Lest we misread Chips's long bachelorhood, his discomfort with women, his devotion to the boys, his "high-pitched voice," and his problems maintaining discipline ("Take up a firm attitude from the beginning," the headmaster counsels), Chips is given, for a brief interval, a wife (4, 7). Lest we find suspiciously unmanly his "mantelpiece crowded with fixture cards and signed photographs of boys and men," or sissified his fussy way of making tea ("All that fuss about making the tea—a typical bachelor," a boy notes), Chips is given not just any wife, but a younger woman with "New Woman" tendencies (19, 21). And if this is not enough to assure us of Chips's fundamental heterosexuality and courageous virility, the new wife, Katherine, becomes quickly and conveniently pregnant. Just as quickly, and perhaps conveniently, Katherine and the child die, and Chips returns to his bachelor digs to become, as he claims on his deathbed, father to thousands of boys.

The narrative stresses Katherine's attempts to humanize Chips, as she encourages him to unbend himself and to be more compassionate with misbehaving boys. But clearly her primary function is to heterosexualize him, even as she argues for a more tolerant (for its time) attitude toward

schoolboy homoeroticism and against Chips's inclination to have one of
the boys expelled for it (45–49). We might say that here again Chips
has "discipline" problems, and as Katherine recoups him for the cause
of heterosexual masculinity, she keeps him from policing too tyrannically
the very boundary that, were it not for her presence, he would appear
to straddle. But it is not for this moment of potential progressivism or
the book's hint of homoeroticism that Chips is remembered and beloved
by generations of Brookfield boys, or that Hilton's novel has been beloved by readers and viewers of its many film versions. As the nostalgia
of the title implies, Brookfield loves Chips because he is a relic, "pre-
War" the boys call him, or, we might say, mid-Victorian—a remnant of
times more traditional and hierarchical, when England had an empire,
and before medical and legal discourses had constructed the homosexual
identity (103).

Boys' schools and men's colleges, of course, trained students for the
exercise of patriarchal power. Women's institutions—ostensibly supposed
to train their students to submit to and reproduce that power—also
created the opportunity for erotic and political subversion of that power.
Responses to this possibility from conservative novelists, which cast girls'
schools and the romantic friendships that thrived there as destructive, go
back at least as far as Clemence Dane's (Winifred Ashton's) 1917 *Regi-
ment of Women*. By the '30s, Winifred Holtby was a minority voice when
she argued for the positive effects of raves or *Schwarmerei* in her novel
South Riding (1936). Echoing the arguments of female educators who
saw raves as an energy that could be harnessed for good, the headmistress
in that novel declares, "I control them all by monopoly and then absorb
them. It's quite simple. We needs must love the highest when we see it. I
take good care to be the highest in my school" (110).[3] Few writers, it
appears, were willing to "save" female teachers invested in their students,
to give them, as Chips is given, a pass to pass. For example, a few months
after the April 1934 publication of *Good-bye, Mr. Chips* in the United
States, another well-known school story, Lillian Hellman's *The Children's
Hour*, premiered in New York. Liberal readings of the play cast it as a
call for tolerance and a critique of prejudice, a reading of the dangers of
moral panics and a lesson about how such panics can start—what flimsy
and interested evidence can be used to incite them—and what destruction
they wreak in innocent lives. It's not an accident that a much-publicized
film version of this 1930s play appeared in the '60s, when the United
States was recovering from, and in some quarters at least, trying to make

sense of, the McCarthy-era witch hunts of Communists and the panicked purges of homosexuals. But I also want to argue that it's not ironic or coincidental that the tendency to read the play as a more generalized political protest against authoritarian thought police has the effect of diminishing the likelihood that readers/viewers will take seriously the possibility that homophobia is political and that it does destroy lives. Allegorical readings enhance lesbian invisibility.

The fact that Martha, the teacher accused by a student of lesbianism, didn't, after all, *do* anything appears to solidify the liberal reading of the play. "You are guilty of nothing," stresses Karen, the teacher with whom Martha runs the school (79). And while this twist might add poignance and tragic irony for some viewers/readers, such pleasures of interpretation are luxuries for gay persons, who must worry, as the play vividly—I want to say deliberately—reminds us, that we can lose our livelihood, not because of something that we do or fail to do at work, but for what we "are." Martha's story, in other words, illustrates the cultural shift from understanding homosexuality as a class of acts to constructing it as an identity, and outlines the disciplinary possibilities that shift makes possible. After confessing to Karen and herself that she has indeed loved Karen "the way they said," Martha provides a self-description painful in its self-loathing and frightening in its totalizing and essentializing character: "I feel *all* dirty" (78, 79, my italics). Disciplinary regimes depend on identity categories. Martha takes up the demonized identity, but, ironically, through her suicide proves herself to be the very thing she has been accused of not being, an upholder of the conventional moral order. Dead, she is once again a good teacher.

With Martha dispatched, life can return to "normal." A remorseful Mrs. Tilford reappears; she now recognizes her horrid little grandchild's villainies. No longer a moral crusader, Mrs. Tilford is penitently eager to help Karen reestablish her professional life and her heterosexual life (Karen had been engaged to Mrs. Tilford's nephew). And while the close of the play is somber, there is some hope that Karen's life is not forever ruined. We are, it seems, supposed to take comfort in Mrs. Tilford's guilty conscience and Karen's possibility for future happiness. Not quite the close of comedy, but close. This ending, however, diminishes Martha's status as tragic victim, a status on which the liberal reading depends. As the exiled one, Martha occupies the place of the villain in conventional narrative; she is positioned as the transgressive/evil force that must be exorcised as a prelude to happy and morally unambiguous closure.

Martha may not have done anything, but Karen is "innocent" in both deed and desire, and for this she is, after much trial and testing (after all, when Martha confesses her desire to Karen, Karen rejects that desire) given the reward of a future. As the school setting emphasizes, there's a lesson here.[4]

Thus *The Children's Hour*, despite its surface progressive politics, is as well a cautionary tale about the necessity of self-monitoring and the closet. When Martha is, as it were, in the closet to herself—"It's funny; it's all mixed up. There's something in you and you don't know it and you don't do anything about it. Suddenly a child gets bored and lies—and there you are, seeing it for the first time"—she is safe from the mental anguish she exhibits when she decides that she "is" a "lesbian" (79). That very ignorance, however, makes her vulnerable to displaying behavior that can be read by others as evidence of her "lesbian nature." In the world of the play's politics, it's a tragedy if your desire is homoerotic because it makes you vulnerable to the bigotries of others, but you must accept the pain of that knowledge about your desire so you can closer scrutinize yourself and better closet yourself. No wonder Martha blows her brains out.

Or perhaps reading Radclyffe Hall's *The Well of Loneliness* made Martha suicidal; it very nearly did me. By the '30s, the notion that lesbianism was pathological was well-entrenched, and in Hall's novel a literary model for lesbianism as painful and doomed became widely, famously, available. Thus fatality is everywhere in Anglo-American narratives of women's education of the '30s and '40s. Dorothy Strachey Bussy's *Olivia* was published under the pseudonym "Olivia" by Leonard Woolf's Hogarth Press in 1949, some sixteen years after Bussy wrote it, apparently as an offering to Gide, whose works she translated into English. The tale is generated from her own experience at Marie Souvestre's school at Fountainbleau (Bussy later taught at Souvestre's school in Wimbledon, where one of their pupils was Eleanor Roosevelt). Olivia's first-person narration retrospectively recounts her attachment to Mlle. Julie (purportedly modeled on Marie Souvestre), who ran a school with her longtime companion Mlle. Cara, and Cara's mysterious death after she and Julie, bitterly estranged, had completed arrangements for the division of their property and Julie's departure from France.

Bussy's narrative employs many of the conventions of girls' school tales: an adolescent girl who, if she has a home at all, finds it drab and confining, and who finds her mother, if she has one, inadequate as both a nurturer and a model for her own womanhood; a charismatic teacher, not necessarily nurturing and often given to conflicting behavior toward the girl (affectionate one day, distant or angry the next), who makes her one in a line of favorites. The teacher introduces the girl to new worlds of learning and realms of feeling. Indeed, much of Olivia's learning and appreciating, as well as her willingness to work at her lessons, are effects of her attraction to Julie—"Those evenings have coloured for me all French literature. How many masterpieces she read us! How many she clothed in the beauty of her voice! How many she passed on to us infused and vivified by the zest of her wit, by the spirit of her genius," Olivia enthuses (79–80). A teacher herself, Bussy understands that eroticism can sometimes be, as it were, a learning aid, a teaching tool. Passion attracts and motivates. Some of the most effective teaching and motivating is, in effect, a process of seduction, whereby the teacher hopes to bring the student to a love of the subject by displaying her own passion for it. Not all students love learning for its own sake. We make the subject attractive by making our own personas attractive.[5]

Olivia's narration focuses on her own feelings and their quick transformations between hope and dread, ecstasy and despair, longing and resentment. The predominant note is pain and confusion. Olivia freely admits her ignorance of Mlle. Julie's thoughts and feelings, although she is always trying to read and understand, with little success, her place in them. In the introduction to the tale, the narrator (is it Bussy who is speaking here or "Olivia"?) is similarly worried and conflicted, desiring to claim importance for the experience and feelings in her narrative:

I have condensed into a few score of pages the history of a whole year when life was, if not at its fullest, at any rate at its most poignant—that year when every vital experience was the first, or, if you Freudians object, the year when I first became conscious of myself, of love and pleasure, of death and pain, and when every reaction to them was as unexpected, as amazing, as *involuntary* as the experience itself. (9)

But she is also concerned that it will be read as an indulgent and sentimental account of adolescent romantic angst.[6] And not just adolescent romantic angst; Les Avons school is a hothouse of erotic and professional intrigue. The mademoiselles had been happily coupled until the arrival of a new German mistress, Frau Riesener, who divides them by convincing Cara that she has been ill-used by Julie and the students. By the time Olivia arrives, both students and staff are divided into Julie and Cara camps. Feeling rejected and hurt by Cara's complaints, Julie apparently seeks consolation in close friendships with an Italian mistress and select students. In response, Cara becomes a professional invalid who turns herself over to the ministrations of the officious Frau. Longing, bitterness, anger, pathology—it's enough to make any girl look again at the comforts and pleasures promised by the het romance myth. Unable to bear the situation any longer, Julie decides to sell Cara her share of the school and start a new one in Canada. Shortly after the contracts are signed, Cara dies from an overdose of her sleeping draught. The coroner rules the death accidental, and the blame is placed on a young woman in whose care Frau Riesener had left Cara, but there is a strong possibility, recognized by all, that Cara had either committed suicide or was murdered by Frau Riesener (the sole beneficiary in Cara's new, post-sale will). Julie dies a few years later in Canada, and Olivia never gets from her the recognition and affection she had so craved.

It's hard to know what to make of this. If Frau Riesener is a murderer, what looks like a tale about the dangers of female passion becomes instead a tale about the destructiveness of greed. If Cara is a suicide, *Olivia* is a cautionary tale that figures lesbianism as painful and, finally, self-destructive. If Cara's death is an accident, *Olivia* still figures lesbianism as doom, and implies that lesbian teachers recruit. However we look at it, one thing is certain—Olivia is well out of it, saddened but saved by Julie's rejection, self-exile, and death. What makes this conventional and moralizing end so odd and emphatically disciplinary is that Dorothy Bussy must have known better. She knew and lived another, less tragic and violent, end to this purportedly autobiographical narrative. In other words, if Dorothy Strachey was enamored of her teacher Marie Souvestre, however painful and conflicted that passion may have been, her later history as a teacher in Souvestre's Wimbledon school duplicates the very alternative narrative I outlined earlier: desire for the teacher is transformed into a desire to be the teacher.[7]

Similarly filled with fatality and ambivalence is Josephine Tey's *Miss Pym Disposes* (1947), in which a student at the all-female Leys Physical Training College falls from a gymnastics boom and dies of a fractured skull.[8] The coroner rules Barbara Rouse's death an accident, but visiting lecturer and psychologist Lucy Pym discovers evidence which suggests that someone had tampered with the apparatus. Her prime suspect is the hard-working, tightly wound, and emotionally vulnerable Mary Innes, universally regarded as the College's top senior, and universally thought to have been robbed of a prestigious post-graduation position at the top girls' school in Britain when the headmistress recommended Rouse for the job instead. Lucy Pym decides, despite advice to report what she knows and let God dispose, to confront Innes with the evidence. Innes confesses responsibility for Rouse's death, and promises to atone for it by doing exactly what she had desperately hoped to avoid—returning to her drab and unexciting hometown and working at the orthopedic hospital there. The magnitude of this penitential sacrifice, to Innes's eyes, is suggested by her summation of the bargain: "My life for hers" (198). Only after this bargain has been struck and her silence pledged does Lucy Pym discover that while Innes may have felt responsible for Rouse's injury, she did not tamper with the apparatus. Rather, Mary Innes's special friend—all the students consider Mary and Pamela "Beau" Nash a couple—engineered the accident. Beau apparently hoped that an injured Rouse would clear the way for Mary. Lucy Pym keeps her pledge to remain silent and thus Beau suffers no consequences. Thinking about giving up psychology, Lucy Pym returns to London.

Detectives in mystery fiction do occasionally decide to take justice into their own hands and let an offender go free; even Holmes does this. Lucy Pym's decision to keep evidence from the police is perhaps made more palatable for some readers because Rouse is isolated—an orphan who even looks like a "stray"—and not particularly sympathetic or morally upright herself (Lucy discovers a cheat sheet Rouse used during her final exams). Only the headmistress mourns her.

The plot invites a reading of the murder as a symptom of the pathology and, given the context, criminality of Mary and Beau's relationship, a sign that their transgressive relationship has generated further, fatal, excess and transgression. A number of details, however, combine to unsettle this reading. First is the text's stress on Beau's sense of easy entitlement. Unlike Mary, she comes from a wealthy family and has the confident bearing of one used to having things go her way. Her butchy nickname, then, has as much to do with class as her gender performance. Lucy finds this upper-class and masculine bearing attractive, but there is a suggestion that this attractive confidence may be problematic. For example, after Beau's mother tells Lucy that "Pam has never worked hard in her life," the narrator interrupts their conversation with the ironic observation: "No. Everything had been served to Beau on a plate. It was miraculous that she turned out so charming" (164). In other words, while plenty of red herrings point to middle-class Mary's emotional vulnerability as the source of the crime, Beau's privilege and consequent inexperience with disappointment play a major part in her decision to arrogate to herself the job of seeing that Mary gets the reward she deserves. A crime committed for passion is recast as a crime of class arrogance.

Second, the college community and Lucy Pym herself are remarkably accepting of Mary and Beau's relationship, and little before the revelation of Beau's guilt suggests that the text sees raves among students as a pathology that must be either rooted out or suppressed. No one sees their special friendship as a threat to school harmony, female duty, or compulsory heterosexuality. Lucy Pym's status as lionized author of a best-selling book on psychology seems to endow her tolerance with a special and exemplary authority, and her popularity with "the intellectuals tired of Freud and Company" suggests that her work is a departure from psychoanalytic theory, and, perhaps, its pathologizing of female homoeroticism. Indeed, watching Beau's tender care of the depressed Mary after the announcement that the prized post had gone to Barbara Rouse, Lucy Pym wishes she had as attentive and considerate a friend as Beau.

To what extent the exemplary status of Lucy's acceptance of Mary and Beau's relationship is compromised by Lucy's later error is uncertain. This is further complicated by the fact that Lucy once had a schoolgirl crush on Henrietta Hodge, the Leys Headmistress: "the little fourth-form rabbit [Lucy], had admired the sixth form Henrietta extravagantly" (2). But this early partiality does not compromise the adult Lucy's judgment of her friend. Indeed, after Lucy concludes that Mary must have sabotaged the apparatus, she blames Henrietta for the tragedy:

And who in the first place had brought that catastrophe?
  Henrietta. Henrietta with her mule-like preference for her inferior favorite. She wondered if Henrietta was sharing Innes's vigil. Henrietta who had come back from [the hospital] so strangely thin and old-looking . . . .
  She had been truly sorry for her friend, bereft of someone she had—loved? Yes, loved she supposed. Only love could have blinded her to Rouse's defects. Bereft; and afraid for her beloved Leys. She had been truly moved by her suffering. But she could not help the thought that but for Henrietta's own action none of this would have happened. (182)

Again the reading of women's attachments as necessarily destructive and pathological is unsettled. Henrietta's fault is not in loving a student, but in loving the wrong student, an unworthy student. What might have been cast as an unnatural or pathological attachment symptomatic of a deviant nature is instead marked out as an error in judgment, a wrong choice.

One of the more remarkable features of Tey's conflicted text, especially for its time, is the way it takes for granted that romantic attachments do occur in women's educational communities. In other words, while the novel warns of possible dangers when judgments are faulty, it also acknowledges these relations as a common, ordinary feature of girls' school culture, and, by implication, casts erotic attachment between women as—if I can use so ideologically loaded a word—natural.

Whatever the ambiguities, however, the student is dead and the teacher's love for her is somehow responsible. And however able I am to manipulate the counter-discourses as a literary critic, besotted students can hardly be consoled.

The flip side of these fatality narratives are narratives in which passion for the teacher is disciplined and placed in the service of traditional female duties like wifehood or nunhood (nunhood being, of course, a socially acceptable, even elevated, alternative to marriage).[9] Edna O'Brien's short story "Sister Imelda" (1981) captures the ambivalence over teacher-student affections I have been tracing here, flirts with the possibility of transcending passion by devotion to a transcendent power, but finally refuses to resolve the ambivalence with either melodramatic fatality or romanticized renunciation of desire for a "greater good" or "higher cause." The narrator is a student at an Irish convent school, and the tale opens with her return for her final year. For the narrator and her friend Baba (the tale's voice of unimaginative, if sometimes perceptive, convention and conventional heterosexuality), "The convent . . . seemed more a prison than ever—for after our spell in the outside world we all felt very much older and more sophisticated" (124). Thus we are never completely sure how much the narrator's keen sense of the new young nun's suppressed eroticism is observed and how much projected. This sensualizing of Sister Imelda may also be an example of the kind of speculation about a nun's (especially one who is young and/or attractive) past and private life, the weaving of fantasy narratives about desire, romance, tragedy, and renunciation that is so conventional a part of Catholic school culture:

Her pale, slightly long face I saw as formidable, but her eyes were different, being blue-black and full of verve. Her lips were very purple, as if she had put puce pencil on them. They were the lips of a woman who might sing in a cabaret, and unconsciously she had formed the habit of turning them inward, as if she, too, was aware of their provocativeness. . . . Some days, when her eyes were flashing, she looked almost profane and made me wonder what events inside the precincts

of the convent caused her to be suddenly so excited. She might have been a girl
going to a dance, except for her habit. (124–25)

Distance and mystery generate desire and narrative. The narrator is
fascinated; Baba, on the other hand, speculates that there is "Something
wrong in her upstairs department" (125).

The intimacy between the narrator and Sister Imelda is from the
start an electrifying mix of pleasure, pain, longing, and dread: "I found
myself becoming dreadfully happy" (127). While walking together on
the convent grounds, the nun does a "reckless thing" and picks a chry-
santhemum and offers it to the narrator to smell; in the classroom,
the narrator's inability to grasp geometry drives Sister Imelda into a
rage and she throws an eraser at her (127). The narrator reads the
outburst as a sign of her special status: "I knew dimly that it was as
much to do with liking as it was with dislike. In me then there came
a sort of speechless tenderness for her" (128). Ambivalence even marks
the small gifts the nun gives her. The recklessly picked and bestowed
flower (ironically, perhaps prophetically, lacking in scent) and freshly
baked jam tarts left over from cooking class—gifts that gratify the senses
and give pleasure—are countered by a holy picture inscribed with a
religious verse and a miniature prayer book—gifts that speak of transcendent duty and the mortification of desire. One of her final gifts, a
holy medal "slipped" into the pocket of the narrator's gym frock, epito-
mizes this ambivalence (137).

I am suggesting, then, that we can never be quite sure what Sister
Imelda is about. The nature of the narrator's conflicted feelings is trans-
parent by comparison. There is the pleasure of receiving extra attention
and being the source of another's pleasure; the satisfaction of finding
someone in authority who, in the narrator's eyes at least, is reckless and
defiant; there is the fearful thrill of transgressing boundaries by their
intimacy. Sister Imelda watches her eat the jam tarts "as if she herself
derived some peculiar pleasure from it, whereas I was embarrassed about
the pastry crumbling. . . . It was one of the most awkward yet thrilling
moments I had lived, and inherent in the pleasure was the terrible sense
of danger. Had we been caught, she, no doubt, would have had to make
massive sacrifice" (130). One hopes, however, that the lesson the narrator
brings away from this scene, as well as the eraser scene, is generated from
transitory adolescent romantic angst rather than mature self-knowledge:
"It was clear to me then that my version of pleasure was inextricable from

pain, that they existed side by side and were interdependent, like the two forces of an electric current" (130).

The pleasure peaks at the end of the fall term, during the Christmas theatricals. School play scenes in which girls play male roles are a convention of girls' school narratives. Generally, the cross-dressing serves both a transgressive and recuperative function; gender roles are revealed as constructions on the one hand and reinscribed as fundamental on the other. Cross-dressing in narratives of same-sex desire can, as well, remind readers of the theatricality of passing. Here the narrator is assigned to recite Mark Antony's lament over Caesar's corpse, but she is consumed by stage fright:

> [Sister Imelda] sensed my panic and very slowly put her hand on my face and enjoined me to look at her. I looked into her eyes, which seemed fathomless and saw that she was willing me to be calm and obliging me to be master of my fears. . . . As we continued to stare, I felt myself becoming calm and the words were restored to me in their right and fluent order. . . . She kissed her crucifix and I realized that she was saying a prayer for me. She raised her arms as if depicting the stance of a Greek Goddess; walking onto the stage, I was fired by her ardor. (132–33)

On returning backstage after her performance, "she put her arms around me and I was encased in a shower of silent kisses" (133). (Are the kisses transgressive or recuperative? Do we see a woman kissing another woman or a woman kissing, given the costume, a man? But the male costume, we assume, is a toga or robe, clothing that to our eyes is more dress-like. And if this leads us back to seeing two women kissing, does the robe-like costume coupled with the nun's long habit invite us to see two nuns kissing?) They exchange gifts—chocolates "bought illicitly by one of the day girls" for the nun, and for the narrator "a casket made from the insides of match boxes and covered with gilt paint and gold dust" (133). The allusion to *The Merchant of Venice* suggests that the narrator will not be very lucky in her love, yet this moment of "intimacy between us" seals the attachment for the narrator (134). Worried that the nun's Christmas might be "bleak and deprived," the narrator asks about her plans. Sister Imelda is "radiant as if such austerity was joyful," which leads her student to fantasize, without much cause, "Maybe she was basking in some secret realization involving her and me" (133).

The pain increases as soon as the narrator returns from the Christmas holidays. Sister Imelda withdraws on the grounds that "it is not proper . . . to be so friendly," that they "must not become attached"

(134). Her casting of the issue as one of propriety rather than pathology is significant, and comforting. She berates and embarrasses the narrator in class and directs her to avoid her in the halls. But Sister Imelda's messages, and perhaps her motives, are mixed. At the same time that she declares an end to their intimacy, she gives the narrator a notebook in which she had copied quotations when she herself was a schoolgirl. In other words, Sister Imelda offers some crumbs to the starving narrator, enough for her to "[cling] to the belief that a bond existed between them" (136). Her small and rare attentions encourage hope that can be placed in the service of duty. Comforting the narrator after an embarrassing failure on the playing field, Sister Imelda counsels that "she must not give way to tears, because humiliation was the greatest test of God's love, or indeed *any* love":

> "When you are a nun you will know that," she said, and instantly I made up my mind that I would be a nun and that though we might never be free to express our feelings, we would be under the same roof, in the same cloister, in mental and spiritual conjunction all our lives. (136–37)

The Catholic context—where suffering is ecstasy, love is service and mortification, and thus salvation is renunciation—joins with the tendency of frustrated desire to desire what the distant object desires. Thwarted desire for Sister Imelda generates desire to be like Sister Imelda, to desire what the nun desires.

The narrator does not, apparently, experience the nun's behavior as manipulative, and it's hard to say if it is, or if it's merely careless, or if it's designed to convince her to discipline her passion and place it in the service of a "greater good." In other words, while Sister Imelda is the major figure in the narrator's emotional drama, it's difficult to know what part she plays in the nun's. Sister Imelda admits that at first she found convent life "awful," and it's unclear if things have improved with time. The narrator notes: "She certainly got thinner because her nun's silver ring slipped easily and sometimes unavoidably off her marriage finger. It occurred to me that she was having a nervous breakdown" (136). The band that signifies Sister Imelda's status as Bride of Christ no longer fits, is too large. The image leaves us wondering whether the nun finds her own vocation too great to bear or whether the religious life, and perhaps the pedagogical life, is not sufficiently nourishing for a woman who can kiss a crucifix and then strike the pose of a Greek goddess, or for a teacher who holds the chalk as if it were a cigarette. And where the narrator fits here is equally unclear. Is her affection an antidote to the emotional austerities of convent life? Is Sister Imelda so involved in her own emotional/spiritual struggles that she fails to register the depth and intensity of the emotions her behavior calls up in the narrator?

The narrator leaves school promising to return in the fall to enter the convent. She doesn't, of course, and goes off instead to the university in Dublin with Baba. She stops writing to her beloved nun and never explains to her why she changed her plans. During the two years after their departure from the convent, she and Baba "never did anything that was good for us. Life was geared to work and to meeting men, and yet one knew that mating could only lead to one's being a mother. . . . 'They know not what they do' could surely be said of us" (142). The betrayal here is twofold: she has betrayed her promise to Sister Imelda as well as her own aspiration not to live her mother's life.

One day, taking the bus with Baba for a double date Baba had arranged, the narrator notices Sister Imelda and another nun sitting in the back, next to the exit:

She looked older, but she had the same aloof quality and the same eyes, and my heart began to race with a mixture of excitement and dread. At first it raced with prodigal strength, and then it began to falter, and I thought it was going to give out. My fear of her and my love came back in one fell realization. . . . The thing was to escape her. (142)

Quaking with anxiety, wiping off her lipstick, the narrator wonders how she can manage to explain her silence and broken promise; when they reach their stop, however, the nuns have already disembarked. The narrator closes her tale with:

I saw the back of their two stable, identical figures with the veils being blown wildly about in the wind. They looked so cold and lost as they hurried along the pavement and I wanted to run after them. In some way I felt worse than if I had confronted them. I cannot be certain what I would have said. I know that there is something sad and faintly distasteful about love's ending, particularly love that has never been realized. I might have hinted at that, but I doubt it. In our deepest moments we say the most inadequate things. (143)

The final view of Sister Imelda, as one of two indistinguishable blank black backs, confirms her status as, at least in part, a field for her favorite student's projections. To the end she remains aloof and unreadable. Confrontation is elided. This love story lacks a climax—the love "has never been fully realized"—as well as closure. This is rather sad and perhaps faintly distasteful, but the admission of banality in the final scene and the narrator's confession that she would probably have said inadequate things are as much a relief to me, interested reader of such narratives that I am, as Sister Imelda's disappearance is to her student. We love—mostly from a distance—and we go on, and some of us try to cultivate a kind of ironic detachment from ourselves, our teachers, our adolescent loves, an ironic detachment that the narrator's final sentence might also suggest.

Dykes, baby dykes, and protodykes have a slightly better survival rate in films than in fiction. The best known girls' school film is probably Leontine Sagan's *Madchen in Uniform* (1931), based on a play by Christa Winsloe.[10] Nearly the entire student body of a repressive Prussian boarding school for the daughters of military men is in love with a beautiful young teacher, Fräulein von Bernberg. A new girl, Manuela, publicly declares her passion for the teacher, and for this the principal, a patriarchal female if ever there was one, orders Manuela confined to the infirmary (of course), where she becomes suicidally depressed. Meanwhile, Fräulein von Bernberg, who returns Manuela's affection, finally rebels against the principal's discipline, declaring, "What you call sin, I call the great spirit of love which has a thousand forms." Manuela tries to commit suicide by throwing herself down the back stairwell, but is saved by the united students and their teacher. The principal, and the patriarchal power she represents, is (for a moment, at least) vanquished. In its uncut version, lesbianism in *Madchen* is not perverse but subversive; it is an anti-authoritarian political force.

The American release of *Madchen in Uniform* was delayed by censors until the film was de-dyked. The version released in 1932, shortly before the premiere of Hellman's play, lacked all the explicit scenes of physical affection between the students and von Bernberg's declaration that love between women is not a sin. If later American films about girls' schools are any indication, this regulatory demand for lesbian invisibility seems to have presided over American film long after the censorship boards. One of the more interesting cinematic versions of the passion-transcended plot—in part because the passion is oblique and the transcendence incomplete—is *The Trouble With Angels*, a 1960s comedy about a convent boarding high school. Directed by Ida Lupino, written by Blanche Hanalis, and starring Rosalind Russell as the Mother Superior, it features Hayley Mills as Mary Clancy, the bright and rebellious troublemaker who, with her friend Rachel, turns the school upside down, makes the Reverend Mother's life a misery, and finally, to the Reverend Mother's pleasure (the Reverend Mother it turns out, is a closet rebel), decides to join the convent.

Filled with Catholic and Catholic school clichés—young Sister Constance, a "flawless beauty," decides to leave the school and go off to teach in a Philippine leper colony, for example—*The Trouble With Angels* is often silly and hackneyed, so it's a bit embarrassing to come out as having been a passionate, but always guilty, viewer of this film in my youth. It's even more embarrassing to realize now that my repeated viewing of it—every time it was on television—should have told me something about myself and my own attractions to women. What then seemed to me to be merely an exercise in gratifying my own desire to rebel against authority, I now read as a clear sign of my own developing dykehood.

The Trouble With Angels is on one level a conservative film about how the motherless Mary Clancy, thanks to the Reverend Mother's saintly patience and affectionate discipline, finds Mother Church and, by implication, God the Father. I doubt this is what so attracted me to it. Although the convent and academy of St. Francis are supposed to be dedicated to the service of a patriarchal God, the world of St. Francis is a community of independent women. There are fewer markers of patriarchal authority in this film than there are, for example, in *Madchen in Uniform*. There is nothing like *Madchen*'s opening montage of pointed phallic towers; in *Trouble* the towers of the old estate that is both academy and cloister (the order's "Mother House") are fewer and shorter and rounder. The opening shots of *The Trouble With Angels*—first on a train and then a school bus as it brings the new students to campus—stress rather the privacy, isolation, and autonomy of St. Francis, its distance from patriarchal power. *Madchen*'s forbidden front stairs and Piranesian back stairs, so carceral and claustral, are replaced by the front staircase of St. Francis, more horizontal than vertically abyssal, and center of bustling community life. No phallic supplement, like the principal's cane in *Madchen,* for the Reverend Mother. No rhetoric about service to power through marriage and reproduction. And although there are statues of Christ on the grounds and in the chapel, the statues the camera keeps returning to are of St. Francis, the kinder, gentler (a bit fey or femme perhaps?) saint. No priest appears on screen; no bishop interferes with school affairs, and the few laymen who do cross the threshold of St. Francis are easily manipulated and controlled by the canny Reverend Mother. Even the casting of

Rosalind Russell (there are traces of the *His Girl Friday* Russell in the Reverend Mother's wisecracking wit and unsuitableness for conventional domesticity) suggests that St. Francis can accommodate, as it will with Mary Clancy, strong and spirited women. After all, the Reverend Mother likens Mary's energetic defiance to her own. What fledgling lesbian would not find such a world attractive?

Madchen takes as its theme the politically transgressive nature and subversive potential of lesbianism. *The Trouble With Angels* is also about the pleasures of transgression, but there is no overt thematizing of "particular friendships" in *Trouble,* a remarkable omission for viewers steeped in Catholic culture and nun stories. But the glaring absence of such a conventional conventual theme incites the desire to find desire and erotic curiosity elsewhere (a symptom, my students would claim, of my critical perversity or, if they knew about my lesbianism, of my sexual "perversity"). The film does not disappoint. One of Mary and Rachel's first pranks is an enterprise called "Cloister Tours," a 3 5-cent tour of the nuns' living quarters, which the Reverend Mother had declared off limits to students. The highlight of the tour, as Mary advertises it in language that recalls the "holiest of holies," is "that mystery of mysteries, where Reverend Mother sleeps." The secret center of St. Francis is the Mother Superior's bed. No wonder Rachel worries that they will burn in hell for "defiling the Sanitorium" [sic].

Many of the scenes underline the student's growth toward adult sexuality. There's a comic trip to a department store to buy bras (Reverend Mother notes the need after observing the students in leotards for their posture and dance class, presided over by Gypsy Rose Lee as Mrs. Mabel Dowling Phipps), and a scene in which the school band marches off to a competition in their borrowed and too revealing uniforms; the camera lingers on their naked thighs. But what interests me most is the way Mary's growing desire to enter the order is represented. There are no scenes of confidential conversation about vocations between Mary and a friend or nun; there are no voice-overs in which Mary articulates her spiritual struggles. Rather, the only way we come to suspect that Mary is struggling with a vocation is through a series of scenes in which a solitary Mary watches a solitary Reverend Mother, who, thrillingly, sometimes watches back. In other words, Mary's vocation is generated from her voyeurism.[11]

The first of these scenes follows on the "Cloister Tours" incident. In the window seat of her upper story bedroom, Mary watches the Reverend Mother strolling the grounds alone. The camera follows Mary's view, zooming in on the nun from above and thus inviting the viewer to take up and identify with what film theory has usually marked as a masculine position, a superior and omniscient position (here, literally from above) that frames and objectifies a female figure. As I suggested earlier, however, this film works hard to free its women from what we might call a patriarchal frame of reference, from the masculine gaze and its appropriative desire, so it's hard to miss the scene's regendering of the scene of desire and of the gaze of desire, its attempt to construct a desiring female gaze that can't be read as "masculinized." The gaze we follow, and with which this lesbian viewer identifies, is a female gaze of desire, as it watches another female sense that desiring gaze and gaze back.

Another such scene takes place in the chapel, during a (priestless) Christmas Eve service. Forced to remain at school for the vacation, Mary sneaks into the back of the chapel and hides in the shadows behind, of course, a statue of St. Francis. The camera shifts back and forth from Mary's view of the Mother Superior (who, when she recognizes that she is being watched, seems pleased and amused, and does a very good imitation of Roz Russell enjoying her sex appeal) to the Reverend Mother's view of an uneasy and reluctant-to-be-seen Mary. Of course the thematization of the gaze reminds the viewer of her own voyeurism and implicates her in it. The camera work, with its rapid shifts back and forth between Mary's view and the Reverend Mother's, has the added, and queer, effect of making the viewer feel (happily for me) trapped in the gaze of both and participating in a triangular circuit of desire.[12] Watching the scene now, I'm surprised that the little lesbian I then was did not decide that she had a religious vocation, too.

The final important gaze scene also occurs in the chapel. The setting, action, and camera work again suggest the implication of erotic desire in spirituality, and thus make possible a reading of Mary's desire to become a nun as the displacement of erotic desire for the nun. This must be one of the hottest mourning scenes in film. The occasion is the death of Sister Ligouri, the Reverend Mother's assistant and, given their warm affection for each other, the obvious choice for Reverend Mother's "particular friend." Unseen and unsensed, Mary watches again from the back of the chapel as the Reverend Mother escorts Ligouri's family from the chapel, closes the door, and returns to the closed coffin, her back to Mary and thus to us. The camera angle then shifts to the front of the coffin and we see the Mother Superior's love and grief as she kneels, leans her body into the casket, caresses it slowly with open hands, dissolves into tears, and buries her face into the top of the coffin. It is painfully passionate. The camera shifts back to the gazing Mary and the scene closes with a shot of the black coffin from above; the crucifix on top of it is ever so slightly askew.

The following scene, chronologically and, I want to argue, logically, is a celebratory graduation scene during which the Reverend Mother announces to the assembled class that Mary Clancy has decided to join the order. As Ligouri leaves, so Mary enters. But all is not universal happiness; Mary's coming out as a postulant runs the same risks as coming out as a lesbian. We are not surprised by the announcement, but Rachel is. Rachel also feels angry and betrayed, and for a time she rejects Mary by refusing to speak to her friend until she is just about to board the train home. Train stations are traditional places for passionate heterosexual good-byes in film, and thus the setting emphasizes that Mary is bidding farewell to conventional womanhood and its demand for marriage and active heterosexuality. The Reverend Mother approaches Rachel, who is ignoring Mary, and tries to convince her to talk to Mary. Calling Mary a "traitor" and contending that she had been "brainwashed," Rachel refuses. Rachel's deep anger and pain suggest that she sees Mary's decision as a personal, as well as, we might say, political betrayal. Not surprisingly, then, her exchange with the Reverend Mother revolves around whether or not Mary has been, as it were, recruited to nunhood by the older woman. The appearance of the seduction/recruitment theme again invites a reading of the scene as an allegory of coming out and recalls the accusation, as old as Sappho, that has so long operated to keep gay and lesbian teachers closeted: that gays recruit and gay teachers convert. How wonderful the Reverend Mother's ringing rejection of the seduction/recruitment scenario and her defense of Mary's strength and independence: "She didn't yield; she chose."

As I grow older and older I am convinced that desire is the central force in teaching, a force that can be dangerous if it is not recognized and controlled but without which the language and literature classroom is a dry and boring place.

Thus comments Elaine Marks in a recent *MLA Newsletter.*[13] I want to add that one way to recognize and "control" desire is to teach about it, to teach students that literature is all about desire, to teach students about the kinds of desire that, as Foucault has observed and this essay has tried to show, have been purged from literature and falsified in history. Students need syllabi that recognize the diversity of their desires and teachers who respect that diversity. Students need teachers who know and are unafraid of their own desire and who can thus respond to students' desire with sensitivity and care. I remember vividly the guilty pleasures and nameless pains of feeling homoerotic desire in the classroom. I wish for my own students guiltless revelry in the pleasures—however they come by them—of texts, and pain, if pain there must be, that can be named and assuaged.

Notes

1. I use this term and other identificatory categories like it under protest in this essay. First, because these categories are constructions used to discipline and regulate sexuality, and thus people like me, and second, because it tells less than people think it does and constructs a fiction of a totalized "I." For the problems with and political practicalities of coming out as a "lesbian" or "gay" see Judith Butler's "Imitation and Gender Insubordination."

2. The classic study of this shift and the conflicting discourses about women's romantic friendships, especially those between teachers and students, is, of course, Martha Vicinus's "Distance and Desire: English Boarding School Friendships, 1870–1920."

3. My thanks to Susan J. Leonardi for directing me to this passage. For a reading of this novel and others concerned with this issue, see her *Dangerous by Degrees: Women at Oxford and the Somerville College Novelists.*

4. In other words, Martha's fate seems to be a demonstration, on the level of erotic object choice, of what Foucault, in his list of the principles of juridico-discursive power allied with the repressive hypothesis he rejects, has called the "cycle of prohibition." According to Foucault: "Its objective: that sex renounce itself. Its instrument: the threat of punishment that is nothing other than the suppression of sex. Renounce yourself or suffer the penalty of being suppressed; do not appear if you do not want to disappear. Your existence will be maintained only at the cost of your nullification" (*History of Sexuality* vol. I, 84).

5. This is less an endorsement than an acknowledgement of this dynamic. Anyone who has read course evaluation forms knows how often what is supposed to be an evaluation of a course comes down to an evaluation of the teacher's personality and, if the teacher is a woman, of how well she meets conventional indices of female attractiveness. Recent discussions with my female colleagues about what students say on evaluation forms have yielded such depressing examples as "good teacher, too bad she's not younger" and "nice body." An anonymous student once described my laugh as "hideously annoying" (I wish for that student humorless professors for the rest of her/his college career). My point here is not merely that students write stupid, sexist, arrogant, cruel, and irrelevant things on evaluations, but that (contrary to the general assumption that the teacher is always corrupt and the student always pure/innocent) students objectify and eroticize their teachers.

6. If Brigid Brophy's novel about a girls' school in France, *The Finishing Touch* (1963), an apparent sendup of *Olivia,* is any indication, Bussy was right to worry that her text might be seen as precious rather than powerful. Brophy's book, as slim a volume as *Olivia,* covers much the same ground but in a comic key. Both schools are run by two women who are, in effect, a couple; one is competent and fairly stable, the other emotionally dependent and chronically ill with headaches, insomnia, and the like. A favorite evening activity at both schools is the charismatic teacher's reading, to select students, of French classics, especially Racine. In both texts a student falls in love with one of the two mistresses. In a 1986 introduction to a reprint of the novel, Brophy writes that the title was her publisher's, that she had originally called it *Antonia* after the main character, schoolmistress Antonia Mount. While Brophy never cites *Olivia* as a model, or rather, target, of *Antonia/The Finishing Touch* (she says in that introduction that her model for Antonia was Anthony Blunt during his days as Director of the Courtauld), the number of parallels between the two texts is striking.

7. Trying to account for the rewriting of history in *Olivia,* Vicinus offers: "Perhaps Bussy revenged herself on the past by such a reordering of events, although she thereby continued the stereotype of the doomed lesbian relationship established by Radclyffe Hall's *Well of Loneliness* (1928). Bussy never thought of her love as deviant, but she interpreted victory as suppression, not expression" (225). The language here is detached and vague enough to support a number of constructions, but the implication seems to be that for personal reasons Bussy chose a way of representing her experience that had the unfortunate and unintended consequence of reinscribing the stereotype of lesbian fatality. I want to reverse this formulation and argue that the cultural determined what could be represented about the personal. Citing *Olivia* with a number of other narratives of lesbian doom and fatality, Blanche Weisen Cook observes, "The truth is that these passionate little girls were not always abused and abandoned. They did not commit suicide. They wrote books about passionate little girls, death, and abandonment" (723).

8. While I have been concentrating here on the varieties of fatality in narratives of student-teacher love in the '30s and '40s, and will go on to talk about later narratives that end less tragically, if rather ambiguously, it is significant that this fatality plot still surfaces in later narratives about female teacher-student love. For example, Mary Wings's recent crime thriller *Divine Victim* (1993) intersperses with its lesbian rewrite of Daphne Du Maurier's *Rebecca* an account of the unnamed narrator's previous affair with her dissertation advisor, the brilliant and beautiful Ilona. Their relationship is a messy and abusive mix of intellectual and erotic competition thats ends only when the narrator, in a rage after Ilona tells her, probably inaccurately, that her dissertation had been approved solely because she was sleeping with Ilona, pushes the car Ilona is sitting in over a cliff. Of course one does not have to be suffering from romantic disappointment to be tempted to murder one's dissertation advisor.

9. Narratives of passion disciplined and transcended, which cast the beloved and loving teacher as moral/spiritual mentor who encourages the student to discipline love into self-discipline and service, rehearse what Vicinus shows was the general line on raves taken by nineteenth and early twentieth-century female educators in England and America. Raves, they argued, were common, and with proper guidance could be occasions for a student's moral/spiritual growth, a

growth toward traditional female service as wife and mother, and for later, reforming educators, social service (225–26).

10. *Madchen in Uniform* is also the girls' school film that has received the most attention from film critics and scholars. See especially B. Ruby Rich's "From Repressive Tolerance to Erotic Liberation: *Maedchen in Uniform*" for a careful, at times Foucauldian, reading of the film that places it in relation to lesbian culture in Germany between the wars, Weimar progressivism, and a growing Nazi repression. Vito Russo's *The Celluloid Closet* recounts the recutting of the film for American release after censors refused an exhibition license because of the film's explicit representation of affection between women and its general sympathy with lesbianism. Ironically, the recut film allowed critics to argue that only homos would see anything homo in it (56–58).

Other important girls' school films are a film version of *Olivia* by British director Jacqueline Audry (1951, screenplay by Colette, herself a writer of girls' school narratives and the writer of the subtitles for the French print of *Madchen*), which was released in the States as *The Pit of Loneliness* (1954), a title that recalls the lesbian angst of Radclyffe Hall's novel and gives it a demonic twist; and a film version of French writer Violette Leduc's *Therese and Isabelle*. Of course the most explicit treatment of female teacher-student love in American film is John Sayles's *Lianna* (1984); the student in that film, however, is a married adult woman who returns to college to finish her degree, which places Sayles's film near, but beyond, my focus here.

11. Elaine Marks isolates female voyeurism as a feature of gyneceum narratives that are sympathetic to intimate attachments between women, and traces a pattern of growing intensity in such scenes from Colette to Wittig (363).

12. The scenes I am describing seem to me to be examples of what Judith Roof, in her critique of the heterosexist trajectory of so much film theory (even feminist theory) has called the "lesbian configuration," which "momentarily detaches the sexual narrative and voyeuristic politics of viewing from their heterosexual premise, disturbing any easy alignment among gender, viewer, and screen image and creating other viewing and identificatory possibilities that may enrich our understanding of how film identification works" (37–38). Although Roof does not mention this film (to my knowledge no writer on film does), my reading of it has benefited from her theorizing.

13. For an interesting collection of essays on this and other related issues, a collection that came out after this essay was written, see *Tilting the Tower: Lesbians Teaching Queer Subjects*, ed. Linda Garber.

Works Cited

Bowen, Elizabeth. *Eva Trout, or Changing Scenes*. New York: Knopf, 1968.

Brophy, Brigid. *The Finishing Touch*. 1963. London: Gay Men's Press, 1987.

Bussy, Dorothy Strachey. *Olivia*. 1949. London: Virago, 1987.

Butler, Judith. "Imitation and Gender Insubordination." In *Inside/Out: Lesbian Theories, Gay Theories*, edited by Diana Fuss, 13–31. New York: Routledge, 1991.

Cook, Blanche Weisen. "'Women Alone Stir My Imagination': Lesbianism and the Cultural Tradition." *Signs* 4 (1979): 718–739.

Foucault, Michel. *Foucault Live*. Edited by Sylvere Lotringer, translated by John Lotringer. New York: Semiotext(e), 1989.

————. *The History of Sexuality, Volume I: An Introduction.* Translated by Robert Hurley. New York: Vintage, 1990.

Garber, Linda, ed. *Tilting the Tower: Lesbians Teaching Queer Subjects.* New York: Routledge, 1994.

Hellman, Lillian. *Four Plays By Lillian Hellman.* New York: Random House, 1942.

Hilton, James. *Good-bye, Mr. Chips.* New York: Little, Brown, 1934.

Holtby, Winifred. *South Riding: An English Landscape.* 1936. London: The Reprint Society, 1949.

Leonardi, Susan J. *Dangerous By Degrees: Women at Oxford and the Somerville College Novelists.* New Brunswick: Rutgers University Press, 1989.

Marks, Elaine. "Lesbian Intertextuality." In *Homosexualities and French Literature,* edited by George Stambolian and Elaine Marks, 353–77. Ithaca: Cornell University Press, 1979.

————. "Memory, Desire, and Pleasure in the Classroom: *La Grande Mademoiselle.*" *MLA Newsletter* 25 (1993): 3–4.

O'Brien, Edna. *A Fanatic Heart; Selected Stories of Edna O'Brien.* New York: Farrar, Straus & Giroux, 1984.

Rich, B. Ruby. "From Repressive Tolerance to Erotic Liberation: *Maedchen in Uniform.*" In *Re-vision: Essays in Feminist Film Criticism,* edited by Mary Ann Doane, Patricia Mellencamp, and Linda Williams, 100–130. Bethesda, Md.: University Publications of America, 1984.

Roof, Judith. *A Lure of Knowledge: Lesbian Sexuality and Theory.* New York: Columbia University Press, 1991.

Russo, Vito. *The Celluloid Closet: Homosexuality in the Movies.* Rev. ed. New York: Harper & Row, 1987.

Tey, Josephine. *Three By Tey.* New York: Macmillan, 1954.

Vicinus, Martha. "Distance and Desire: English Boarding School Friendships, 1870–1920." In *Hidden From History: Reclaiming the Gay and Lesbian Past,* edited by Martin Duberman, Martha Vicinus, and George Chauncey, Jr., 212–19. New York: Meridian, 1990.

Wings, Mary. *Divine Victim.* New York: Dutton, 1993.

VANESSA D. DICKERSON

The Teachings of Small Smothered Lives

The Erotics of Instruction in Henry James's
The Turn of the Screw

Teaching at a small, private, predominately white, conservative liberal arts college in the South, I have found without fail each year among student evaluations of my courses some strong objections to the discussion of allusions to, or references to sexuality in my classes. I was taken aback when I read the first student protestations, since I had never come across such resistance before: most eighteen- and nineteen-year-old students appear eager, given the requisite analytical skills, to identify such references in their discussions of literature. I had never even heard about other professors who had stirred similar reactions in their students. But then, I had never asked.

After the initial shock of reading these evaluations, I simply shrugged them off, attributing them to personal quirks and hang-ups, but suspecting that they were evidence of ultra-conservatism, of provincialism and insularity, of my arrival in the Bible Belt. I still think my dismissal of these scattered denunciatory comments was and is, in the short run, appropriate and sensible: however, it may be that, in the long run, my response was too pat, too uninteresting, itself too provincial. This is to say that when I begin to explore the implications of those students' comments, all sorts of provocative meanings and nuances present themselves. For instance, I now wonder to what extent students' negative response to sexual references in the classroom relates to more global concerns about making sex education a part of the grade or secondary school curriculum and about sexual harassment on campuses; I wonder how our national concern about AIDS and its attendant issues of sexual taboo, restraint, and abstinence may factor into the reactions of those students who tended not to want to hear about the sexual dimension of a text. Perhaps I had not properly, so to speak, turned the Freudian screw. There is, after all, if I may play on the title of an essay by Mark Spilka, a way one ought "not to do it."[1] Perhaps I had presented these ideas with too great a satisfaction, thinking, like Strother Purdy, somewhere in the depths of my being, "that sex does not go away for being hidden," that "no one can be a master of the novel without including the terrible power physical love exerts," that "any work of fiction purporting to delineate human experience that fails to demonstrate its sexual components is inferior to one with a clearer specification."[2] Perhaps I had presented the sexual references too playfully and irreverently, had not been "clinical" enough in my mention of sexuality.[3] Still, I could not but wonder whether these students would have been so troubled or resistant to my connection of the sexual with the intellectual now and then had I not been a female and a black female at that. What did the students perceive to be the relation between femaleness and nurturance and sexuality? To put it another way, would they have been as unreceptive to the Freudian allusions of a white male professor?

I am more convinced now than ever of the importance of such questions, especially in light of the recent experience of a well-known and respected white female professor who is publicly raising similar questions about women's relations to sex in the classroom. Accused of sexually harassing two female students, Jane Gallop, in a reexamination of the definition of sexual harassment, both touches on the difficulty and questions the desirability of separating the erotic from the intellectual (she notes "an atmosphere in which sexual policy is so widely construed as not only to punish and restrict harassment but also to chill other relations, productive relations where it is not so easy to separate the erotic from the intellectual or the professional"), even as she recognizes how "our society can conflate women with sex and make women bear a disproportionate share of the burden of human sexuality."[4]

At the turn of the century, "Victorian sexual ethics were thrown," according to Lloyd Fernando, into a "turmoil," a turmoil the effects of which I and, I would speculate, Jane Gallop find reverberating in our different but related classroom experiences. This is to say that our society has "never fully escaped the strongly persistent Victorian notion of sexuality as intrinsically base and despicable, unhappily coarsening to feminine nature."[5] This "intrinsically base" sexuality becomes doubly "despicable" when it is associated with youth, with children. Does it follow that sex and the classroom are remote entities that ought to be kept at a remove from each other because they put children, even young adults, at some sort of risk? These are all compelling questions and speculations which I do not propose to address directly here. Instead, I raise them as an orientation to, more specifically as prologue and epilogue to, my reading of Henry James's *The Turn of the Screw*. This reading is enhanced, I like to think, by the question it too addresses about teacher-pupil relations, about the place of erotics in the classroom.

James's novel about ghosts, about ambiguity, about point of view, about the nature of evil, about "erotic ambiguities," affords some interesting insights into the relations between teacher and student. It also provides some insight into the position of the Victorian child and female, two figures who were oddly enough diminished at the same time that they were protected and, in the case of the female, even put on a pedestal by men.[6] Both were dependents required in essence to, as Martha Vicinus would put it, "suffer and be still."[7] While the ideal Victorian woman was by law of coverture no better off contractually than a child herself, was indeed to work only in the home, where she, as angel in the house, administered to the care and comfort of husband and children, the child's role too was as strictly prescribed: children were "raised to accept discipline and learn not to complain," to control "displays of childish high spirits," to behave like "miniature adult[s]."[8] Though it is true that male children were allowed more freedom and privileges educationally and socially in expectation of their coming into adulthood, on the whole it is true that both young children and women were in a sense neatly crinolined and tightly corseted for most of the nineteenth century.[9]

In *The Turn of the Screw*, Henry James cleverly explores the "teachings of . . . small smothered life" by representing the interactions of a governess—a female officially responsible for indoctrinating children out of their more freewheeling and animalistic impulses, for "civilizing" and stilling by instilling them with moral lessons—and children, or, as David McWhirter maintains, "mature young adults who are not 'excused' from the simple humanity of sexual longing by virtue of their age . . . or their questionable mental state," or, I might add, their gender.[10] This use of one silent or subdued figure to screw down others is yet another turn of the screw in a work that even contextually turns the screw by virtue of its publication in the 1890s, a period during which governesses, according to Katharine West, "were in their heyday" and "as much in demand for small boys as for little girls."[11] The 1890s, the decade during which James consolidated "diverse thematic patterns . . . to produce the uniquely

Jamesian child,"[12] was also the decade during which women were busy reconstructing themselves and their lives by becoming not only attuned to sexuality, but also, to the even greater horror of some individuals, by becoming what neither woman nor child was expected to be—sexually frank.[13] Having "reached maturity and found his calling at a time when the air was thick with theory and controversy about women," the author of *The Turn of the Screw* was anything but oblivious to the sexual revolution that saw the advent of the New Woman, "a literary phrase," as Sandra Stanley points out, "actually popularized by James."[14] James was also, however, aware of one figure from his childhood that appears to stand opposite the New Woman—the Victorian governess, whose role "as the guardian of middle- and upper-class values" was "a function still persistent in English families he came to know." As conservative and clear-cut as the governess's role appeared, the governess herself was, James recognized, more complex, an often "unhappy" or "neurotic" woman, "a dangerous figure lurking somewhere in the Victorian consciousness," and "making for class instability."[15] Interestingly, though the governess in James's *Turn of the Screw* is hardly a pioneering New Woman, she does figure as a Victorian woman whose domestic duty and professional task come to revolve intensely, if not wildly, around issues of sexual frankness—especially where children are concerned.[16]

   The Turn of the Screw is about the opposite of revolution and frankness; it is about stultification. More specifically it explores the condition of the female and her charges impossibly positioned by the teachings of their small smothered lives. The first indication we get of woman's position is in the structure of the narrative itself. The governess's story is complexly and tellingly framed or fixed by that of a male, Douglas, who proves the proprietor and master of the tale, lending the governess's story "a coherence and prestige" it would otherwise not have, coming as it does from a quasi-servant, a female at that, who may be construed as hysterically in love.[17] Oddly enough, one of the ways the framing narrative establishes Douglas's position as the more trustworthy and prestigious narrator among the group of storytellers gathered to tell and to hear ghost stories is by the use of a handmaid or disciple, in this instance another female narrator, who serves Douglas by framing and introducing his story in a way that establishes his remoteness, the remoteness that inspires awe and reverence.[18] This is to say that during the course of the frame it becomes clear that Douglas is himself a teacher whom his disciple, the character who ushers in his tale, perceives as a guru of sorts, one extremely adept at contextualizing, embellishing, and directing the attention of his audience to the history he wants to present. At different points, Douglas shows himself a master of speech and stage, as he stands "before the fire" and "look[s] down at" a "converser." He "with quiet art, prepar[es] his triumph," and successfully teaches a lesson to the female whom he singles out as the one person present who can fully appreciate what he was about to share. "'You'll easily judge,' he repeated: '*you* will'" (1, 3). She does; Douglas's fireside pupil is rewarded both in the hearing and ultimately the owning of the governess's story.

The handmaid is the only one who can approach this man so preeminently in possession of the real thing. She is the pupil with the critical acumen to discern the precarious position of the governess. Douglas laughs when the listener he has continued to fix "fixed him too," anticipating the governess's dilemma: "I see. She was in love" (3). Douglas, who is pleased with this insight, not only confirms her response, but also elaborates: "You *are* acute. Yes, she was in love. That is she *had* been. That came out—she couldn't tell her story without its coming out. I saw it, and she saw I saw it; but neither of us spoke of it" (3). At this gathering, Douglas's insistence that only he and the individual he continues to fix can see into the life of the governess suggests a kind of academic intimacy that resonates with all the erotics that will emerge as the governess recounts her experiences.

The disposition of the governess's story adumbrates the governess's position. Framed by a male's narrative which itself is "embroidered" by what appears to be a reverent female acolyte, the governess's story, if not actually smothered or buried, is so situated that it has virtually to be emancipated, unpacked, brought out of containment and concealment.[19] When Douglas discloses the existence of the manuscript, he begins what amounts to a resurrection of the text, which is brought to the circle of listeners over time and miles. There can be no immediate rendering of the story; it is not a mere piece that is passed on by word of mouth. It is written down. It lies at a distance; Douglas has to send to town for it: "It's in a locked drawer—it has not been out for years" (2).

Douglas's narrative literally governs, orders, disposes of, controls the governess's story; it represents Douglas as a benign and chivalrous guardian, the most notable, if not the ultimate keeper of, a female narrative with an erotic content that Douglas himself is set on deflecting or putting by just as capably as he, "without a smile . . . also without irritation," puts by the "inference" of his own romantic involvement with the governess, who had "sent me the pages in question before she died" (2). In the masculine frame of *The Turn of the Screw*, Douglas's remoteness, his silence, and what is more, his silencing and absenting of the text, merely hint at the stultification and smothering that inform the governess's story. Thus, Douglas's silence and remoteness are mirrored in the figure of the bachelor uncle, who employs the governess and then distances himself from both her and her charges, locking them away at Bly with the requirement that they all, but especially the governess, be as silent and contained as the manuscript locked away in Douglas's town drawer: "That she should never trouble him—but never, never: neither appeal nor complain nor write about anything; only meet all questions herself, receive all moneys from his solicitor, take the whole thing over and let him alone" (6).

Douglas the silent silencer is textually redeemed when he resurrects the manuscript, thereby freeing up the governess's story, allowing her "to speak," if still through him; however the governess's patron and employer, who neither breaks his silence, nor crosses the distance, nor invites further contact, remains the reprehensible jailer of the poor souls at Bly. Douglas has assumed a "burden" of intimacy, if not love (a secret so compelling, a text so precious it had to be written down and locked away); the bachelor uncle has disburdened himself.[20] Relegating himself to invisibility and inaccessibility, he ironically becomes even more present to the governess, haunting her thoughts, lurking in her libido, titillating her consciousness with his prime directive (to keep herself, as well as little Miles and Flora, out of his sight or invisible), which consists of his exorbitant demand on her person and time, underscoring the forbidden act. Miles and Flora's uncle has not so much disregarded the emotional needs of the governess, as most employers of governesses tended to do, but rather he has played upon them.[21] Having declared his intent to be the specter of an uncle, the governess's patron directs her to Bly, where she will find not only more ghosts, but ghosts that are sexualized.

When the main narrative opens with the governess's arrival at Bly, where she is to take responsibility for eight-year-old Flora and ten-year-old Miles, we are to understand that the governess is effectively put in the "indeterminant position" of being simultaneously authorized if not empowered, muted if not gagged.[22] Hers is a supremely ambiguous situation.[23] The most notable and clear-cut idea we have of this young woman, who had led a small smothered life as the inexperienced daughter of a country parson, is that she is "governess." This generic term desig-

nates throughout the novel her function, her being, her significance, even
as it clues the reader into the phenomenon of naming or not naming. As
Linda S. Kauffman notes, "in this tale a great deal remains unnamed"
(e.g., the female narrator of the frame, the uncle, Miles's secret). Kauffman, identifying naming as "another form of possession," concludes that
"what really remains unnamed and, thus, unpossessed in this strange
story, is love" (189). This may well be the case, but for the purposes of
this essay the most compelling issue is what it means that the governess
herself remains unnamed. While being named may positively be associated with possession, and while being named may also be seen "as a
positive integration of the individual into the community," it is not clear
that, for the governess, "acts of naming" are unequivocally positive.[24]
For while the name can signify identity, possession, and community, it
may also contain, limit, label, and expose. Without a proper or a family
name, a part of the governess remains hidden, not fixed or fastened down.
Without a proper name, she becomes constructable either as one possessed of some unpublicized, unseen, private kernel of her self (she is not
"reduce[d] . . . to a single and fixed value"), or as one dispossessed of a
part of herself, a part so unseen, withheld, repressed, and ghostly that it
cannot be identified.[25] She herself by virtue of her withheld name contrib-
utes to the novel's famous or infamous ambiguity.[26]

The issue of naming not only affects the governess's role in the narrative, but also has epistemological and pedagogical consequences for her
teacher-pupil relations. Her strong reluctance to engage in naming, to
engage in what she calls the "monstrous utterance of names" (53) can
only affect the content and style of her interaction with her students.
Naming is associated with knowing, and naming and knowing are functions of a scientific teaching in turn associated with clarity and order.[27]
To the extent that she feels that she cannot or ought not to speak or to
utter certain names in or out of the classroom; to the extent to which she
cannot name and thus reveal her knowledge and thus, in part, her self; to
the extent that she must withhold, be silent, James's governess is disen-
franchised in her own classroom; her teaching compromised or at least
obscured. So that while she who narrates the tale in which she is the
central consciousness remains as unnamed as the uncle who, as a repre-
sentative of the absent but all-powerful father, need not be named, it is
not clear that her namelessness effects a similarly powerful aura.

Certainly in the classroom (and out of it, for that matter), where the
governess shrinks from the monstrous utterance of names, her teaching

takes on a tone better characterized by the word "wile" than "wield" as she humors, coaxes, and distracts her students in an effort to steer them clear of sexuality. Her efforts are not spent in bringing light to her pupils. Instead she may be said to stop teaching and start contriving ways to obscure knowledge, specifically knowledge about sexuality. Acting as a human "screen" (28), the governess allows "the element of the unnamed and untouched" to become, between her students and herself, "greater than any others" (50). Her fear lest she "should violate as rare a little case of instinctive delicacy as any schoolroom probably had ever known" (53) evinces an emphasis on scruple, conscientiousness, discretion, and propriety that finally prove debilitating, driving, as it does, a wedge of distrust and suspicion between the governess and her pupils and intimating how those responsible for the enlightenment of youth must finesse the boundaries of truth, light, ambiguity, and obscurity.

When the governess assumes the position at Bly, she does what other women would not do because "the conditions had been prohibitive. They were somehow simply afraid. It sounded dull—it sounded strange" (6). The young governess, however, succumbs to "the seduction exercised by the splendid young man," and in her idealism, feels herself romantically rewarded by the touch of the young patriarch's hand, rewarded for making herself the handmaid of his freedom. In doing so, she does not place herself among the ranks of the New Woman who in the 1890s insisted openly on her own sexuality, on her own autonomy. Instead she behaves like those Victorian women who sacrificed their autonomy and mobility for the sake of financial security, maternity, usefulness. She in essence forfeits or relinquishes her name not only for money, but also for an erotic attachment which she can never as a respectable Victorian woman own, for a passion which she as the designated teacher and "mother" of the two children at Bly must, as her calling requires, govern if not deny. She, true enough, finds in the service of the "splendid young man" a "different affair from [her own] scant [paternal] home" (7), but one different from the world of solid engagement that she leaves behind. The upshot of this untenable position is a latently erotic "succession of flights and drops, a little see-saw of the right throbs and the wrong" (6) that inform her contact with her pupils.

One critic remarks that "we hear practically nothing about the academic lessons she [the governess] offers Miles and Flora."[28] We do, however, learn a great deal both in and out of the classroom about the dynamics of the governess's instruction and her relations to her pupils.

Although "Regular lessons . . . certainly suffered some wrong" (9), as the governess herself confesses during her first days at Bly, time in the classroom constituted, after all, only a part, not the whole of the duties of the governess, whose entry into a household usually proved more constrictive and burdensome than expansive and liberating.[29] The governess in James's story undertakes "the whole care" of her pupils without any trace of master or mistress and is atypically happy to do so: "To watch, teach, 'form' little Flora would too evidently be the making of a happy and useful life" (8) declares the governess, as she prepares to have the bed of the angelic little girl moved into her own room (8).[30] Interestingly enough, like the mother mentioned at the beginning of the framing narrative who sleeps with her little boy only to find that she cannot dispel his fear of ghosts, but rather, "encounter[s] also herself . . . the same sight that had shocked him" (1), the governess who is in effect a surrogate mother to Miles and Flora, must confront the only other parents the two children have known since they have been banished to Bly—the ghosts of Quint and Miss Jessel.

The children have experienced a sequence of absent specterized parents, not only in their biological parents, who die, but in their uncle, who adopts them and then vanishes; in the uncle's valet Quint, who as one critic points out may be seen "as a projection of the Master's [the uncle's] potentiality"; and in Miss Jessel, "dishonoured and tragic" (59), the governess's predecessor.[31] Unlike these other adults, the governess is present and unquestionably responsible.[32] Indeed, in more ways than one, the young governess proves she not only has the superior character, but also that she is the "superior servant."[33] She is granted authority over the other servants at Bly, graciously enlisting the sympathetic ear, if not the complete understanding of the housekeeper Mrs. Grose, in whom the governess notes what would have been unusual in the housekeeper of the day, "An odd recognition of my superiority—my accomplishments and my function" (46).[34] More importantly, she demonstrates her superiority by strictly following the law the employer has laid down. She shows herself a better mother figure than he, a father figure.[35] He responds to his charges with neglect and with physical abandonment that underscores Flora and Miles's first and tragic loss of their real parents.

The governess responds to her charges, at least initially, with an enthusiasm and awe that make her more alive and expansive. She is struck by an innocence and purity, a something out of this world, not of this world, especially in Miles (13). As a result of such delightful discoveries, which are heightened by the fact that she takes great latent and erotic satisfaction in pleasing the absent uncle, the governess feels herself charmed and transported into a state "that had not been one of the teachings of my small smothered life": she "learnt to be amused, and even amusing, and not to think for the morrow. It was the first time, in a manner, that I had known space and air and freedom, all the music of summer and all the mystery of nature" (14). Like any good teacher, she learns from her students. She begins to experience what Millicent Bell terms "hedonism," but what can also be read as emotional empowerment.[36] But she does so only for a brief moment as she becomes increasingly preoccupied with the legacy of what appears to be the poor parenting of the two former servants and delegants of the uncle-employer. The contaminating effects of the lascivious dead couple's tutelage are so insidious that they are not only bodied forth in the return of the repressed, in the very ghosts of Quint and Jessel, but also, according to the governess, manifested in the very children themselves. So that while Flora and Miles, the most clever and exuberant of pupils, "got their lessons better and better," the governess still "overscored" their behavior in and out of the classroom, with "prodigious private commentary." As she puts it, "I thought strange things about them" (38–39).

Her "office" ultimately becomes to avoid the pitfalls of the bad servant that John Locke, the "father of the Enlightenment in educational thought," begins to identify in his treatise on education—the servant who keeps children in check with stories of ghosts and goblins.[37] Mindful that she "should continue to defer to the old tradition of the criminality of those caretakers of the young who minister to superstitions and fears" (46–47), the governess discovers that Locke's admonition about ghosts and superstitions does not fully describe the situation at Bly. In fact, the governess awakens one night to find her charges sporting in the dark with ghosts; this indeed is just one turn of the screw. The second horrific turn is that the history of Quint and Jessel eroticizes the ghosts. That history becomes, by virtue of the governess's efforts to make it otherwise, a central subject (51). The governess's mission becomes to protect the children from encounters with their eroticized past, to foster an innocence of things sexual, to exorcise a knowledge with which neither youth nor women were ever in the Victorian scheme of things to be overly conversant. It is not just that the "governess's viability as a narrator thus depends upon the repression of her sexuality," but that her viability as a teacher also comes to depend upon the repression of sexuality.[38] The governess sets about s/mothering the children's sexual impulse, the impulse that so lately bestirred itself in her own youthful self, an impulse that Victorians set against the moral impulse, but one which the New Woman came to see as a harbinger of autonomy and growth. The governess's teaching becomes the teaching of one herself hampered, if not harassed, not so much by ghosts themselves per se, as by ghosts that underscore a cultural censorship and curtailment of sexuality, especially in the children, before whom she must not speak of "one of the most powerful instincts nature has placed in the heart of man."[39] The governess seeks to supplant the erotic history of Quint and Jessel by offering a part of her own modest story.[40] The children listen eagerly to her stories about her father, brothers, sisters, cat, dog, home, village. But again, as the governess herself suspects, hers is the teaching of a small smothered life and does not hold out the complexity, the reality, the truth that the children, but especially Miles, who is entering his adolescence, seek. In their "chatter" about "*my* life, *my* past and *my* friends," in their chatter about dogs, cats, and furniture, Miles, Flora, and the governess "go round" skirting the beefier issues of sexuality and maturation, leaving the governess with a "suspicion" that her students, who have been to class with Miss Jessel, are, "with an art of their own," pulling her strings and watching her "from undercover" (51).

Compelled to keep away from and thereby to circle the forbidden subject of sex, forced into the position of "a character who can express and enact passion only through an obsessive vicarious concern with the passional lives of others,"[41] the governess increasingly feels an inadequacy and ineffectiveness as a teacher that is especially pointed up in her relations to the boy Miles, who has been at school with the masters, but who has been sent home for reasons that are never disclosed. She detects a "small ironic consciousness on the part of [her] pupils" that tries her strength (50). While the governess eventually declares that sexual knowledge puts Flora beyond her purview ("at such times [during Flora's contact with the ghost of the infamous Miss Jessel or Quint] she's not a child: she's an old, old woman" [69]), it is twelve-year-old Miles, with his "respectfully easy" references to the governess as "my dear" (55), who occasions the governess's doubts about her classroom authority. "Miles's whole title to independence, the rights of his sex and situation, were so stamped upon him that if he had suddenly struck for freedom I should have had nothing to say" (54–55). His knowledge—both that acquired at school with the masters and that acquired with Quint (with the assistance, I might add, of Miss Jessel)—is a patriarchal and sexual knowledge to which the governess has no public access: having no "inkling" of what has transpired at Miles's school, she remains "in the dark" (63). This knowledge, Miles's gender, and his prospects, coupled with the governess's comparative ignorance, render Miles's "secret precocity" all the more formidable: it "made him, in spite of the faint breath of this inward trouble, appear as accessible as an older person, forced me to treat him as an intelligent equal" (63).

Unable to speak frankly like a New Woman about sexuality, the governess cannot with the teachings of her small smothered life repossess Flora and Miles in any way that is more healthy than Quint and Jessel's possession of the children. Flora, who comes to fear the governess as the real, frightful ghost, as the real harasser, takes a fever and has to be sent away from Bly.[42] Rejected by Flora, the governess, in one last frantic effort to repossess Miles, figuratively s/mothers the child in an erotic embrace that is partly "ushered in by our non-observance of the regular custom of the [censored] schoolroom," (79) what one could term, if I may borrow a phrase from Jane Gallop, "the pedagogy of shocking performance" (18).[43] The final meeting of the governess and Miles is laden not only with issues of sex, but also with issues of authority and of a control predicated on the maintenance of the governess's leverage, which depends on her ability to repel the "revoltingly" unnatural—the sexualized ghosts. By preempting Quinton, the governess hopes to "reach [Miles's] mind," to take a recalcitrant student firmly into hand (85, 81).

In the encounter between the governess and Miles, James represents the female who dares utter the unnameable, who dares to tackle the issue of sex directly as one who is a far cry from a schoolmarm. She is a wild animal. The language James uses in the final scene of the book does more than portray the governess as ravisher or child molester, it depicts her as one beastly as a tiger, as "With a single bound and an irrepressible cry," she "spring[s] straight upon" young Miles, who, having done things [things so unspeakable the masters themselves never divulge them] at school, now is breathing hard with "unspeakable anxiety" as the governess confines him against his will (87, 88).[44] The governess recalls that during this climactic moment when she pounces between Miles and the ghostly libertine and "hideous author of our woe," Quint, that the "wildness of my veritable leap only served as a great betrayal" (88). For, in her effort to obscure the sexual, in her battle, "it may be imagined with what a passion" (88), to cast it out, the governess has ironically engaged a mental battering that is, like the language James here uses, just as erotic, and finally just as damaging, as the erotic extremes to which Jessel and Quint have gone.[45] As Lloyd Davis has so astutely observed, the language "discloses" the very sexuality it is meant to repress.[46] In the end, sex is neither circumlocuted, nor is Miles saved, at least not in any literal or vulgar way, as "his little heart, dispossessed, had stopped" (88). Dispossessed of the sexual impulse, of sexual knowledge, the body ceases to function and Miles is of no use. He is freed, but to what and to where? His demise is one of the most painful ambiguities in this text, which finally, no matter how obliquely, affords the opportunity to focus on gender, sexuality, and instruction in such a way as to shed light on my own experience as a black female instructor.

With no intention of reducing the complexities of *The Turn of the Screw,* I find that James's text proffers a timely review of some pedagogical conditions that are relevant to today's classroom. James's story should, for instance, remind us how language powers teaching to the point that what we say or do not say in a classroom takes the measure of the richness and dearth of the classroom experience and reveals the possibilities of human existence. James's story reminds us that the classroom is a place for—among other things—speech, and that women have traditionally not been granted the privilege of speech independent of the doctoring or swaddling of men. James's story also suggests that even when a woman speaks, claiming her own voice, she has often to do so in the face of an audience historically conditioned to stop its ears, as women are to be seen and not heard. Finally, one of the subjects James's novel suggests, which is problematic for the female, especially the female who professes to explore and share the fullness and multiplicity of ideas and human meanings through language and literature in the classroom, is sexuality. The social and historical strictures of voice and body are, of course, even more stringent for the black female, who, either denied a voice or granted a voice criticized as sassy, and who, stereotyped as a lascivious and lewd hottentot, finds that her voice and body historically made her ineligible for membership in the Victorian cult of true womanhood, a cult which defined itself in opposition to the black female.

What my reading of *The Turn of the Screw* comes down to is an understanding that the governess who dared in her nineteenth-century milieu to broach issues of sexuality in her relations with her charges teetered on the edge of a precipice. While the female today who raises issues of sexuality in her classroom may not be so impossibly positioned, she is still likely to experience some difficulty, some static, as gender can still problematize the female instructor's ability to engage in meaningful and constructive relations with students when sex is the topic. Factor in race and region, and a black female professor in a Southern white conservative classroom may very well find that the phrase "turn of the screw" takes on yet another interesting dimension.

Notes

1. See Mark Spilka's "Turning the Freudian Screw: How Not to Do It," in *"The Turn of the Screw": An Authoritative Text, Backgrounds and Sources, Essays in Criticism,* ed. Robert Kimbrough (New York: Norton, 1966), 245–83.

2. Strother B. Purdy, *The Hole in the Fabric: Science, Contemporary Literature, and Henry James* (Pittsburgh: University of Pittsburgh Press, 1977), 149, 150, 157.

3. I am indebted here to Robert Heilman via Spilka, who borrows the phrase "commonplace clinical record" from Heilman's "The Freudian Reading of *The Turn of the Screw,*" *Modern Language Notes,* LXII (November 1947): 443.

4. Jane Gallop, "Sex and Sexism: Feminism and Harassment Policy," *Academe* (September–October 1994: 18, 19–20). In our society the African-American female, even more so than the white female, has been conflated with sexuality, and in a markedly negative way. In fact, the black female has not just been conflated with, she has been accused of sexuality, stereotyped as Jezebel and whore.

5. Lloyd Fernando, *"New Women" in the Late Victorian Novel* (University Park: Pennsylvania State University Press, 1977), 138.

6. I borrow the phrase "erotic ambiguities" from Mark Spilka's "Turning the Freudian Screw: How Not to Do It," p. 245. James's *The Turn of the Screw* has occasioned a plethora of critical readings, from Edmund Wilson's Freudian reading to Shoshana Felman's deconstructionist approach to the text. For an excellent review of the criticism, see the *Case Studies in Contemporary Criticism* edition of Henry James's *The Turn of the Screw,* ed. Peter G. Beidler (Boston: St. Martin's Press [Bedford Books], 1995), 127–296.

7. Martha Vicinus, ed., *Suffer and Be Still: Women in the Victorian Age* (Bloomington: Indiana University Press, 1972).

8. Alice Renton, *Tyrant or Victim?: A History of the British Governess* (London: Weidenfeld and Nicolson, 1991), 119, 120.

9. Perhaps no figure experienced the harshness of social prescriptions for the maintenance of a virginal character in the child and female more intricately than the governess. See Lloyd Davis's analysis of the virginal character in the work of Henry James, *Sexuality and Textuality in Henry James: Reading Through the Virginal* (New York: Peter Lang, 1988). Though Davis does not make specific reference to the governess in *The Turn of the Screw,* when he comments that "S/he [the virgin] is placed in a situation analogous to that experienced by the child" and that the "virginal character is also absorbed in an epistemological quest" (8, 12), he might just as well be referring to not only the governess in James's ghost story, but to the figure of the governess.

10. This phrase, "teachings of . . . small smothered life," which also figures in this essay's title, is taken from Henry James's *The Turn of the Screw: An Authoritative Text, Backgrounds and Sources, Essays in Criticism,* ed. Robert Kimbrough (New York: Norton, 1966), 14. All further references to *The Turn of the Screw* are taken from this edition.

David McWhirter, *Desire and Love in Henry James: A Study of the Late Novels* (Cambridge: Cambridge University Press, 1989), 87.

11. Katharine West, *Chapter of Governesses: A Study of the Governess in English Fiction 1800–1949* (London: Cohen and West, 1949; Folcroft, Penn: Folcroft Library Editions, 1974), 170.

12. Muriel G. Shine, *The Fictional Children of Henry James* (Chapel Hill: University of North Carolina Press, 1969), viii.

13. Lyn Pykett, *The 'Improper' Feminine: The Women's Sensation Novel and the New Woman Writing* (London and New York: Routledge, 1992), 200. Pykett writes of a "preoccupation with sexuality" and a "sexual frankness" that "also caused the New Woman writers to be linked to the residual forms of 'pernicious literature' and French naturalism of the 1870s and 1880s, while also linking them to the emergent forms of 'Ibscenity' and sex-problem literature that developed around the turn of the century."

14. Alfred Habegger, *Henry James and the "Woman Business,"* (Cambridge: Cambridge University Press, 1989), 9: Sandra Stanley, "Female Acquisition in *The Spoils of Poynton;*" in *Keeping the Victorian House: A Collection of Essays,* ed. Vanessa D. Dickerson (New York: Garland, 1995), 143.

In *Hole in the Fabric,* Strother B. Purdy reminds us that "James's career ran right through the erotic decadence of the European *fin de siècle* . . . James was forty-seven in 1890 and did his best work from 1897 to 1904; he knew Swinburne, Wilde, Whistler, and Beardsley; he wrote for the *Yellow Book* (or published in it); he adopted a personal catechism as strongly derived from Walter Pater as that of any of his contemporaries. Yet his work is as unmarked by their popular flirtation with diabolism and the challenge to a God-ordered world in erotic extremity as if it had been written in another century" (136).

I suggest that *The Turn of the Screw* cannot so quickly be determined a text unmarked by one of the other ideas that arose during this period—the idea of the New Woman.

15. Millicent Bell, "Class, Sex, and the Victorian Governess: James's *The Turn of the Screw,*" in *New Essays on Daisy Miller and The Turn of the Screw,* ed. Vivian R. Pollak (Cambridge: Cambridge University Press, 1993), 96, 98.

16. A recent essay, a contemporary case study of James's *The Turn of the Screw,* may help to bring the governess closer to, if not into, the fold of the New Woman. Priscilla L. Walton, in "'What then on earth was I?': Feminine Subjectivity and *The Turn of the Screw,*" in *The Turn of the Screw* by Henry James, ed. Peter G. Beidler, pp. 253–67, construes the governess as one who tries, albeit unsuccessfully, to open up a place for herself outside patriarchal boundaries.

17. In *"New Women" in the Late Victorian Novel,* Lloyd Fernando writes, "We need not assume that these views [about the inequities in the marriage contract] were original to Mill—most of them in one form or another were part of the stock of arguments advanced on the subject by leading feminists of the time—but they gained immensely in coherence and prestige through being enunciated by him" (12).

Priscilla Walton in an excellent essay ("What then was I") that reads *The Turn of the Screw* "as an exemplar of the problematic nature of feminine representation . . . and feminine subjectivity" (253–54) sees the frame, or what she terms the prologue, as an instrument for the delegitimization of the governess: "The governess's story . . . has been structurally trivialized as a result of the prologue," (260) argues Walton. I do not disagree with this assessment here. I also recognize how "the governess requires male validation" (257), a validation which does not completely or successfully validate the governess's narrative at all. However, in this essay I focus more on Douglas as a master/teacher who stands before not only a select audience, but also and especially before a female "pupil" (the unnamed narrator) as an advocate for the governess's story: he orchestrates and controls even as he emancipates.

Finally, Walton's interpretation of *The Turn of the Screw* is problematized if one accepts the idea that the unnamed narrator of the frame is a female. For if, as Walton contends, "the governess . . . is initially objectified as a character in Douglas's story" (256), then Douglas himself is in turn objectified in the story of the unnamed female narrator (as unnamed, I should point out, as the governess herself), who ultimately owns, transmits, and relates both Douglas's and the governess's stories.

18. There is some debate about the gender of Douglas's admirer, but I tend to side with Linda S. Kauffman in "The Author of Our Woe: Virtue Recorded in *The Turn of the Screw,*" *Nineteenth-Century Fiction* 36 (1981): 176–92. See also Terry Heller, *The Turn of the Screw: Bewildered Vision* (Boston: Twayne, 1989) 21, and Michael J. H. Taylor, "A Note on the First Narrator of 'The Turn of the Screw,'" *American Literature* 53 (January 1982): 717–22.

19. Taking into account James's preface as well as the prologue, Priscilla Walton finds the "female narratives are doubly buried . . . first by James as the more adept teller of the unnamed woman's story [James's source for *The Turn of the Screw*], and later by Douglas and the narrator within the tale itself" (255). This burying may well prove more complex than Walton suggests by joining, if not collapsing into one, the narratives of Douglas and the unnamed narrator. The complexity is evident when one understands the unnamed narrator to be a female, even if a female finally supportive of the patriarchal discourse.

20. In "The Author of Our Woe," Linda S. Kauffman determines that the governess "has only one reader in mind when she composes her narrative": she writes for the uncle.

21. Renton writes that "Even where governesses were treated with respect, simple disregard for their emotional needs was widespread" (*Tyrant or Victim?*, 73).

22. The manuscript becomes the governess's effort to empower herself, to find her voice, to take authority and ungag herself, especially if, as Linda Kauffman argues, the governess has not just the authority the master grants her at Bly, but "also . . . supreme authority as *author*" and chronicler of her own virtue (185).

Priscilla Walton would have it that this attempt to gain authority through authorship is already severely compromised by Douglas, whose framing narrative "renders her suspect and undermines the authority of her narrative" (259). Undermined author though she may be, the governess, deconstructionist Shoshana Felman points out, is also a reader "whose reading alone indeed commands the situation, clutches at power as sense, and at sense as power." Felman, "'The grasp with which I recovered him': A Child Is Killed in *The Turn of the Screw,*" in *The Turn of the Screw,* ed. Peter G. Beidler, p. 199. In "Class, Sex, and the Victorian Governess: James's *The Turn of the Screw,*" Millicent Bell writes of the governess's view of herself as a "[moral] 'authority'" (Bell's interpolation); however, in the course of the essay, that "moral" authority becomes questionable as Bell represents the governess at various points as a hedonist, as the double of the disreputable Miss Jessel, and as an adult who has fallen in love with the child, Miles (106–107). David McWhirter also offers a good discussion of authority, an authority he at one point calls "improvisatory"(136). See McWhirter's "In the 'Other House' of Fiction: Writing, Authority, and Femininity in *The Turn of the Screw,*" in *New Essays on Daisy Miller and the Turn of the Screw,* ed. Vivain R. Pollak (Cambridge: Cambridge University Press, 1993). The point, as I see it, is that the governess has no unequivocal authority.

23. She is truly in what Bonnie S. Anderson and Judith P. Zinsser identify as an "indeterminate position—somewhere between a servant and a lady—called forth from both her employers and her fellow workers" in *A History of Their Own: Women in Europe from Prehistory to the Present,* vol. 2 (New York: Harper & Row, 1988), 193. See also M. Jeanne Peterson's "The Victorian Governess: Status Incongruence in Family and Society" in *Suffer and Be Still: Women in the Victorian Age,* ed. Martha Vicinus (Bloomington: Indiana University Press, 1972). Here Peterson contends that "one can go further [than status and role] and suggest that the real discomfort [of the governess's situation] arose not from lack of definition but from the existence of contradictory definitions of the governess's place in society"(10). In "'What then on earth was I,'" Priscilla Walton also briefly considers "the contradictory significations of a governess's position"(257). Ambiguity describes the condition of the middle-class single female who undertook governessing: "neither servant nor family member, she found her position in the household ambiguous and uncomfortable, her wages minimal, and her tenure uncertain" (Leslie Parker Hume and Karen M. Offen, introduction to part III, in *Victorian Women: A Documentary Account of Women's Lives in Nineteenth-Century England, France, and the United States* [Stanford: Stanford University Press, 1981], 281).

24. See Michael Ragussis's *Acts of Naming: The Family Plot in Fiction* (New York: Oxford University Press, 1986), 8.

25. Ragussis, *Acts of Naming,* 10.

26. As Shlomith Rimmon declares in *The Concept of Ambiguity—The Example of James* (Chicago: University of Chicago Press, 1977), p. 116, "*The Turn of the Screw* has been so firmly linked with ambiguity that even people who have not read it know that it is somehow supposed to be ambiguous."

27. In *Acts of Naming,* Ragussis writes about "English empiricism" that seeks "the name as the means whereby science can classify and reveal all things in perfect clarity and order" (5).

28. Bell, "Class, Sex, and the Victorian Governess: James's *The Turn of the Screw,*" 97.

29. See Renton's, *Tyrant or Victim?,* 108, 119.

30. In *Chapter of Governesses,* Katharine West also notes how "this unnamed governess undertook her duties in a spirit sadly lacking in most of her kind" (181).

31. Bell, "Class, Sex, and the Victorian Governess: James's *The Turn of the Screw,*" 106. Bell begins here her discussion of the doubling in the text.

32. Stanley Renner, "'Red hair, very red, close-curling': Sexual Hysteria,

Physiognomical Bogeymen, and the 'Ghosts' in *The Turn of the Screw*," in *The Turn of the Screw* by Henry James, ed. Peter G. Beidler.

33. Renton, *Tyrant or Victim?*, 67.

34. Katharine West observes in *Chapter of Governesses* that "many a maid, nurse or housekeeper rightly or wrongly resented the influences of the governess . . . (18).

35. Walton, in her essay, "'What then on earth was I?'", sets up an interesting opposition between Mrs. Grose as the figure of the good, responsible mother and Jessel as the figure of the bad, irresponsible whore, with "the governess's own place in the narrative . . . indeterminate"(265). My understanding of Walton's idea is that, struggle as she may to set up a place outside these patriarchal constructs, the governess is caught in a binary trap. I opt to see the line drawn between Mrs. Grose and Miss Jessel as a continuum that allows the governess to be both/and, not one or the other. Furthermore, though Mrs. Grose has some matronly and nurturing role in the text, it is subordinated to the maternal role of the governess. After all, the governess, who assumes officially and personally the cares, feelings, and duties of the absent parents, is even recognized by Mrs. Grose as the superior not only in her accomplishments, but also in her function as governess—one of a class of single women, as Walton herself notes, "employed to act as mother substitutes" (257).

36. Bell, "Class, Sex, and the Victorian Governess: James's *The Turn of the Screw*," 107.

37. John Locke, *John Locke on Education*, ed. Peter Gay (New York: Teachers College, Columbia University Press, 1964), 100.

38. Walton, "'What then on earth was I,'" 260.

39. I borrow this phrase from a medical treatise on contraception by one "Dr. Louis F.-E. Bergeret . . . chief physician of the Arbois Hospital." See *Victorian Women: A Documentary Account of Women's Lives in Nineteenth-Century England, France, and the United States*, ed. Erna Olafson Hellerstein, Leslie Parker Hume, and Karen M. Offen (Stanford: Stanford University Press, 1981), 190, 192.

40. In "The Author of Our Woe," Linda S. Kauffman may be said to describe the governess's narrative, as it is delivered by Douglas, as one long erotic sigh. The part of the governess's story that is not modest, the part that reveals her own erotic longings, must not be spoken, but rather is committed to paper, then processed by the male Douglas, who contains and controls the presentation of her sexuality.

41. David McWhirter, *Desire and Love in Henry James: A Study of the Late Novels* (Cambridge: Cambridge University Press, 1989), 8.

42. Thomas Mabry Cranfill and Robert Lanier Clark, Jr., *An Anatomy of "The Turn of the Screw"* (Austin: University of Texas Press, 1965), 169. Cranfill and Clark believe that the governess harasses Flora and Miles.

43. One critic has argued that the governess literally asphyxiates Miles. See Terence J. Matheson's "Did the Governess Smother Miles? A Note on James's *The Turn of the Screw*," *Studies in Short Fiction* 19 (1982): 173. Gallop, "Sex and Sexism: Feminism and Harassment Policy," 18.

44. Though Millicent Bell does not call the governess herself a child molester, she suggests than the governess has violated a sexual "taboo even more outrageous than love between the classes" by falling in love with young Miles. Bell continues, "To suspect Miss Jessel and Quint of molesting Flora and Miles—

either homosexually or heterosexually—is to fill in another way, the blank of their undenoted evil by something well known in Victorian as in our own times" ("Class, Sex, and the Victorian Governess: James's *The Turn of the Screw*," 107).

Interestingly enough, Miles, whom James has represented as precocious, as the governess's equal, gets his share of animalistic description. James casts him as the young pup, or at least as one whose movements are for a moment like those of a "baffled dog" (James, *The Turn of the Screw,* 88).

45. Alice Renton uses the phrase "mentally battered" in *Tyrant or Victim?*, 121.

46. Lloyd Davis, *Sexuality and Textuality in Henry James: Reading Through the Virginal* (New York: Peter Lang, 1988), 16. Davis uses the apt expression "circumsexualocution" to describe James's language.

MARY ANN CAWS

Instructive Energies

Expensive Energy

Like other expressions of the self, the energetics of the work place has its privilege and its price. In the workplace as teachplace, the privilege may tend to get swallowed up, either in the hallowed tradition of didactic seriousness or the hollowing-out exhaustion of personal communication *ad libitum*. So the problem arises of conservation, and that seems, somehow, allied to conservatism, the c-word. Better to stick to the l-word and all it entails, granted. But that does not relieve the problem.

Now we know that sources of energy are personal, like everything else. My personal sources relate to one specific passion, that is to say, the visual. My metabolism is related to art, even as my job concerns the text. I am not now, although I started out by being, an art historian. I am also not now, although I also started out by being, a philosopher. What I am is a teacher of literature cum critic and cum slides, with passions on some other sides, including art and philosophy.

Visual Passion

My main source of energies, then, the ones I call on in lecturing or writing situations because it is there that they like to respond, is an interdisciplinary one. Very often, this has to do with the visual, often in connection with the verbal, sometimes not. For instance, I might want to make a point that I have already sketched out with a few written texts, discussed, shared, read aloud. Maybe it's about how a diagonal reading can be used, specifically in a poem, to make more interesting parallels between syntax and imagery than the ordinary left-to-right, down a line, left-to-right pattern the Western eye is used to following.[1] So I demonstrate in a painting how such diagonals are stressed, either in straight lines or in serpentine ones—as in the mannerist weavings back and forth of Tintoretto's *Leda and the Swan,* for example, comparing it then with Yeats's poem by the same name. Then I compare it with some other Ledas and some other swans of literature and art, and then perhaps extend the branchings into other kinds of swans, black and white: of Baudelaire and Mallarmé, of Ruben Dario and Neruda and Thomas Mann, before the curve of that neck reaches back into art, and Leda has her time to develop. For I think energetics is about developing: the self, the mind, those of others, in the classroom and museum and library.

As the students see the snake-like weavings and loops of the painting and the poem, their own interior dynamism comes to the surface, albeit shyly. Their frequent surprise at their own capabilities generally delights them, and me. I am convinced by repeated experiences of the multiple ways that a group seemingly disparate in its talent and its interest can suddenly find itself focused with intensity on the same image, in an energetic collective participation.

In part, this is evident above all where, as in a literature class, the visual is more unfamiliar than the verbal. The power of difference, into which we've all spent a good bit of our time dipping, is never to be underestimated. This is startlingly manifest for those of us who sometimes teach in other languages than English: you sound different in another tongue, so that you are.[2] The foreign is already more seductive, already more other, already more appealing because less everyday.

The same is true, of course, of translation. The erotics of translation, on which I have reflected frequently,[3] has the appeal of the other in the same, of the uncontainable in the everyday container that *claims* or pretends to contain it sufficiently to be understood. In a further example of crossover energetics, I claim that this effort of containment must be taken also in the foreign-based sense of the claim: that is, "to pretend" as in the French for "to claim"—"prétendre," since we are speaking of translation. Translation is erotic because it works both ways. That is energetics also. It works in foreign languages, brought near to home, in the near confines of the classroom.

And for an English teacher, another way of othering, of inhabituating, is located in the foreign world—foreign to the tongue, at least—of the eye. The erotics of the eye, however well-known to be urgent in the way of sexual interchange, is often underused when it is a matter of the art object, other than human.

Why Study with a Woman???

A most endearing question was once posed to me by one of my more forthright students among the lovely long-haired barefooted bluejeaned young women at Sarah Lawrence, where I taught for one exhausting semester in the daytime while teaching at Hunter College in the evening and nursing my baby in between. I was doing my writing in the middle of the night, before the baby woke up at three, when else?

"Why should anyone study with a woman?" she asked. I understood immediately exactly what was to be understood, without *too* much difficulty. It wouldn't have taken a great deal of just plain unsexy energy to get that one. It is, of course, what many of the contributions to this volume will no doubt study: female students and male professors have something going sometimes—to understate the oh-so-obvious case. But here, any of the clear and present answers I could have given to the lovely young thing, or the protests I could have made on behalf of the woman-kind she was presumably to participate in at least some day, if not at that moment in the fullest sense, would have seemed to me at the time unsuited to the occasion. Surely I was supposed to give some witty reply? I was too tired.

But we aren't always tired, even when we're older. And here's my answer to the remarkably painful question, why study with a woman? Energy, just pure unadulterated *energy*, can be attractive. Even grown-up, aging energy. Even when it isn't male. Do I mean seductive, erotic, *winning*? Is it fun to manifest? To watch? It seems to be, sometimes, all of the above. Its very manifestation appears to strengthen everyone without the drawbacks of competition. Energy is delightful, doing no harm. It can nourish everything else, including feeling. BUT, coming from a woman of whom, alas, much is expected, maybe too much, it can wear you out.

Let me begin with that, as my first cautionary tale.

A Tale of Payment

In her desperately convincing piece called "'How Many of Us Can You Hold to Your Breast?': Mothering in the Academy,"[4] Diana Hunme George discusses a not-so-very-often-discussed topic: what she calls "the danger of the different voice." The different voice is of course that of the female, and in our workplace, it works overtime. It has to do with playing the intercessor between, say, the student and another (often male) professor, with forgiving everything and healing a great deal, with standing not just *in loco parentis* for our students but, specifically, in the place of the mother. "The overvaluation of the different voice" creates problems, draining spirit and energy, with its price attached: "the continued muting of our words and works" (229). Having finally refused the Victorian virtue—thanks, in part, to Virginia Woolf—of being the Angel in the House, we have had to become the Angel in the Academy (227). Well, it's exhausting stuff, and you just might find yourself longing for a tiny taste of the demonic, to get back to yourself at least for a moment.

Even as energy is presumably attractive, it wears (you) out. Now *that's* not so attractive, in the long run. It means that the very privilege of and privileging of the innate impulse to doing a lot, a lot of the time, has to be watched out for and, finally, paid for, sometimes quite dearly. Liveliness may end up by a premature dying out.

Elsewhere, Two Anecdotes

I am teaching in France, some interrelations between art and literature, and finding it difficult to arouse the students into their own language. They are used to listening; their professors are used to talking. I believe, and say aloud, that perhaps *looking* will help speech: it does. I ask questions about the different angles of seeing—and as the weeks go by, the angles become more differentiated. The students, advanced doctoral candidates at that, grow accustomed to speaking and speaking up, to looking, to conversing.

Still in France, at another university, when the slides are projected higher on the screen than they should be, there is no pointer provided for my lecture. After a moment of despair, I find a chair in the audience, drag it forward, and climb on it to point at the top part of the projected image. The audience of students who are not my own, faculty who are not my colleagues, has become a group of spectators, laughing at my awkwardness and with my enthusiasm. They seem delighted.

The next week, they ask the regular lecturer why she doesn't stand on a chair.

A Second Cautionary Tale: The Errors of Energy

My second cautionary tale is specific, but as veridical as the first, more general one of the nurturing woman in the academy was general and veridical. As with anything, it does not pay to be too sure. And yet, it certainly does not pay to be timid, a trap I tend to fall into. Shyness may lead to chaos. Both ways are full of risk.

I am to give a talk in Canada on a few problems of teaching comparative topics and literature in general, combining the usual processes with art. I want—since it is Canada—to illustrate my talk with Canadian art. In the beating rain and cold, I walk to the National Gallery to see the Veronese and the Poussins, as well as some Canadian art, hoping to pick up some slides. I see the Canadian artists whom I particularly like: Jack Bush, Riopelle, Emily Carr. There are no slides available, but I feel refreshed and energetic, ready. Under the rain, I dash into a taxi to the campus, arriving at the wrong building to give my talk.

Once I get to the right building, I find the room gratifyingly packed, excited about showing the two slides I have chosen to begin with in order to speak of conflicting readings. But it is late, and they have been waiting. I stride to the back of the room, put the slides in the projector, and look for my bag with my talk in it: it is nowhere to be seen. I can *show*, but I can't speak. I have arrived before without my slides, but I have never arrived, as it were, speechless. There is always a first time. This is that time. I am crimson.

I seize a book bag from the front table—clearly not mine—and panic. Accompanied by someone in the audience, I hasten to the ladies' room, then back to the wrong building in which I lingered and lunched, when I thought it was the right building, finding my bag nowhere. Returning to the room to apologize, miraculously and ridiculously, I find it right there, against the wall, where I had put in the slides. My anxiety must be manifesting itself again. It is, just as plainly, part of my energy, as the latter is a large part of my way of being, teaching, caring; even when I am most careless, I am no less expressive of myself.

So I give my talk about multiple interpretations and possibilities, about reading a world both visually and verbally together, embarrassed but impassioned, happy to be able to say anything at all. Afterward, a young woman thanks me for "letting her know how to be." How important it is for us, she says. It will be for me also, once I find out how to know it, and be it.

A Third Cautionary Tale: Teaching and Its Trials

We are sitting, three colleagues, myself, and an advanced student being examined on her knowledge of literature and philosophy, around a table in a seminar room whose only window opens onto a yellow brick wall. On the blackboard is written, in a careful hand, to the right of a series of diagrams:

BE SURE, AT ALL TIMES, TO STATE YOUR PREMISE CLEARLY!

and under it is scrawled:

so this is logic?

Something strikes me as very funny about that setup, with the answer as a put-down, relatively successful, to the unwitting solemnity of the initial command. I try to bring my attention back to the matter at hand. It is, alas, neither funny nor slated for success.

The candidate is a budding comparatist who wishes to write a thesis entitled, if I have understood it correctly, "Certain Philosophies and the Work of Samuel Beckett." The part I am supposed to examine her on is not philosophy, but Beckett, of whom I am particularly fond, as is she—who's not?—and about whom she seems to know relatively little.

Some critic, she had said in her written proposal, had pointed out the link with Schopenhauer, and I am eager to hear that discussed. Well, not eager, let's be honest about this, but willing. She has not provided us with the name of the critic, nor with any suggestion of the link proposed. I ask for details, say the topic would be a good place to begin, and give what I think is my most reassuring smile. You know: the kind that reveals how you are interested, patient, sure that we are on our way to a fascinating discussion.

—I have a problem, she says, twisting a button on her blouse, with Schopenhauer.
—Ah, I repeat, mustering my most patient smile, and wondering in that case why she would have brought up the comparison.
—You have a problem with Schopenhauer. Now we are on to some-

thing, surely. What is it exactly? Do you think Beckett might have had the same one? A different one? *(You are being nasty, I say to myself. Cut it out.)*

Silence. "Perhaps your problem is with Beckett," I am thinking, determined not to ask. My non-nasty self is getting the upper hand. Good.

—Well, would you like to talk of some other philosophers and Beckett? *Any* other philosopher, I add, looking at her vacant expression.

Silence.

—Take anyone. I pause, and continue hoping, now that I am in my patient mode. Take any relation between Beckett and someone.

Silence. I am plainly not able to summon forth answers in this case. *What* is the problem? Whose problem is it? I have chosen to go first, wanting to put her at ease, this stumbling student with the vapid smile, and am determined to have it work. Too determined.

—O.K. Take Joyce and a philosopher, and show how the relation might differ between that combination and, say, Beckett and some thinker. Anyone. *(Am I am going too far out of the way? Will my colleagues think I am being sarcastic?)*
—So can I talk about Leibniz? I don't have a problem with Leibniz.
—Sure, go on. *(Triumph. I was right to pursue it this way. Attagirl, me.)*

I look at my colleagues: Michael, with his lavender tee-shirt bringing out the blue of his eyes behind his horn-rimmed glasses; Albert, with his longish light grey hair and sparkling eyes—even his nose is witty. Two hundred other people and I have always admired Albert. The third member of our company I know less well. That's probably a good thing; I have heard him state his conviction that women have inferior brains, in a tone of voice that could not be described as ironic. I find myself wishing the candidate were male, not wanting him to have ammunition for his persuasion. Damn. He smiles to himself at my question, tossing his head back until its blond waves rest on his green corduroy jacket where it meets the chair. His neck is crimson. I expect my face is too.

—My dear, he says, uttering my name like some sort of medicine. Let me see if I can rephrase your most challenging questions. They are perhaps a bit too complex. Might we not rather see it this way? The point was, and even is, if I am not sorely mistaken, to invite Ms. Peders—Jane (here comes his smarmy smile—oh lordie, are they involved? you know, eros raising its as it were head even here? my mind is taking a loop, get back to the question, right?)—to discuss certain philosophers and not certain relations, if you see what I mean.

But of course I see what he means, all right. Erotics in other people's classrooms, aesthetics in mine, is that the way it goes? My face still burning. OK, OK, I'll make nice, as Michael sometimes tells me to.

The candidate is looking relieved: let's get away from this crazy woman and her snide questions and back on the pleasing the man track, shall we? I look around the table, deciding to let go. Let's just do the general kind of question and call it quits.

—Right, Ms. Peders, so sorry; why don't you just tell us what you find most interesting about this topic?

—Oh, you know. It is important for the modern psyche.

I wait. That can't be *it,* that cannot be the end of what she was going to say? I have to help her save some sort of face.

—How? How is it important? *(That seems fair to ask, doesn't it?)*

She picks up the question, her face lighting up:

—Maybe we can even say, for modernism. I believe that is true for Derrida and everybody. Lacan, Kristeva, you know, everybody.

I knead my hands together under the table. Mustn't snort, be polite, attentive, kind. Think of a question she can grip. My mind goes blank.

—Could you elaborate, please? asks Michael.

I am grateful to him for asking. Every time I ask anything, the ground sort of scoots away under my feet.

—Oh, you *devil!* she simpers at him.

I am feeling ill. I want out. That's admitting defeat. I want to make a point: how to do it? That: you can't just flirt, wink, and simper your way through what is supposed to be a serious trial of the intellect and the imagination. On the other hand, I am beginning to feel like a prude. Is this what my energy has turned into, a condemnation of the erotic interplay of others? Heavens, I say to me, get a grip on yourself.

—Ms. Peders, I start over. Perhaps . . . *(why am I always starting with "perhaps?"—it sounds so tentative.)* Look, let's talk about Beckett. What is your basic approach to whichever text you feel most comfortable with? Which genre do you find yourself attracted to?

I hate myself for this dummy questions, loaded with traps. Give her enough rope, I am thinking . . . "Attraction," I am thinking. Even here, the charged vocabulary sneaks in. Or do I just read it as charged? Is it me? My heart is pounding, of all times.

To my utter surprise, Ms. Peders turns out to be more knowledgeable than I could have guessed, once she settles down to a text. She has chosen *Watt,* my all-time favorite, and is actually saying things I never thought of.

My mind goes back to long ago, when I was in exactly her position. At Yale, feeling out of sorts, sure no one understood my projects, my way of thinking, when suddenly I was given the occasion to choose, to talk about the poet I found most compelling; the world opened up. The faces around me, I'll never forget the moment, seemed to change their dull, cynical, and uncomprehending blankness to vital witnesses of thinking beings. I never understood the alteration or tried to: the key was in my choice and not my perception.

What was happening here, in my own place, my own classroom, with my own colleagues, with myself was what had happened to me all those years before. I had continued because of that moment.

What could I say? Afterward, I took Ms. Peders aside and smiled at her hesitant face: it was up to me now.

—Jane, I'm so sorry. You just proved you have it in you; I couldn't see. What about a cup of coffee?

Charging Up Again

Now I'd really like to say, going back to the nurturing role we women energy advisers are called on to play so often, that I really loved that cup of coffee. It wouldn't be altogether true, though, and here is my point. Energetics such as I have defined them are likely to prove, like apologies for the lack of sight or power or anything else, exhausting. They are not always fun, or erotic even, not for yourself or anyone else either. It would be a terrible fate to always and only exhaust others, as, for instance, Edith Wharton exhausted Henry James with her "desolating, raving, burning and destroying energy," as he termed her insatiable whirling about. It's better to contribute something than to destroy anything, and if burning brightly means burning up or out, you'd better watch it. Desolation is no damned good.

But it's essential to charge. That's part of the price of teaching, learning, and being, and the privilege I began with. Anyway, if you *have* to exhaust someone, in the classroom or anywhere else, it might as well be yourself. If you've gotten this far, I say to myself, you can take it.

So that's the final point I want to make. There is a responsibility attached to the erotics of instruction as there is to the erotics of translation and to the energetics of anything at all. These things we give don't come without a price for the giver or the getter. In that, they are like any other privilege, meaningful.

Notes

1. See, for a diagram of these patterns, the initial chapter in Claude Gandelman's *Reading Pictures, Viewing Texts*. (Bloomington: Indiana University Press, 1991), pp. 12–13.

2. We have only to read Alice Kaplan's convincing *French Lessons* (Chicago: University of Chicago, 1993) to see how it works.

3. As in "From Rape to Rectitude," in *Teaching Language Through Literature*, Modern Language Association Conference Volume XXI, no. 2, (April 1982): 12–21; and "The Ethics of Translation," MLA San Diego, December 28 1994; and University of Manchester, April 4 1995.

4. In *Listening to Silences: New Essays in Feminist Criticism*, ed. Elaine Hedges and Shelley Fisher Fishkin (New York: Oxford University Press, 1994), 225–44.

JAMES R. KINCAID

Eroticism Is a Two-Way Street, And I'm Working Both Sides

Editors' Note:

We don't mean to grumble, but an essay like this makes us wonder why we embarked on this project in the first place. We planned it as a service to others, knowing we would gain nothing (not a raise, not even departmental favor) from all our hard work. But we were willing to offer ourselves so that others might learn from our editing.

And then we get this from Kincaid. Let us speak plainly here: colleagues who read this essay confirmed our opinion that it should on no account be published; but lawyers we paid for advice said we'd be mad to cross Kincaid, with whom they had prior (and calamitous) experience, other editors having recoiled as violently as we from his submissions and awakened to find themselves ensnared in litigation that drained everything but their life blood. Coincident with his other defects, these attorneys said, were a fierce "animal cunning" and "low dogged ferocity" that would make it hell for us were we to do what we otherwise would have done and you perhaps think we should have done anyhow. But it would have been our asses in court, not yours; so shut the hell up.

That doesn't mean you have to read this essay, of course, only that we have to print it.

Before turning our pages over (oh God!) to Kincaid, we feel we should provide a one-sentence abstract (that's all it'll take) for those who are curious (why?) about what he has to say and for those (and there will be a couple) who will actually try to read it. The essay explores the faucet theory (either all the way on or all the way off) of eroticism by way of a pointlessly confusing now-you-see-it, now-you-don't analysis of classroom passion as (a) an urban legend touched with absurdist pathos and (b) just one node in that vast tingling network of eros, which is what (after all) life *is*, the author concluding that a happy relativist erotic scale (like those carnival fun-house love-thermometer squeezie things, we gather) would serve us better than our current absolutisms (Well, duh!), and adding a mean-spirited coda suggesting that the subject of this volume is a foolish and actually dangerous red herring, for God's sake! Signed—The Editors.

A False Lead

A friend, cowering now in anonymity, wrote me as follows:

You hear what that Barreca and Morse are doing now? "Erotics of Instruction." Honest to God. It's true! I mean, this is maniac land. It really is worse than theory and that gender stuff. Never thought I'd find anything worse than those. Erotics of Instruction, which is only Part I, to be followed by The Erotics of the Bursar's Office, The Erotics of Space Allocation, Scheduling, Parking Management. What a non-topic! Issues of moment cry out from every corner, and these two go after sex where there isn't any. Can you, Kincaid, imagine anything less erotic than teaching? I know I can't, and used to be before my fall I could if I tried find something erotic in everything, but now I see things as they are, which is not erotic at all. But never mind me, what about Barreca and Morse? Correct me if I'm wrong, but these people do actually teach, don't they? What I want to know is what in hell they're doing that they imagine incites arousal! On second thought, that's just what I don't want to hear, since it'll all be a lot of filth and wild fantasy besides. Am I right? Correct me if I'm wrong, but this is just an excuse for people to dream about students pining for them, getting all electrified in Intro to the Short Story, am I right? Well, that's sickening. And pathetic too, since their classes, I'm sure, are just as flaccid as mine and yours. Admit it straight out, I say! If Morse and Barreca can't keep their minds off smut, let them write about what goes on at the MLA! Hell, I could contribute a long chapter myself, and you too, I happen to know. Remember those two we met at the Houston convention after we left the Victorian session cause you said if you heard Hillis Miller prattle one more time you'd. . . .

Nothing in the last sentence is true: Morse and Barreca are each of them quite capable of keeping their minds off smut and some have witnessed them doing so; my friend (a Victorian scholar) spends his MLAs attending cash bars and seeking attention; I did nothing in Houston to be ashamed of, and I certainly never spoke ill of Hillis Miller, who is a dear old friend with lots of influence.

Anyhow, this opening section you're now reading (entitled "A False Lead," which should tell you a lot—know what I mean? know what I mean?), this opening section is an attempt to develop my friend's assertion that the whole idea of erotic teaching is a sad and silly phantom. Let's see what will happen if we take this guy (from a large Eastern school) seriously (which will be a new twist): "erotic instruction" is a fable so sadly paranoic it is heart-withering. Utterly ignored and alone, the gluggy

nerds of this world, our teachers, flap their arms, yap, and survive by
nursing the delusion that the young people yawning before them not only
admire their minds but itch for their bodies. Let's see what we can do with
my friend's (suspiciously wild-eyed) notion that eroticism does not exist
at all, at least not in teaching.

Here we go . . .

The other essays in this volume are all exercises in the spreading
of what folklorists call urban legends and the rest of us call bull. What's
more, the editors know it and admit they have got together this collection for no better reason than to "meet a need," i.e., wedge out a
gap and then mash something into it. Thus, you see, this volume aligns
itself with "Guide to Sublime Ohio Vistas," "Let's Go: Des Moines,"
and "The Wit of Catharine MacKinnon." But if it were only a matter
of trying to hawk vacuity, we (I could say "I," but I know you're with
me on this) would heave a sigh and say that times are tough and that
everyone must publish. But it's worse (much) than that: in a cynical
appeal to our baser self, our (I'm choosing my words carefully here)
erotic hungers, this volume suggests that this non-subject is also arousing, subversive, a secret-waiting-to-be-blabbed that is scandalous and
ever so animating.

Maturity, you and I agree, is, at bottom, an erotic realism, the graceful
and becoming acknowledgement that Sophia Loren will not, after all
these years, come to the door and tear our clothes from us, right off us,
all of them. No she won't. Had she been likely to do so, she would have
done it by now. She isn't coming. Stop thinking about whether she should
have come or whether she would have come had she had any sense or all
the time you wasted preparing for her or whether you are not justified in
writing her a very angry letter. We (You and I) are mature and have put
away childish things. We laugh at the idea of Sophia Loren coming to our
door, though she is still so heart-stoppingly beautiful and would have
such a good time with us were she somehow only to drop by when she is
here and she wouldn't after all have to stay so long (she is often in Los
Angeles, you know, and so am I).

I need a new paragraph, as that last one is taking on a life of its own,
an inconvenient thing but not uninstructive, so I let it stand for what it
shows us about the working of the mind when it's really going. Maturity
amounts to accepting what's what, the old spilled milk that's all that's left
of your dreams, the shattered rainbows and golden dawns turned into
smog-screened acid drizzle—and not only accepting but finding strength

in what is left behind, what Ruskin termed the philosophic horniness. Here's maturity for you: we each of us live at the center of an erotic cosmos that is inhabited by us alone. Others have their own cosmi, you see; but they don't make contact. In fact, they speed apart from one another in an expanding, increasingly empty universe; it's the sexual big bang. Put more simply, you may find me alluring (an example, but a telling one); but, I will not be aware of your (nearly overpowering) feelings, and thus will muster no response. That's the way it is. No use howling, at least if you're mature.

But howling is more mature than retreating to cuckoo-land, where the editors of this volume lilt around cheeping about sex in the classroom. They are locked into a mental space where they also watch griffins coupling and mermaids strip. I do not think you will hear mermaids singing in this volume. It is an invitation to regress (that's not too strong a word) to a time when we really did imagine that someone at the door meant Sophia had come to her senses, had said yes to life and to me. Even when we went back to work after an encounter with the Jehovah's Witness, we didn't give up, fed our titillating daydreams. Those of us willing to abandon such puerility will have nothing to do with such fantasies, will make do with the sexual possibilities, however sad and wizened, God has seen fit to place in our path.

Be right back—someone's (oh jesus!) at the door.

Clarity Coming

What I mean is this: there are two ways to approach the subject of "sleeping with the teacher." One is to adopt the position taken above: it's preposterous. Another is to suggest that pedagogy IS eroticism through and through and that only relatively trivial things like old habits and cultural prejudices keep teachers and students clothed and off one another as it is.

Both of these approaches are flawed, I'm here to tell you, though I know you probably have placed yourself in one or the other camp. If you have, goodbye. If not, read on and I'll give you a third position, one that will make you free and capacious, maximize your pleasure as well as your probity, secure your intellectual and moral superiority to all those around you.

Absolute Passion

My friend's position, however, is not so pathological or so useless to us as it might seem or as this scholar himself (his first initial is N.) indisputably is. Let's keep exploring its utility. My friend (above average height) does note the odd absolutism that often infects discussions of sex and sexuality, the way in which people are driven into all-or-nothing corners. You've noticed that. Essentialism is one sign of this: otherwise smart and educated (alert, with-it) people say, without a blink, that somebody *is* gay, or straight, or a pedophile—as if such species thinking were not in the least suspect.

You and I know better, which is why a closer look at my friend's especially naive absolutisms might be instructive: it will reveal to us how the less sophisticated view things, and it's always good to know that. So, let's give a little more play to the idea that erotic instruction is merely an urban legend. You with me now? I'm anxious to be clear, and I've been told I'm not always, so I am taking great pains here, even with this editor/biographer's views (which should result in charges being filed, especially when what he did in Houston is taken into account). What we're still on is our first point. We haven't left it, despite its lack of weight. The present section tries to look calmly and with a skeptical but open-hearted intelligence on the idea that classroom eroticism is a non-issue, blithering nonsense.

Students and Teachers Burn for Truth, Not One Another

Here's how my friend, were he of another order, might go about developing persuasively his guess, based doubtless on his own gray life, that classroom eros is a legend, a rumor, bunk. He could cite the *Symposium* (I think it is) and other well-known sources for the cultural construction of the pedagogue, tracing it carefully through Rousseau and Thomas Arnold and Horace Mann and—I needn't go on as you are all as capable as I (probably not, but we'll pretend) of supplying the big names and a précis of their views. What would become immediately apparent is that the original (Greek, anyhow) erotic construction of pedagogy (better just say "pederastic" and be done with it) has yielded over time to the "familial," where Teacher is not Lover, but Dad or Mom. Hence the incest baggage and something the very reverse of erotic, except in the field of the unconscious, which is not our concern here, of course. For us, it's enough to observe what everyone knows: when the folks walk in, sex flies out the window.

To reinforce this incest taboo, all sorts of narratives are told about how teachers are dry, wizened, sterile—capable only of comic imitations of passion. Nothing is funnier or more disgusting than the idea of the math teacher copulating with the woman who does physics and gym. They have no equipment. Just so: Ichabod Crane and all the comic opera buffoons and the schoolmasters in Fielding and Smollett and Wing Biddlebaum and Aschenbach, the last two rendered in a different tone but still supporting my point. My point is that, however virile flesh-and-blood teachers (you, me) may be, the part they are required to play allows them only bumbling impotence. Our culture provides but one erotic script for the pedagogue, and it's a farce.

Now, you may think that I am confusing comic plots with real life, but I'm not. It's you who are confused. I'm saying that our practices and bodies conform to the requirements of the parts we are assigned. That much is clear as pie. We (you, anyhow) have no sexual inclinations, send out no vibes and get none back, because you have adapted, as you must. It's all there in Darwin. This is not a matter of nerdiness merely; it's social selection, a matter of survival of our cultural tales. Look at how we dress: always with an eye to the unalluring. Look at the bodies we foster: shapeless and uncomfortable. Both are designed to make the idea of sexual intercourse never present where we are: our clothes are such as no one would ever want removed; our bodies those no one would ever want to clamber on. That's just the way it is.

One qualification: the teachers of the very young are often knockouts, men and women alike. Gorgeous kindergarten teachers are the rule; but they become progressively less thinkable as sexual partners as the students get older and more capable of thinking that sexual partners are what they'd like to have. By junior high it's a mockery, by high school preposterous. Graduate education is an exposure to full-scale god-awful revulsion; it's a wonder the highly-educated propagate. Those who go on to be deans and presidents enter another species altogether, a reptilian order where cross-fertilization with the human is not to be thought on.

Look at our fantasies too. This is a good test. What gets talked about when everyone is drunk, say, or in the coffee room, or lying big-time somewhere else, like a poker party? I submit that in all my years of having confidential friends, I have never heard so much as a convincing fantasy, a lie that was told with any hope that it would be believed. One runs into the same academic folktales, and even these are pathetic. Here's one of the longest-lived and most popular. I'll tell it now because it collars the way even academic eros, at its most phantasmatic and unrestrained, amounts to an acceptance of our anti-erotic role:

This really beautiful student came into my office two days before the final. Now I mean to tell you s/he (it don't matter) was really goddam beautiful. [Notice the poverty of descriptive language—very revealing.] Well, this beautiful young thing said, "Oh, Dr. Kincaid, I'm so very anxious to do well in your course." S/he got closer and closer to me as s/he said this. "Are you?" I said. "Yes I am," s/he said. I was silent. "I really want to please you," s/he said smiling up at me. "Do you?" I said. "Yes I do," s/he said. I was silent and s/he smiled up at me again. "I'd do anything to please you, anything to get a good grade." "Oh?" I said. "Absolutely anything!" s/he smiled. "Anything?" I said. "Oh yes," s/he moaned; "anything!" So, you know what I did? I turned from him/her and closed the venetian blinds and then I turned back around and faced him/her and I said, "Are you sure you'd do anything?" "Yes, Dr. Kincaid, and I meant"—here s/he smiled up at me again—"ABSOLUTELY ANYTHING." I let his/her words hang in the air like a shimmering summer shower or petal of rose and then I got closer to him/her and I said in a low husky voice—I was quite close to the beautiful thing—"Study!"

That's very funny; but forget that and concentrate on what it reveals. This is the sort of story Freud identified as typical of the humor of the downtrodden: recognizing the disabling part one has to play and caricaturing it, exaggerating it and thus beating your opponent to the punch. It's not that we dare claim eroticism for ourselves; we say, in effect, "I know, I know—but I don't give a damn; and to prove it I'll tell a humiliating joke against myself that's wittier than anything you can come up with." And that's all we have, you see, even as legend. So maybe my friend is right.

If so, we may ask, then, why all the fuss? Where do all the current stories about erotic classrooms come from, what is the source of the worry about teachers and students going at it? In a world that believes in alien abduction, recovered memory, Satanism, and Newt Gingrich, perhaps nothing should surprise us; but all these things are food for sober reason compared to the idea of randy teachers and (fantastic!) students randy for them. So the question remains, where do these stories come from? The simpleton enthusiasm of our editors, eager to publish on any subject whatever, cannot entirely explain away even the existence of this volume. So, once again, where do these stories come from? The answers are so many and so uninteresting, I'll list them:

1. From neurotics like my fiftyish friend who, despite protestations, are unable not to tell sex stories, the more unlikely the better: sex among air traffic controllers, during bungee jumps, in veterinarians' offices.

2. From right-wing cockatrices like Rush Limbaugh, who hate sex and academics equally and can imagine nothing more damning than coupling them.

3. Bitter academics who have come to feed on self-hatred and get pleasure in nothing but dirtying their own nest. I am not sure there are any of these, but there might be, and if there are, they'd tell these stories for sure.

4. Mischievous students who find the idea hilarious. I think this is the major source of all this hoo-haw.

5. More mischievous students who don't find the idea funny but know that, like the music they pretend to admire, it irks their elders.

6. A general public so anxious to talk about sex between children and adults, so obsessed with the idea and image, that no improbability is too great, no absurdity too palpable.

Well, this is the best case that can be made for my friend's thesis. It's a weak case. It stinks. But you wouldn't maybe have known that had it not been aired.

Eroticism Is the Air We Breathe

Let me repeat that: eroticism is the air we breathe. This slogan is meant to stand for the very opposite of my wizened friend's view that there is, in effect, no such thing anywhere, that it's all, like multiple orgasm and literary theory and wee people who live amongst the ferns, a lie. Now, in this section, we'll swing to what is really just another absolutism, but certainly a more engaging one than my friend's wilted nonsense: that everything is erotic and we'd be better off (you would, certainly) if we'd just what the hell admit it.

Let me draw on my own experience here, though I mean nothing personal by this. Right now there's this elderly man doing some work for me and Mrs. K on the house we live in, we having hired him not because we're rich and are used to having others at our beck and call but because my wife is very unhandy, doesn't even try to fix things. But it's not my wife's klutziness I am addressing but her erotic qualities or, more exactly, those of our (not that I mean "our" in any possessive way) handyman, call him Millard. Millard is very old I think, or at least very beat-up, unshaven, and dappled, like a cow. Internal liquids escape and drip from him; hairs grow from his eyelids; inside his mouth are swamp things; his clothes sag and reveal unspeakable butt-cracks even where no butt could possibly be. Millard has trouble adjusting the volume control on his voice, which is either pitched at inaudible-murmur or jet-take-off-deafening. Millard tells dirty jokes and winks; he once actually wiped his nose on my shoulder; he smells a lot like the shrimp I once buried for three weeks because my Dad told me as a joke it'd make good fish bait that way and I believed him.

Millard, I say it proud, is erotic. I'm watching him outside the window right now, doing something to himself with a rake and I say it's erotic. I can hardly keep from rushing out and joining him. Millard is erotic and so is mother and so are students and so is W. E. Gladstone, James K. Polk, Henry Kissinger, Janet Reno, Macaulay Culkin, Julia Roberts, Geraldo, Orrin Hatch, Strom Thurmond, Storm Davis, George Eliot, George Gissing, George Brett, Barbara Bush, Barbara Stanwyck, Barbie, Barbarella, Mary Todd Lincoln, and Mary Mother of God. And to prove it just try to think of the people you try to think of when you don't want to get aroused, the images of the unerotic you call up to calm yourself and then what happens is you find yourself getting all aroused anyhow which proves my point that there's nothing that isn't erotic even Shelley Winters if we just admit it and that it's all OK and we should relax and allow a kind of low-voltage eroticism (which is all even young teachers can hope for) to give a little tingle to our lives in each and every moment of them, including the classroom.

I think that pretty well catches what can be said for this point of view. There really isn't anything more to say. Still, I think we can stand some expansion on the idea that everything is erotic, since it's a view that, however giddy and frivolous, isn't heard too often. For that reason, what if we tried to map out the erotics of the classroom, even if there aren't any?

Here goes: as Judy Blume has shown and as every boy and girl in the sixth grade knows, blackboards are the most pornographically arousing things there are. Just go to one at age twelve to work a math problem and see what happens—zing! This is true in its way for girls, I've been told, though I wouldn't presume to describe it exactly, not wanting to speak for the feminerotic, as I've no call to do and know it. Blackboards, then, are one thing. Another is desks in rows. Desks in themselves are neither uppers or downers, but the rows are another thing: they suggest both infinite order and yet crawly-space secretive possibilities both between the rows and underneath the constituents (desks) of those rows, if you see what I mean. Even if you don't see it, I know you feel it.

Perhaps that's enough of that. The mapping business isn't too persuasive, but I'll let it stand since it looks sophisticated. But more important are exotic classroom smells: pencil shavings and oiled floors, musty cloakrooms leaking odors out into the room, the smell of someone peeing himself/herself, the tick of the clock, and the portrait of George Washington with the clouds under him. I realize that the tick and the painting are not smells, but they're atmospheric; I realize too that the famous Washington portrait is unfinished, not cloud-beruffled; but all kids think it's clouds, so that's what matters: it's only when shades of the prison house begin to close that we don't see the clouds any longer—or see up the teacher's dress either, all classrooms offering that view, a view which is not in itself erotic, certainly (except to my friend), but part of a hazy, static atmosphere that is itself erotic.

People who say they really do think lots of sex is going on between teachers and students are thinking about this smudgy, sun-filtered atmosphere: warm and drowsy, protected and never-changing, vaguely Eastern in its exoticism and its serene indifference to anything but its own comforts. Like the Western imaginings of a harem, the classroom we evoke in our minds wraps itself in its own perverse self-sufficiency, like a photograph so enticing and achingly ungraspable we wish we had not seen it. (The writing here in this part is especially affecting.) The classroom retreats for us into an imaginative construction we can treasure and condemn, hug close and cast off, welcome into our house and spit on as foreign, turn back the covers for and . . . [That's enough!—Eds.] It is this teasing, too close to home exoticism that so shocked Oscar Wilde's jurors, who may have been far less concerned about buggery than about Alfred Taylor's rooms: incense burning, drapes never opened, thick carpets, more sofas than were strictly necessary—and always, always the same. Who wouldn't find it necessary to find sex there, find it and speak out against it? Otherwise, how could we live with ourselves?

Just so, the schoolroom. I think that nails it, but you might think that the development of this particular argument has not gone on long enough. (The argument, you recall, which we're ventilating even though we don't support it, is that all things are erotic.) Perhaps we have focused too strongly on the issue of atmosphere, leaving out, more or less, the human actants, as we might say, the two (or so) it takes to hobble and gobble.

Can it be said that teachers are erotic, that term being understood according to the best understandings available, or that students are, for that matter? I am speaking here of the material things, the people and the bodies they're in: can we say they are erotic or regard one another in this manner? Think of, say, Ms. Johnson or Mr. Kettle (taught shop) or, on the other hand, of Melissa or Scott. Erotic? Come on!

Conclusion to This Section and Transition to Next

So, it's clear that these absolutisms meet, the snake swallows his tail: saying that everything is erotic is much the same as joining my friend in declaring eroticism a gyp. We cannot live an intelligent or satisfying life going around supposing everything we come upon is alike arousing or that nothing is. The first person would get nothing done—or only one thing done—and the second would accomplish much, perhaps, but joylessly.

The answer is that we need to think about sex not in terms of fixed categories and essences and that sort of thing, but in terms of scales and degrees and swings here and there and dynamic shifts and changes. We need to think of all things that way, but sex is obviously most in need of relativizing and temporalizing. Alfred Kinsey, even when he was observing WASPS, saw that their activities and being and sexual preferences and doings could not be caught and held stationary, like—well, insects on a pin. If this is true of insects, how much more true it is, naturally, of human goings at it. Kinsey firmly and properly rejected all categorical thinking on sexuality as muddled and disabling:

It would encourage clearer thinking on these matters if persons were not characterized as heterosexual or homosexual, but as individuals who have had certain amounts of heterosexual experience and certain amounts of homosexual experience. Instead of using these terms as substantives which stand for persons, or even as adjectives to describe persons, they may better be used to describe the nature of the overt sexual relations, or of the stimuli to which an individual erotically responds.[1]

---

1. Anybody here? This is just a test to see if footnotes are ever noticed. If you are actually reading this, please call both the editors (collect, during business hours) and tell them. Their view of footnotes—"just put anything down or ignore them altogether; nobody reads them"—struck me as cynical and unscholarly, wholly at odds with my own rigorous training. But I agreed to this test. The quotation, in case you care, comes from Kinsey's *Sexual Behavior in the Human Male*, I think, which was published in Philadelphia, W. B. Saunders, in 1948. The quote's from way in the back of the book, past p. 600 (I read it all); try 617 or 618.

Taking Kinsey's enlightened relativism and "charting it onto the current trajectory of our desires" (I read that in *Representations*), we get this: eroticism and erotic responses are wildly various and change constantly; what's more, they exist at different levels and at different degrees simultaneously. Eroticism is a little like the color red in a full-spectrum, three-dimensional kaleidoscope being whirled madly. (What a simile!) It is, thus (eroticism) always present but also always about to vanish and also always anticipated. Erotic (red) impulses and guesses bang around with contrary feelings like indifference (yellow), fear (purple), and repulsion (blue). They may exist or not in various shadings at various levels of consciousness and unconsciousness at the same time, the spinning sorting out different possibilities that will allow us either to act or not to act.

And jumbly-tumbly as this superb figure of the kaleidoscope is, it still gives us an image of our desire that is too stable and far too simple. Desire is not a bit of glass. Desire often takes its shading and owes its existence to other feelings, often is camouflaged, often is pumped into being by an effort of will much more massive than is suggested by the turning of a kaleidoscope's barrel. Just ask my friend (who lives in a big city, very big) about that. Let's say, as a figure not to replace but to complement the kaleidoscope, that desires swim into our ken like flecks of sunlight across and through the ocean. You see that desire always is there and always is not, can always be called into being or denied, that it lives in and among us, on one hand, inescapably, and, on the other, only because it is invited—most cordially, cordially.

Conclusion

To focus, then, on desire as it's activated in the classroom is, in one sense, mildly interesting, since the classroom provides a balmy-exotic setting and a good many people together, so that desire will float in and out and around, sure enough. But this is also true of a grocery store or Magic Mountain or the AAA office where they do TripTiks. You may (I hope not) be thinking that the classroom is different because of the power imbalance. Don't be thinking that way. Power has become so laden with sexuality that it is, in our culture, eros itself. It has also, power has, been made metaphysical, and that does a lot of harm. Power is only a word, only a word. We've learned to do without "hopefully," and soon we will drop "problematic," so surely we can forget "power." Power doesn't exist in nature, only in our own degraded imaginings: free yourself from this phantom. Well, I'm sure that won't do the job on those who believe in power, belief systems being hard to rock, but I tried. I tried in other writings of mine to argue this point carefully and it hasn't worked, so I'll just blurt it out here.

Classroom eroticism is certain to be there, sure, just like anxiety, fear, repulsion, boredom, and even curiosity, affection, and good-will. To isolate it, however, as this volume has tried to do, is foolish, futile, and foul.

Foul? Yeah, since it draws attention away from issues that matter. On one hand, we are being skinned alive by right-wing anti-intellectuals now in power: virtually all our values and best procedures are in jeopardy: theory, multi-culturalism, research itself, government support for the arts and humanities, experimental work, gender studies, queer studies, university presses, journals, small colleges, large universities, new jobs, any jobs, and intellectual freedom. On the other hand, we have access to previously undreamt-of possibilities opened to us by new theoretical developments, curricular experiments, more smart people in the discipline, and cultural studies.

In such a climate and in such a world, to join in the mob, yelling and snorting, waving a banner that proclaims "Stamp Out Classroom Sex," or "Classroom Sex Now!" as if this were an issue either way, as if it mattered, as if something were there to attend to, as if it were the one thing needful—oh my! Wragg is in custody!

Hell's fire, we do have problems, positive human attractions and their occasional misfiring not being high on the list. To elevate them is to drag a red herring across a trail that is otherwise leading us to important and maybe sweet territory. It's like pretending that the sexual abduction of children, a trivial issue, is THE problem, allowing us to ignore the millions of children who are hungry, without hope, beaten or even murdered, neglected, and actually thrown away. It's like complaining to the purser on the Titanic about the quality of the coffee. It's like being annoyed about the hay fever that kicks up on you in Eden.

If we stopped being afraid of eroticism and stopped equating it with power, we might find a passion we liked, one with which we could spend time, make friends, enjoy, and stop bashing one another with. Such a turn of events would be a boon for everyone, even my dreary friend.

The "Editors' Note" at the beginning of this chapter was, in fact, written by James Kincaid himself.

GERHARD JOSEPH

Bartleby and the Professor

In thinking about the dynamics of the classroom when the issue reaches a level of conscious design, I try as a teacher to fashion a place that is psychically neither too far away from nor too close to students, one that is neither too coldly professional nor too intrusively personal. Either extreme, I've usually assumed, will lead to pedagogical ineffectiveness—if not to some downright disaster or other. Of course such a statement of policy assumes that a teacher pretty much sets and controls the psychic distance, that the predesignated, conventional quality of his or her role will make it possible to assert an authority, to fix by an act of individual will a relatively stable semester- or year-long attitude. But as the erotics of our private rather than merely professional contacts should teach us, such a sense of unidirectional control is usually self-deceptive, even in the most apparently passive and cooperative of classes. Passivity or cooperation can of course mask all sorts of student reservation that the teacher's ego may prefer to ignore. But some classroom experiences, especially those in which a quirkily rebellious student within an otherwise "cooperative" group asserts him or herself, highlight the illusory nature of the teacher's pedagogical mastery more than others. And I use the word "mastery" to throw up the question of whether the pedagogical model outlined above is, as a matter of fact, a gendered one.

I had given Jane—let's call her that—a D in the previous class she had taken with me, a sophomore survey of English literature in a branch of the City University of New York. A smart, hostile, African-American, working-class young woman, she had refused to do any of the papers I had assigned ("I'm sick of writing about white male authors," she said— this in a course that went from Beowulf to Jonathan Swift in the pre-feminist, pre-multiculturalist classroom of the early seventies) and had instead handed in moderately successful if highly idiosyncratic papers on literary subjects of her own devising. When toward the end of the semester I announced that the college had scheduled our final examination for 8:30 in the morning on a set day, Jane said that there was no way that she could write intelligibly at such an hour and that I would have to reschedule the exam—or at least give it to *her* later in the day. Needless to say ("needless to say?"), I refused and told her that I would just average an F in with the rest of her work if she did not turn up. She didn't, I would not give her the makeup she insisted on—and hence the D, which probably ought to have been an F, I now imagine I thought at the time. At least, I said to myself, I was rid of this particular albatross once and for all.

Wrong: one of the very first persons to sign up for an American literature survey I gave the following year was Jane. And her immediate, first-class response to my syllabus, which included *The Adventures of Huckleberry Finn,* was to try to circulate a petition asking me to find a substitute for this "blatantly racist" novel. I responded with a writing assignment asking the class to consider whether in the light of Mark Twain's continuing use of "nigger" and treatment of Huck and Jim, there was any substance to Jane's characterization of the novel. I feel she's wrong, of course, that "racist" is too categorical a term but, I also think there's something to be said about the complexity of Twain's feelings about race, if only in the light of the re-infantilization of Jim in the last third of the book when Tom Sawyer—and his regressive adolescent spirit—enters it once more. Jane's was therefore an arguable reading (and one that has a pretty respectable critical pedigree) that I tried explicitly to address in my assignment. But this was yet another paper that she refused to write. Or rather "preferred not to," for I had begun to associate her in my mind with Bartleby the Scrivener, the law copyist in Herman Melville's great story (also on my syllabus), who mysteriously refuses, with reiterations of these words, all request for cooperation by an increasingly frustrated and comically angry employer—with whom *I* had begun to identify.

There's more, but the pattern of professional assignment, student rebellion, and professional parry must by now be clear. What seems less clear—certainly to me—is why I responded as I did. For the entire experience has for me a kind of personal and pedagogical resonance, a powerful cluster of meanings whose full implications I hardly understand but some of which I can surely articulate. Why, I can hear certain colleagues—and, for that matter, students—asking, didn't you assert greater control, have a more disciplined sense of your discipline, in the

face of such continuing challenge and provocation? Why did you sup-
press the anger *you* clearly must have felt, partially masked even in the
present screen-memory as self-deprecating irony and self-congratulatory
"tolerance" for a Crazy Jane (to work in yet another literary allusion
that may serve to aestheticize and thus anaesthetize something painful,
something humiliating)? A lifelong passivity that translates readily
enough into the passive (or not so passive) aggressiveness of this very
narrative? A liberal guilt at class, gender, and/or racial "oppression"?
As a matter of fact I did once when I thought her especially disruptive
angrily ask Jane to leave the classroom: she refused, on the grounds that
she had "paid good money" and was not going to be forced out. What
does one do then? Call security? (In the event, I did cancel the class in
mid-hour and have a brief reconciliatory talk with Jane thereafter that
served to paper matters over between us until the end of the semester.)
For her part, why did Jane keep at it with me? Why come back for
another round (and I employ the boxing metaphor to suggest both the
mutual antagonism and the sense of regulated sport that I now feel
characterized our confrontations) with an instructor who had already
given her a D?

   Despite my self-doubt and suppression at the time and in the current
retelling, I thus consider my exchanges with Jane and the failure of control
attendant thereon deeply instructive, whatever she may have taken away
from them. For they did foreground for me, even at the time and in as stark
a fashion as possible, the ideology behind my teaching—the authoritative
stance of an older, white, middle-class, male professor, a purveyor of
literary truth by way of a fairly well established Western canon, vis-à-vis a
younger, black (now "African-American"), working-class, woman student. What was unusual and disturbing and—yes, exhilarating—about
Jane was the uncompromising tenacity with which she kept bringing to the
surface what is usually kept implicit in the urban classroom within which I
teach: the complex hegemonic interweave within the teacher-student economy of older and younger, of male and female, of white and African-
American, of Anglo and Latino, of middle and working class (and which of
these pairs, if any, was in our individual confrontation primary I cannot
fathom). Without apparent fear of my greater power institutionalized in
my control of grades and demonstrated by that earlier D, she just kept
challenging, from the depths of her own psychic and cultural needs, my
psychic and cultural authority as coherent Subject who is Supposed to
Know. That Lacanian specter of armored self-certitude I ran into as a

theoretical construct some years later, but Jane prepared me for its mystifying form. And I would want her to understand, wherever she is, that, alongside my puzzlement and anger (muted into this narrative) as a counter to her complex feelings, I'm grateful for the dialogue—whatever its contradictory, open-ended meanings.

DEBORAH DENENHOLZ MORSE

Educating Louis

Teaching the Victorian Father in Trollope's *He Knew He Was Right*

I begin with two scenes from my recent past: In the first scene, a burly, muscled student named Michael Holly is standing outside my bedroom window, throwing pebbles at the windowpane. After I throw open the window, he calls up, "Oh, Professor Morse, Denholm Elliott has died! I knew you would want to know! He died of AIDS—isn't it terrible?" This Michael's passion reminds me of the passionate Michael Furey in Joyce's *The Dead,* the boy who stood out in the wind and rain, in defiance of the weather, and of conventionalities. Michael Holly was standing under my window, in an erotic posture familiar from Romeo through Stanley Kowalski. He was there because, in a sense, he loved me. I was his English teacher, his erotic fantasy, and his friend. He knew that we would, together, grieve for Denholm Elliott, the Welsh actor who specialized in playing the father figure in films like *A Room with a View, Bleak House,* and *A Child's Christmas in Wales.* Michael Holly and I had come to know and respect each other in the milieu of the classroom, and we knew that we would mourn the death of creativity, of artistic brilliance, of the perfect, sensitive, disarming Father.

In the second scene, a tall, diffident, blond student knocks on my door, and then enters unthinkingly before I say "Come in." I am slightly irritated, but I tell the young man, whose name is Tim Martin, to sit down. He asks to be in my upper-division Victorian fiction course, and he is a freshman. I ask him to state his case, and he speaks for ten minutes—about his education in England, about his love of the Victorian novel. I let him in the course, breaking precedent. Two years later, after he has taken three courses from me and transferred to Columbia University, he visits our family in England. We sit on the floor of a tiny, cramped, and wonderful Cambridge bookstore while reminiscing about our friendship and talking about Dickens and Trollope. We hug goodbye as he leaves for London, and marvel at how we have come to be so close after our inauspicious first encounter. I know his story well now, his story of grief for the father, his father, a famous *Time* magazine correspondent, killed in the Vietnam War.

My own father was a doctor, a pediatrician; by all accounts, he was a very brilliant man, the protege of Brennaman, "Father of Pediatric Medicine." He was chief resident at Michael Reese Hospital in Chicago for six years before World War II, when that was an honor conferred on the most promising of young physicians. Early on in his career he identified a new disease, wrote articles, invented a machine to help premature babies live longer. I am vague about much of this, which feels like myth although it is in fact truth. My father never spoke of these things, but Brennaman came to visit us, as did many other notable physicians. I do remember that we often went to medical conventions with my father, and he attended them without us as well. I would hear from friends of my father's, other doctors—indeed, I still hear these things from them when I visit Modesto, California, my hometown—that my father always knew the answers to the questions after lectures, and that everyone, including the lecturer, ended up listening to my father. I don't think, in fact, that I ever saw a photograph of him at a convention that didn't show him talking animatedly while a ring of fascinated men surrounded him. He was so brilliant and witty and knowledgeable that he was, quite simply, irresistible. Everyone found him to be so, both men and women. On top of every other gift he possessed, he was darkly handsome and very kind. Friends who see his photograph ask about the movie star—Ronald Coleman? His glamour cast an aura about all my childhood.

When I was not quite sixteen, my father died very suddenly. One night we were laughing at the dinner table, the next morning he left to see patients at the hospital, and that afternoon he was himself a patient. I never saw him alive again. That was the hard thing, the thing that needed remedying, transforming, replaying. He was still alive in my memory, but I couldn't look at his kind, intelligent brown eyes or hear his resonant baritone voice reassure me about the one million insecurities I had as a high school sophomore. He had been my teacher, my counselor, my friend, as well as my father and my pediatrician. As a younger daughter with a beautiful, assured, and truly brilliant older sister, I needed his admiration desperately. When he was alive, I was convinced—most of the time—that I too was smart, pretty, and creative. He saw my particular gifts, valued my singing and writing and even cheerleading, asked me to look at medical journals with him so that he could share his own interests. Without him, I wasn't sure I was worth so very much.

My period of mourning, of looking for the perfect father surrogate, had begun. Once safely off to a big university, I met my first and only professor/lover, although he was one among a number of professors in college and graduate school with whom I shared an erotic attraction. He was in his mid-thirties, dark and handsome, and seemed to me then to be brilliant and virile to an almost magical extent. I went braless to class and wore long hippie dresses made from Indian bedspreads and spread my waist-length Pre-Raphaelite hair out around my shoulders in a manner that might have been erotic but was probably comical in his eyes (and others') as well. I was sleeping with another man in the class, so the atmosphere must have been pretty charged. He understood that this liaison was highly pleasurable but temporary, that he would never be my father. He had several daughters of his own, whom he adored. Later, after our passionate affair, I married someone my own age, and he married someone a good deal older than me. We all had lunch together and I threw up because I was pregnant. My professor called me "daughter dear," and we all laughed. We had never fully consummated our union.

I wrote him many letters, full of love and wit and literary criticism, perhaps the best letters I ever wrote. He burned them in a fit of guilt about the wife from whom he was separated when he wanted me, even though he left her before we ever met. I used to write to him in my head all the time, framing all of my consciousness in anticipation of his response. I wanted him to regret me, to think about me as the one who got away. The thing is, I never did get away from loving him, from hearing the words he wrote to me: "I do feel close to you. I haven't wanted to hurt you. But I should have let you know, sooner, what you needed to know."

In graduate school, I got a crush on a young professor who was writing on Anthony Trollope. Under his influence, I began to read Trollope's fiction, in which so many daughters need to resist their fathers. That interested me because it was so alien to my experience: I never got to rebel against my father, because he died just when I was getting ready. Perhaps I could play out that part of my teenage rebellion by writing about the stalwart Mary Palliser in *The Duke's Children* or the intransigent Alice Vavasor in *Can You Forgive Her?* My first book told the Trollopian daughter's story as it evolved in Trollope's great urban chronicle, the Palliser series. I was compelled, in writing that text, not only by the fervent will to resist the Father that both Mary and Alice embodied, but also—perhaps primarily—by the story of Glencora McCluskie, an orphan who did not rebel against her domineering relatives. I became interested in Trollope's insistence on the reeducation of Glencora's husband, the Duke of Omnium, patriarch of the Palliser novels. In the early Palliser novels, he must learn to be a more loving and egalitarian husband; by the final novel of the series, *The Duke's Children,* he must learn that his late Victorian children need to forge their own histories—not relive his. The lessons are bitter ones, but the sense that he makes some accommodation to changing values is signified by the Duke's gracious presence at their wedding ceremonies, despite his lingering inward grief and vexation, his sense of "all that he had suffered."

And yet I realized, in writing about the rebellious daughter, I was myself enacting in the classroom and in my professor's office the narrative of the most dutiful of daughters. My professor had himself become my surrogate father as well as mentor and erotic fantasy, and I could not please him enough to satiate my great need for his approval. I studied twelve hours a day for eighteen months for my preliminary examinations for the Ph.D. Exhausted, I did not excel, but did fine and easily passed. My professor's disappointment was so manifest that I broke down in tears and cried for two hours straight. Now, twelve years later, I am fascinated by the Victorian father/mentor. Perhaps I am ready, now that *I* am the mentor, to focus more centrally on the reeducation of the authority figure in Trollope.

Trollope's *He Knew He Was Right* was written during the period directly following the first two novels of his urban Palliser chronicle, in which the locus of English political power is explored. *He Knew* dissects the obsessive will to power of a member of the Victorian elite. In successive vignettes, we see how Louis Trevelyan, Victorian gentleman par excellence, the perfect husband and father, refuses to learn what Trollope's thinking women and men have to teach about the possibilities for more liberated relationships between the sexes, between the generations—and, perhaps, within the Empire. Ultimately, Trevelyan's resistance to his instructors in compassion, love—and feminism—leads to his own madness and death.[1]

Louis Trevelyan, exemplar of the English upper-class gentleman, ninth wrangler at Oxford, is explicitly introduced on the first page of the novel as "a very pearl among men" (5). We expect him to be the hero of the tale. But in a much more extreme sense than Arthur Fletcher of *The Prime Minister,* another Trollope hero who is similarly described as "the very pearl of the Fletcher tribe," the white and shining "pearl" among Victorian men is not such a treasure after all. Experienced readers of Trollope might immediately hear something in Trollope's encomium that makes them wary of Trevelyan's perfection. As Frank O'Connor astutely comments in his essay on Trollope's narrator in *The Mirror in the Roadway,* "His favorite device is to lead his reader very gently up the garden path of his own conventions and prejudices and then to point out that the reader is wrong. This is not very like the behavior of a typical mid-Victorian gentleman."[2] Trevelyan decides, shortly after he is married, that he "should like to have his own way completely" (7). His inability to coerce his innocent wife Emily into admitting that she has committed adultery eventually leads to his isolation in the Italian countryside at the desiccated Casalunga, and then to his death near London, origin and emblem of the raving lunatic he has become.

Trollope critics have not fully analyzed the link between sexual dominance and racial mastery that is central to Trollope's novel. The irrational, obsessively jealous figure of Louis Trevelyan should be seen not only in terms of Victorian gender relations but also as a constructed element in a more global context, Victorian imperialism: the Cambridge-educated Trevelyan goes out to the Mandarin Islands to bring his dark wife, Emily Rowley, to London. And it is in London, the heart of English civilization, that Trollope sets his tale of obsession and madness.

Trollope's narrative strategies in *He Knew He Was Right* include evoking other stories of obsession that link race and gender. Trollope often figures Trevelyan as his Shakespearean prototype, Othello;[3] in one of numerous echoes in the text, Trevelyn laments "the pity of it" to his hired city detective, Bozzle. However, Trevelyan is very much a diminished Othello, neither war hero nor tragic dupe of an evil Iago. Trollope depicts Trevelyan's madness as the petulant ravings of a child, while the rebellion and sufferings of his dark, passionate wife take on a kind of tragic grandeur. As Jane Nardin comments, "Trollope is able to present Louis' grim decline in farcical terms . . . Ostensibly a man's tragedy, the novel is in fact the tragedy of a woman" (Nardin 204–5). Through his warped vision of himself as unquestioned authority figure, Trevelyan brings about his own insanity and death; the final chapter of the novel begins starkly, "At last the maniac was dead . . . " (733).

The image of Louis Trevelyan as raving "maniac" might recall the "madwoman in the attic" in Brontë's *Jane Eyre,* another narrative that underlies *He Knew He Was Right* and which gives point both to its gender critique and to its questioning of imperialism.[4] One might look at Trollope's text as a conscious reinscription of Brontë's novel: the well-bred Englishman marries a dark, passionate girl whom he cannot tame, a woman who is carefully described as Other. Although Emily is in fact daughter to the Governor of the Islands, she is described as rather like Brontë's Bertha Mason: "a very handsome young woman, tall, with a bust rather full for her age . . . dark . . . brown . . . and very strong, as are some girls who come from the tropics" (9). Trollope seems to foreshadow the Rochester of Jean Rhys's *Wide Sargasso Sea* in passages such as that in which Louis Trevelyn thinks, early on in his marital troubles:

He thought he could remember to have heard it said in early days, long before he himself had had an idea of marrying, that no man should look for a wife from among the tropics, that women educated amidst the languors of those sunny climes rarely came to possess those high ideas of conjugal duty and feminine truth which a man should regard as the first requisites of a good wife. As he thought of all this, he almost regretted that he had ever visited the Mandarins, or ever heard of the name of Sir Marmaduke Rowley. (37)

Those "high ideas of conjugal duty and feminine truth" are what the "Indian Messalina" of Brontë's text is lacking as well, we recall. Trevelyan's speech reminds us of the erotics of instruction in *Jane Eyre:* the best-known governess of the English novel is instructed in Romantic love by her domesticated Byronic hero, and ends up teaching him about true Christianity and Victorian marriage. It might be well if we pause to look at Brontë's text for a moment, to see in what senses it is a feminist precursor to Trollope's novel. Essentially, Jane refuses the Romantic teachings of her beloved Rochester, his assertion that no one will be harmed if Jane lives with him out of wedlock. They can decide their own morality, he claims, to which she responds with her famous speech in which she states that she will "keep the Law given by God; sanctioned by man" (344). In the next scenes of that novel, after her journey from Rochester's Thornfield to Moor House, she encounters the intransigent St. John Rivers, who tries to shape his mentor relationship to Jane so that she will marry him and go to India as a missionary. He instructs her in a joyless religion filled with duty, and wills her to name their working partnership an erotic union, although, as he tells her, "You were formed for labour, not for love" (428). Her happiest hours of instruction are in fact the time she spends learning German from her female teachers, her intellectual cousins, Mary and Diana Rivers, characters based upon Anne and Emily Brontë. It is only when she is teacher, wife, and mentor to Rochester, reading to him in his blindness, that Jane is truly fulfilled.

In Brontë's novel, the dark girl goes mad and is imprisoned. Then she throws herself from the battlements of Thornfield, dashing out her brains. In Trollope's novel, the Englishman goes mad and figuratively imprisons himself, all the while travelling restlessly away from London in peripatetic wanderings that ironically serve only to codify the identity forged in that city. In the end, Louis Trevelyan returns to London to die, destroyed by his own imperial self, his fine intellect destroyed, his body fevered and broken.

From the outset of the novel, Trollope makes us aware that Trevelyan has been instructed by his society to think that his privileged life is his birthright as an upper-class Victorian man, and, more intimately, as the sole heir of a widower, a successful professional father. He has no family obligations, and hence "no man could be more independent or more clearly justified in pleasing himself than was this lover" (5–6). There is also the intimation that he has not had a mother for some time, which perhaps helps to explain his misapprehension of the feminine. Trollope's words are quite consciously chosen in this regard, so that we will know that Trevelyan has been miseducated by his culture, and is now misinformed. In the following scene, he has just been cautioned by an old family friend, Lady Milborough, about Colonel Osborne's attentions to his wife:

But it was intolerably bitter to him that he should be warned about his wife's conduct by any living human being; that he to whom the world had been so full of good fortune,—that he, who had in truth taught himself to think that he deserved so much good fortune, should be made the subject of care on behalf of his friend, because of danger between himself and his wife! (25)

At the beginning of the couple's quarrel, Trevelyan has some doubts about the lessons he is teaching himself. After he has offended his wife by asking that Colonel Osborne not visit so very often at the house, Trevelyan reconsiders his perhaps too hasty chastising of his wife. He imagines another, more erotic and tender scenario in which he would gently teach his wife about the dangers of the "ancient Lothario," Osborne:

She had never before felt herself to be insulted by her husband. As soon as the word had been spoken Trevelyan had left the room and had gone down among his books. But when he was alone he knew that he had insulted his wife. He was quite aware that he should have spoken to her gently, and have explained to her, with his arm round her waist, that it would be better for both of them that this friend's friendship should be limited. There is so much in a turn of the eye and in the tone given to a word when such things have to be said,—so much more of importance than in the words themselves . . . But he was one to whose nature the giving of any apology was repulsive. He could not bear to have to own himself to have been wrong. (10)

It is significant that Trevelyan is not only well educated at one of the two great universities, but that he is still actively engaged in scholarly pursuits. He is a student even yet, a man who values reason and logic, who is writing a scientific article on the "waves of sound." It is therefore all the more terrible when his monomania on the subject of Emily's chastity and obedience slowly derange his intellect. Yet looked at from another angle, this retreat to his study, "among his books," is a retreat from emotion. There is something in the scene that recalls Edgar Linton in *Wuthering Heights*, shutting himself up in the library while his pregnant wife Catherine starves herself into delirium in their bedroom. Trollope's narrator tells us that "had he gone to her now and said a word to her in gentleness all might have been made right. But he did not go to her" (18).

It is not long before Trevelyan is uninterested in teaching himself to relent toward Emily. Gradually, his demand that his wife entirely submit to him becomes a belief in her guilty intercourse with Osborne. A number of characters in the novel try to intervene during the course of the marriage's dissolution, but Trevelyan is no longer receptive to any lessons except those that teach him what he is already sure that he knows: that his wife is not only obstinately disobedient, she is an adulteress. Early on in the quarrel between Trevelyan and Emily, Hugh Stanbury, his best friend from college days, tries to make Trevelyan see reason in one of the most telling of the novel's scenes of instruction between men. Trevelyan refuses to hear Stanbury, who has come as an emissary from Emily. Trevelyan speaks first:

"If you'll take my advice, you'll keep your hands out of this. It is not but that I regard you as being as good a friend as I have in the world; but to own the truth, I cannot put up with interference between myself and my wife."

"Of course you understand that I only come as a messenger."

"You had better not be a messenger in such a cause. If she has anything to say she can say it to myself."

"Am I to understand that you will not listen to me?"

"I had rather not."

"I think you are wrong," said Stanbury.

"In that matter you must allow me to judge for myself . . . " (71)

Stanbury has now been alienated from Trevelyan, and has become a "partisan" of the wife. As Stanbury parts angrily from his friend, he thinks, "I believe that no woman on earth could live with him . . . It was always the same with him,—a desire for mastery, which he did not know how to use when he had obtained it" (71–2). This comment suggests an analogy of Trevelyan to a willful child, a comparison that is often made in the novel.

One of the questions raised by my students as we study *He Knew He Was Right* is "Why are there all the scenes of Louis confronting different people?"[5] Certainly, Louis's increasingly adamant refusals to listen to reason are documented in the novel through his verbal encounters with a succession of characters after Hugh Stanbury: Lady Milborough, Lady Rowley, Sir Marmaduke Rowley, the family friend Charles Glascock, little Louie Trevelyan, and finally, Emily Trevelyan. In part, these characters serve as witnesses to his mental breakdown, as they attempt to instruct him in other possible ways of thinking and feeling, other constructions of the duties of men and women, man and wife, father and son. In one quite painful scene, Trevelyan sits with his quiet, cowed little son Louie in an upper room of the house at Casalunga in the dry Italian countryside. Trevelyan tries to be kind, to set out toys for the child's enjoyment, but he no longer knows how to communicate even with his child, who is too miserable to learn anything from his father, even if Trevelyan were able to reach outside his deranged state for long enough really to connect with another mind:

But the toys remained where the father had placed them, almost unheeded, and the child sat looking out of the window, melancholy, silent, and repressed. Even the drum did not tempt him to be noisy. Doubtless he did not know why he was wretched, but he was fully conscious of his wretchedness. In the meantime the father sat motionless, in an old worn-out but once handsome leathern armchair, with his eyes fixed against the opposite wall, thinking of the wreck of his life. (623)

Toward the end of his life, Trevelyan is capable only of interior monologues rather than any true dialogue with another human being. He spends his hours imagining his great self-abnegation in bestowing his goods on his sinful wife at his death. He views himself as a kind of Christ figure, but Trollope makes it clear that Trevelyan can no longer even love.

He is entirely self-focused, as the description of him imagining himself as martyred husband in the chapter ironically titled "Self-Sacrifice" attests:

He put out his thin wasted hands and looked at them, and touched the hollowness of his own cheeks, and coughed that he might hear the hacking sound of his own infirmity, and almost took glory in his weakness. It could not be long before the coals of fire would be heaped upon her head. (625)

Set against Trevelyan's colloquies with himself, his solitary madness, are the many fervent conversations during the course of this long novel in which characters often determine the shapes of their lives. One of the structuring devices of the text is the confrontation, although another is the more intimate discussion of values, such as the following discussion between Emily Trevelyan's sister Nora Rowley, and Hugh Stanbury's sister, the thorny spinster Priscilla Stanbury. As the discussion takes place, Nora has just refused to marry the Honourable Charles Glascock because she in truth loves the poor but dynamic Hugh Stanbury. Nora speaks first:

"I don't want to go back to the islands, and to lose myself there, and to be nobody;—that is what I mean. And I might have been so much! Could one step from the very highest rung of the ladder to the very lowest and not feel it?"
"But you have gone up the ladder,—if you only knew it," said Priscilla. 'There was a choice given to you between the foulest mire of the clay of the world, and the sun-light of the very God. You have chosen the sun-light, and you are crying after the clay! I cannot pity you; but I can esteem you, and love you, and believe in you. And I do. You'll get yourself right at last, and there's my hand on it, if you'll take it." (135)

Priscilla Stanbury, a woman who considers herself by virtue of her difficult, independent nature to be outside the erotic circuit, becomes a spiritual mentor to Nora in her dilemma. This scene between women who will be sisters-in-law is one of a number of quite moving scenes occurring between women in the novel; in these discussions, women define what they have learned about their culture's attitudes toward women, about how difficult it is to be even an upper-class woman in Victorian society. Nora Rowley is afraid of being "nobody," a sentiment echoed by Dorothy Stanbury at another point in the novel. In an earlier scene between Nora and Emily, Nora sounds much like that future Trollopian heroine, Isabel Boncassen (*The Duke's Children*), when she speaks with dark irony of a woman's life as "perhaps better than being a dog . . . but, of course, we can't compare ourselves to men" (35). Originally, there are three pairs of sisters in the novel (four, if we include Camilla and Arabella French in the comic sub-plot): Nora and Emily

Rowley, Priscilla and Dorothy Stanbury, and Caroline and Olivia Spalding. By the end of the novel, the "sister" bonds connecting the characters have multiplied and strengthened, as Nora is to become sister-in-law to Priscilla and Dorothy, and is bridesmaid and confidante to Caroline. This greater sororal community is in sharp contrast to the isolation of the madman Louis Trevelyan.

Trevelyan's imperiousness is mocked through the man he imagines to be his "rival," the dandified Colonel Osborne, a Member of Parliament and old family friend of Emily's father, Sir Marmaduke Rowley, Governor of the Mandarins. Like Trevelyan, Osborne is an upper-class gentleman of leisure, with his time wholly at his own command. His freedom allows him to pursue the gratification of his ego through charming young married women, despite the cost to them or their husbands. Although Col. Osborne is in the House, and men think "that he might have been something considerable," Trollope pointedly says of him that it has "suited him better to be nothing at all" (13). The nullity of his character despite the M.P. after his name, despite society's perception that he is a Somebody, underlies Trollope's gender critique.

In a world in which women constantly lament the lack of opportunity to be someone, to do something, Col. Osborne's choice to be "nothing" resonates. The intelligent, gentle Dorothy Stanbury says: "A man who is nobody can perhaps make himself somebody,—or, at any rate, he can try; but a woman has no means of trying. She is a nobody, and a nobody she must remain" (ch. 51). In one of Trollope's most satisfying comic plots, Dorothy Stanbury refutes her own gender dictum, and emerges as a "somebody" when she resists her Aunt Stanbury and loves the energetic, kindly Brooke Burgess. Dorothy's mother, Mrs. Stanbury, asks her elder daughter Priscilla: "Don't you think she is very much changed?" Priscilla wisely responds: "Not changed in the least, mother; but the sun has opened the bud, and now we see the fruit" (441).

Colonel Osborne, although a cipher, is renowned among the "good, motherly, discreet women" of London as a predator, "a serpent, an hyena, a kite, or a shark" (13). His analogue in Dickens is Deportment Turveydrop in *Bleak House*; he is all style and no substance, but his moral vacuity is not simply lamentable, it is destructive. London is a dangerous site for women, a place in which the Col. Osbornes of the world congregate and prosper, in which sexual predators are given society's imprimatur. Moreover, Colonel Osborne is not only an M.P., but the intimate friend of Emily Trevelyan's father, Sir Marmaduke Rowley, Governor of the Mandarins. Hence, Osborne has been allowed into the bosom of the family by the Father/Governor; the Family and the colonial family are implicated in Osborne's power and status. It is Osborne, finally, who arranges that Sir Marmaduke will be part of a colonial commission in London that will allow him to return to England for a number of months.

All of this suggests a kind of complicity within the power structures that rule England, its colonies—and its daughters. Returned from the Mandarins to London, Sir Marmaduke is faced with the havoc that his old friend Osborne has wrought on Emily Trevelyan. Significantly, it is at the Acrobats, the gentleman's club to which Sir Marmaduke, Trevelyan, and Colonel Osborne all belong, that Osborne manages through twisted logic to defend himself against the accusations of his old comrade Sir Marmaduke, the colonial governor. This is a male-defined space in which upper-class men can exercise their extraordinary freedoms in this culture, including the liberty to call profane desire by the name of sacred duty. Thus Colonel Osborne defends his pursuit of Emily into Devonshire with the exclamation "What the deuce! Because a man like that [Trevelyan] chooses to take vagaries into his head I am not to see my own godchild!" Trollope's irony is patent as he describes Sir Marmaduke, who "tried to remember whether the Colonel was in fact the godfather of his eldest daughter, but he found that his mind was quite a blank about his children's godfathers and godmothers" (486).

In contrast to Trevelyan's will to mastery is the desire to respect and love a woman that is shared by a number of men in the novel: the middle-aged Charles Glascock, the feminized, diffident aristocrat who marries the strong-willed American Caroline Spalding; Brooke Burgess, London banker, a man with "as sweet a mouth as ever declared the excellence of a man's temper" (235), who forms a marriage of equality with the penniless Dorothy Stanbury; and most prominently, the quintessential urban man Hugh Stanbury, reporter for a penny paper, the London Daily Record.

If we consider Trollope's "feminized" men—the men who end up married to the women they love, in relationships that are unions of equals—we see how each serves as a foil to Trevelyan. Charles Glascock is the wealthiest and highest ranking man in the novel, heir to a title and a great estate. He is one of Trollope's many middle-aged, kindly, seemingly unheroic heroes, a man who is in truth masterful because he is reasonable, witty, and sweet-natured. After he is rejected by Nora Rowley, who loves the penniless reporter Hugh Stanbury, Glascock falls in love with another strong-minded woman, the American Caroline Spalding. In the chapter "Mr. Glascock is Master," he combats Caroline's arguments against their impending marriage. Her arguments are based on the inequality of rank between an English peer—Glascock becomes Lord Peterborough and inherits Monkhams, an old and glorious estate, during the course of the novel—and an American girl, even one who has an uncle who is an American Minister, as does Caroline. Glascock argues simply that he and Caroline love one another, and that their love is the greatest reason why they must marry. Their worldly stations do not really matter to him.

In a passage that might in another context suggest male condescension, Trollope writes: "She felt that he was altogether too strong for her,—that she had mistaken his character in supposing that she could be more firm than he. He was so strong that he treated her almost as a child;—and yet she loved him infinitely the better for so treating her" (607). Although the contemporary reader of Trollope will likely feel uncomfortable with the language here, I think that Trollope is illustrating both the strength and the capacity for nurturing that Glascock possesses. He is a diffident man in most of the novel's situations, a man whose quiet wit deflates the pomposity of both egoistical men and women in the novel. His role as nurturer climaxes in the late chapter, "Mr. Glascock as Nurse," in which he takes charge of poor Louie at Casalunga, shepherding him from his demented father to his loving mother. In that context, Glascock is forced into confrontation with the mad Trevelyan, and his politic handling of Trevelyan's rantings places his compassionate strength and calm reason in sharp relief.

Brooke Burgess too is middle-aged, and "rather inclined to be stout. But he would boast that he could still walk his twelve miles in three hours, and would add that as long as he could do that he would never recognise the necessity of putting himself on short commons" (234–35). About Mr. Brooke, as the servants call him, the diffident Dorothy Stanbury thinks that "next to her brother Hugh he was the most good-natured looking man she had ever seen" (234). Brooke Burgess has the insight to see the beauty in the shy Dorothy, and to help her to develop the natural gifts of her loving nature and quick mind. Significantly, the love of Dorothy and Brooke heals an old family feud, and is elastic enough to include the deep love that Aunt Stanbury has come to feel for her kind niece.

Hugh Stanbury is Trevelyan's best friend from his Oxford days, and thus is portrayed as a kind of foil to the increasingly crazed Trevelyan.

While Hugh has trained to be a gentlemanly barrister, he wholeheartedly embraces the rough-and-tumble life of a big city newspaperman, an attitude that affronts the upper-class sensibilities of Trevelyan, who "professed that he did not think much of the trade of a journalist, and told Stanbury that he was sinking from the highest to almost the lowest business by which an educated man and a gentleman could earn his bread" (29). Trollope tells us that although Stanbury is "somewhat hot in spirit and manner . . . very sage in argument, pounding down his ideas in politics, religion, or social life with his fist as well as his voice . . . he possessed the sweetest temper that was ever given to a man for the blessing of a woman" (32), words that presage Trollope's description of that other Trollopian hero, Brooke Burgess.

Hugh's balanced sanity and his longing to love rather than to dominate provide hope that the city will be transformed by the energies and ideals of a new kind of Englishman. As Stanbury thinks to himself in the chapter significantly titled "Hugh Stanbury Smokes His Pipe," a title that points to the issues of masculine identity at stake in his musings, "the poetry of his life was, in fact, the capacity of caring more for other human beings than for himself. The beauty of it all was not so much in the thing loved, as in the loving" (190). It is this love that Trollope hoped to substitute for mastery in the relations between man and woman, and between Englishman and his colonial subject. As Victoria Glendinning states in the most recent Trollope biography, after quoting this same passage: "Anthony Trollope was a loving man. That is not so common."

Hugh tries to instruct Trevelyan about a more egalitarian relationship between man and woman, husband and wife. When Trevelyan informs his friend that he has hired a detective to follow his wife, Hugh condemns this, stating "As far as I can see, women go straight enough nineteen times out of twenty. But they don't like being,—what I call looked after" (148). Trevelyan responds defensively, "And did I look after my wife more than I ought?" Stanbury replies warmly, "I don't mean that; but if I were married,—which I never shall be, for I shall never attain to the respectability of a fixed income,—I fancy I shouldn't look after my wife at all. It seems to me that women hate to be told about their duties" (148). Although Hugh takes on the role of feminist mentor to Trevelyan in this scene, he is also a compelling presence in a slightly later scene in which he tries to shame Osborne into leaving Emily Trevelyan alone after Osborne has followed her down to Nuncombe Putney, thereby causing further trouble between husband and wife. Stanbury speaks first:

> "You best know whether you have seen her or not."
> "I have seen her."
> "Then I shall take leave to tell you, Colonel Osborne, that you have acted in a most unfriendly way, and have done that which must tend to keep an affectionate husband apart from his wife."
> "Sir, I don't at all understand this kind of thing addressed to me. The father of the lady you are speaking of has been my most intimate friend for thirty years." After all, the Colonel was a mean man when he could take pride in his youth, and defend himself on the score of his age, in one and the same proceeding. (174)

As Trevelyan falls away from Stanbury's influence, he becomes closer to his new comrade, the detective Mr. Bozzle. As with that first detective of English fiction, Dickens's Mr. Bucket in *Bleak House*, or with the most famous of fictional English detectives, Conan Doyle's Sherlock Holmes, Mr. Bozzle is the consummate urban man, knowledgeable about the ways of the city, its manners, mores, geography. Trevelyan's degraded mind does not see how ironic his condemnation of Stanbury's newspaper reporting seems when he becomes intimate with Bozzle, a paid informant who seeks damaging evidence that Emily Trevelyan is a adulteress. Finally, Bozzle aids Trevelyan in abducting her child Louie, as Emily and Nora travel with the child and his nurse from the East End of London to the West End. Trollope carefully describes the route the complicit cabman takes in diverting the group from St. Diddulph's in the east (where the Rowley sisters have been staying with their uncle, the Rev. Outhouse) to Marlebone in the west of London, to Gregg's Hotel in Baker Street:

> None of the party in the cab knew anything of the region through which they passed. The cabman took the line by the back of the bank, and Finsbury Square and the City Road, thinking it best, probably, to avoid the crush at Holborn Hill, though at the expense of something of a circuit. But of this Mrs. Trevelyan and Nora knew nothing . . . Had their way taken them along Piccadilly, or through Mayfair, or across Grosvenor Square, they would have known where they were; but at present they were not thinking of those once much-loved localities . . . Surely the man should have gone on along the New Road, now that he had come so far out of his way. But of this the two ladies knew nothing,—nor did the nurse. It was a dark, windy night, but the lamps in the streets had given them light, so that they had not noticed the night. Nor did they notice it now as the streets became narrower and darker. They were hardly thinking that their journey was at an end, and the mother was in the act of covering her boy's face as he lay asleep on the nurse's lap, when the car was stopped . . . They heard the rattle of

another cab as it was carried away at a gallop round a distant corner;—and then some inkling of what had happened came upon them. The father had succeeded in getting possession of his child. (459)

What Trollope stresses in this long passage describing the Louie's kidnapping is, first, the almost dreamlike—and ultimately nightmarish—quality of the journey and its end in the loss of the mother's beloved child. Second, the kidnapping father, Trevelyan, has become conversant with the darkness and the convolutions of the city streets, and is familiar now with their meanness, implicated in the crime of kidnapping—a crime, Trollope is ever reminding us, that is viewed by Victorian law as the father's legal right. The abduction must happen in London, in the city that embodies the consolidated power that has given Trevelyan his prerogatives under the law: "And the policeman was of opinion that as the boy had been kidnapped on behalf of the father, no legal steps could be taken either for the recovery of the child or for the punishment of the perpetrators of the act" (460).

Finally, Nora Rowley and Emily Trevelyan "know nothing" of all this city geography, of the East End and all the city that lies between St. Diddulph's and the West End regions—Mayfair, Grosvenor Square—where they have lived their former privileged existence, a life determined by their gender and social class. The dangers for women inherent in that seemingly perfect social world have now become manifest as Emily's child is kidnapped in the city regions outside the West End perimeters, eerily linking Emily's victimization with that of the lower classes among whom she finds herself after the abduction. Nora and Emily, the child and his nurse—all dependent on men to support them—travel from the protection of the uncle, Mr. Outhouse, to the refuge of the father, Sir Marmaduke Rowley, and are waylaid and robbed by minions paid by the father, the madman Louis Trevelyan.

Trevelyan tries one final time, on his deathbed, to instruct his erring wife, although by now he can only declaim. He returns at last to England so that Emily can nurse him. As Emily tells him that she spoke of her failure in her wifely duties only to get him to leave Casalunga and come to England, he accuses her of lying, and cries out, "with the look and the tone, which had made her sure that he was a madman": "The craft and subtlety of women passes everything! . . . And so at last I am to tell you that from the beginning it has been my doing. I will never say so, though I should die in refusing to do it" (730). There is only one desire left in Emily Trevelyan: to be acquitted of the charge of adultery. It is this erotic content that is elided in the final days with Trevelyan, the subtext of his tirades about his wife's disobedience. As Trevelyan is dying, Emily seeks one last time to be absolved, to be pronounced a faithful wife by her crazed husband:

> "Can you say one word for your wife, dear dear, dearest husband?"
> "What word?"
> "I have not been a harlot to you;—have I?"
> "What name is that?"
> "But what a thing, Louis! Kiss my hand, Louis, if you believe me." And very gently she laid the tips of her fingers on his lips. For a moment or two she waited, and the kiss did not come. Would he spare her in this the last moment left to him either for justice or for mercy? For a moment or two the bitterness of her despair was almost unendurable. She had time to think that were she once to withdraw her hand, she would be condemned for ever;—and that it must be withdrawn. But at length the lips moved, and with struggling ear she could hear the sound of the tongue within, and the verdict of the dying man had been given in her favour. He never spoke a word more either to annul it or to enforce it." (733)

The biblical name Emily uses—harlot—signals Trollope's considera-tion of this scene in a sacred context. The judgment given so cryptically by Trevelyan marks him, despite all his Christ-like posturing and imagin-ings, as spiritually deficient. There is no mercy here, no generosity, only the legalistic judgment that has doomed Trevelyan from the start of his marriage. Emily is "acquitted" (the title of this chapter), but she is not treated with love or with mercy. And it is Trollope's dark lesson to his culture that the absence of love begets death. Against all the joyful marriages that close the novel, this grim scene is played out. But there is hope that the authority of the new Victorian fathers—Hugh Stanbury, Brooke Burgess, Lord Peterborough—will be based on a commitment to loving equality between men and women.

Notes

1. Two influential feminist critiques of *He Knew He Was Right* are Ruth Roberts's pioneer article "Emily and Nora and Dorothy and Priscilla and Jemima and Carry" in *The Victorian Experience: The Novelists*, edited by Richard A. Levine, pp. 87–120 (Athens: Ohio University Press, 1976) and Jane Nardin's section on the novel in her more recent book *He Knew She Was Right; The Independent Woman in the Novels of Anthony Trollope* (Carbondale: Southern Illinois University Press, 1989).

2. "Trollope the Realist" in *The Mirror in the Roadway* (New York: Knopf, 1956).

3. The best discussion of the Othello parallel is in Simon Gatrell, "Jealousy, Mastery, Love, and Madness: A Brief Reading of *He Knew He Was Right*" in *Anthony Trollope*, edited by Tony Bareham (London: Vision Press, 1980).

4. The insight about Trollope's reinscription of Brontë's novel was a communal one, arrived at in my upper-division Trollope and Gaskell seminar in the Spring of 1994. I must especially cite Rebecca and Christine Enos for their brilliant contributions on this subject, and on my other Trollopian subjects as well.

5. Again, I must cite my Spring 1994 Trollope and Gaskell seminar: Amy Adam, Cindy Chao, Christine Enos, Rebecca Enos, Ashley Jantzen, Erin Kuhls, Gwen McDowell, Maria Litzendorf, Tracey McLachlan, Meghan McNeill, Mary Reed, Kelli Rettig, Kathi Roberts, and Bonnie Wilson.

ROBERT POLHEMUS

A Jamesian Sentimental Education

What Maisie Knew: French Literature,
Sacred History

Desires, images, and concepts joining together the roles of teacher, father, and lover have made their lasting marks on our Judeo-Christian heritage, as the Bible shows and tells. The Adam and Eve creation story, the sexual history of patriarchs such as Lot, David, and Solomon, the erotic Song of Solomon and its Christian allegorical interpretations, and the theology of the Trinity and of the Virgin Mary all offer examples of the mysterious intertwinings of religion, erotics, kinship relations, and moral pedagogy that permeate our cultural and literary traditions. The nineteenth-century novel in English explored in depth relationships between teacher-father-lover figures and figures that—seizing on Dickens's resonant epithet "child-wife" in *David Copperfield*—we might call *child-wives*.

My subject is pedagogy in James's great and infinitely suggestive novel *What Maisie Knew*, specifically some of the things that the narrator imagines Maisie Farange and her stepfather Sir Claude learn from and teach one another—and that James imagines they teach himself and his readers as well. Sir Claude is, in Maisie's mind, her favorite teacher of many in the novel and her desired father-lover. Maisie, if she knew the non-Jamesian argot of twentieth-century pop music could certainly—when, in the last chapter, she has "a mental picture of the stepfather and pupil established in a little place in the South [of France]"[1]—call her "English teacher Daddy-O"; Sir Claude, however, in the end, calls the quality of life he thinks he has produced in Maisie "the most beautiful thing I've ever met—it's exquisite, it's *sacred*." Often Maisie, her education neglected by her divorced, remarried, promiscuous parents, wonders who'll give her her lessons. Her step-parents—Sir Claude, her mother's husband, and Mrs. Beale, her ex-governess and her father's wife—

brought together by their concern for the child, but soon plunged into adultery with one another, answer that they will take Maisie to "courses," "on subjects": "All the most important ones. French literature—and sacred history." "All alone?" asks Maisie. "Oh no; I'll attend them with you," says Sir Claude. "They'll teach me a lot I don't know." "I'm going to look thoroughly into the whole thing," he says (117–18).

I want to fasten on the words "French literature and sacred history" and Claude's casual "a lot I don't know" and make them serve as a kind of shorthand—synecdoche—to help get at the highly complex contents of the novel's teaching and knowledge. Let me stipulate that, for my pedagogical purposes here, I use "French literature"—taking into account the connotations that the term would have had in the fin-de-siecle English world—to mean erotics (the adjective *French* adding the kind of transgressive sexual twist to *literature* that it does when it modifies such nouns as *kiss* or *letters*); it connotes, that is, a literary affront to Victorian moral convention and middle-class decorum, a risqué but revealing sentimental education into the nature of personal relationships and sexual desire (obviously I'm including turn-of-the-century Viennese case-history literature as part of the generic "French literature" here). In literature France, to the English-speaking, is the land of sex, of exile from sexual propriety, of erotic transgression and taboo. And let me also now stipulate that I take "sacred history" to mean inquiry into the historical relevance of scripture and the modern search for some kind of credible faith. My general argument, which may sound lame, but, relying on a lot of wordplay, may not be quite as banal as it at first seems, echoes Sir Claude, and it is that *What Maisie Knew* is out to teach us a lot we didn't know.

In previous work, I've tried to show that the nineteenth-century English fiction was a means for imagining forms of faith that would augment, replace, or play off orthodox religious visions and scripture, and that one of the most important of these forms was the imaginative rendering of what I call faith in the child: an emotional conviction, almost religious in nature and prevalent in modern civilization, that meaning, hope, value, and even transcendence can be found in children and our relationship to them. Specifically I've argued that Dickens in *The Old Curiosity Shop* (1841) created the Victorian moral and aesthetic equivalent of a literary gothic cathedral, and that the figure of the child Little Nell, on the brink of puberty, surrounded by a strange, complex, and menacing eroticism, became a holy literary Virgin for a secularizing

Protestant culture; she, like her later Dickensian sister Florence Dombey, for example, and like George Eliot's little Eppie in *Silas Marner*, and like Maisie as James saw her, concentrated, as did the traditional Virgin of Roman Catholicism, religious feeling and faith in nurturing ideal-ism—*Notre Jeune Fille* instead of *Notre Dame,* but sacred nonetheless. Nell leaves her home when sex and the moral corruption loose in the world threaten to violate and destroy her virtue. Greed and male sexual desire menace her childhood, her virginity, and her immaculate goodness, and she must flee into homeless wandering until she finds, in what Dickens presents as a holy, sacrificial apotheosis, her final home in the church, under whose stones she is buried and of which she becomes a part. From her issues a faith that the symbolic power of the pure girl child inspires in others, particularly sinful men such as the redeemed hedonist Dick Swiveller, who takes a poor bastard servant-child, nick-named "the Marchioness," as his ward, educates her, and then in the end marries her. Nell, with her promise of redemption and fresh hope for the world and the future, is brought in to revive the spiritual potency of the old, dying, patriarchal faith, impotent to command in the new world the same kind of belief and authority it once had. She seems to be conceived of as a child-wife of a failing God, a little virgin who shall lead, regenerate, and redeem. Maisie can be seen as an avatar of both Little Nell and the Marchioness. We can also conceive of her placed in a historically revealing group of literary girls within a budding grove standing somewhere between the sexually pure Nell and the sex-re-pressed-and-obsessed neurotic Dora of Freudian fame.

James, writing in the preface to *What Maisie Knew*—this prophetic novel about child-custody issues, child abuse, cross-generational pas-sions, and the coming age of divorce—discusses his own faith in the imaginary girl:

Truly, I reflect, if the theme had had no other beauty it would still have had this rare and distinguished one of its so expressing the variety of the child's values. She is not only the extraordinary "ironic centre" I have already noted; she has the wonderful importance of shedding a light far beyond any reach of her compre-hension; of lending to poorer persons and things, by the mere fact of their being involved with her a precious element of dignity. I lose myself, truly, in apprecia-tion of my theme on noting what she does by her "freshness" for appearances in themselves vulgar and empty enough. They become, as she deals with them, the stuff of poetry and tragedy and art; she has simply to wonder, as I say, about them, and they begin to have meanings, aspects, solidities, connexions—connexions with the "universal!"—that they could scarce have hoped for.

He also writes, using highly suggestive imagery:

To live with all intensity and perplexity and felicity in its terribly mixed little world would thus be the part of my interesting small mortal; bring people together who would be at least more correctly separate; keeping people separate who would be at least more correctly together; flourishing, to a degree, at the cost of many conventions and proprieties, even decencies, really keeping the torch of virtue alive in an air tending infinitely to smother it; really in short making confusion worse confounded by drawing some stray fragrance of an ideal across the scent of selfishness, by sowing on barren strands, through the mere fact of presence, the seed of moral life." (Preface 25–6)

Briefly, my broad sense of *What Maisie Knew* is that: 1) historically, it renders an intensifying fascination and identification with childhood and the condition of children; 2) it expresses a new passion to comprehend and give voice to the developing consciousness of a particular, individualized child; 3) it makes clear the strong cultural desire to sacralize and aestheticize children, to identify faith with childhood, and to honor girlhood as a radiant center of social redemption and potential virtue; 4) it makes the well-being of children a touchstone of good; 5) it portrays childhood as a time-doomed and menaced state of being and the girl-child as an adorable, beautiful, but also vulnerable and desirous figure, requiring on her behalf vigilant adult endeavors of responsibility; 6) it works to provoke and shape new consciousness of child abuse and it confronts the fact of child-custody abuse; and 7) it eroticizes the consciousness of childhood—our adult consciousness and the rendered child's consciousness.

About the novel's pedagogy—troped by subjects of French literature and sacred history—I want first to stress the French connection: if we understand the unfolding narrative of Maisie's childhood as a sentimental journey through a world of sexual double entendre, then France, motherland of the double entendre, where Sir Claude takes the pubescent thirteenish Maisie, is the crucial symbolic site and stopover on her not-so-grand educational tour. (In fact—and of vital significance—he brings her only as far as Boulogne, just at the edge of France.) There, writes James, taking Maisie's point of view, "once or twice, on the jetty, on the sands, he looked at her for a minute with eyes that seemed to propose to her to come straight off with him to Paris" (252). Maisie soon after propositions him with the offer to abandon Mrs. Wix, her tutor in conventional morality, and live with him alone if he will give up and leave his mistress Mrs. Beale, the stepmother. Maisie begs him, in a remarkable passage, to run off with her to Paris, the heart of France (254), "the *real* thing, the thing that . . . one does . . . abroad" (182). She had already learned from him in England "the implication of a kind of natural divergence between lovers and little girls" (164), and, at the Boulogne Station, Sir Claude, buying pink books for Maisie and yellow for Mrs. Beale, tells the girl "in an interesting way that these were the natural divisions in France of literature for the young and for the old." He is tutoring her about France, and, miraculously, she even learns from him to speak her own brand of French, the proverbial language of love. Those divisions and divergences, from her point of view, now, have been used to exploit little girls and have given all the advantages to older people for the sake of the mysterious sort of "love" they indulge in. Looking at the Paris train she says, "I wish we could go. Won't you take me?" When, tempted but doubtful, Sir Claude talks to a porter about departure times and tickets, James moves to French and Maisie's astonishing precocity:

> "*Monsieur veut-il que je les prenne?*" the man said.
> Sir Claude turned back to her. "*Veux-tu bien qu'il en prenne?*"
> It was the most extraordinary thing in the world: in the intensity of her excitement she not only by illumination understood all their French, but fell into it with an active perfection. She addressed herself straight to the porter. "*Prenny, prenny. Oh prenny!*" (254)

Taught by Sir Claude, she speaks, literally for a moment, as a subject of French literature. The passionate cry "*prenny*" from this abused, used, abandoned, patronized, love-hungry, and wonderful child rings out as both deeply moving and disturbing, and just as moving is Sir Claude's white-faced fear of himself and his hesitant, tacit renunciation of her "*prenny*" and what it signifies. Moving too is what follows: her reiterated desire to be with him only and his nearly passive but definitive refusal to *take* her any farther, to keep her in custody for his own ends, to possess her. In this long, climactic chapter, James takes Maisie and the wonder she inspires to what he calls "the end, to the death—the death of her childhood, properly speaking . . . . " (28). Since she can't have Sir Claude on her own terms, she leaves him in France and returns to England. James imagines for her at the last the voice to express her mind—"I love Sir Claude—I love *him*" (264)—the authenticity to know what she wants— "I'll go straight out with you and not come back till she has gone, . . . I'll sit out on that old bench where you see the gold Virgin . . . While you break with Mrs. Beale" (256)—and, when she can't get it, the will to act in what she sees as her own best interests: "'Good-bye,' said Maisie to Sir Claude" (266).

Nothing in this hard book has provoked more reader resistance, repression, and insensitivity than the girl's longing for the Paris trip and her express wish to leave her other guardians behind and be alone with Sir Claude, and nothing matters more than that outburst in French and that untaken journey. If he acquiesced to Maisie's wishes, we would be beyond unconscious libido and Freud, whose Dora, when Herr K. touched and kissed her, was about the same age as Maisie; we would be right smack in the middle of *Lolita*—and its road-show of sexual, generational, pedagogical chaos. The common critical response is either to ignore Maisie's desire, downplay it, deeroticize it, or to condemn it and distance it as corrupt, the natural outcome of her sordid upbringing. We might, however, do well to read allegorically here: to move successfully out of childhood, the girl must go to the edge of the forbidden realm with the father-lover, then move away from him back into her own territory. In the end, her "French lessons" from Sir Claude are positive and necessary.

Maisie describes a daughter's struggle to learn what she needs to know to survive irresponsible parents and keep hope, faith, and charity alive. Her mother and father reify her as a connubial missile to hurl at one another, and then as a material obstacle to their pleasure and financial well-being. Before Sir Claude involves himself in her education, she is the subject and object of intense lessons in child abuse: "Hadn't she lived with her eyes on it from her third year? . . . She knew as well in short that a person could be compromised as that a person could be slapped with a hair-brush or left alone in the dark . . . ." (141). In the first chapter James shows the little girl "handled, pulled hither and thither and kissed" by her father and his friends: "Some of these gentlemen . . . holding her on knees violently jolted, pinched the calves of her legs till she shrieked— her shriek was much admired—and reproached them with being toothpicks. The word stuck in her mind and contributed to her feeling from this time that she was deficient in something that would meet the general desire" (39–40). Early lessons for Maisie "pop" out of that passage: e.g., that she is an object, that girls are cute bundles of fresh flesh, little things for men's fun and patronization; that she is inadequate because she does not physically meet some aesthetic standard; that her feelings don't matter; that her purpose is to fulfill some general desire (which might be perceived as the generalized sire—i.e., patriarchal design).

It is a needy little victim Sir Claude finds, and I can do no more than crudely list what he, laid-back *l'homme moyen sensual* and womanizing Not-Mr. Chips though he may be, teaches Maisie, formally and informally, in the course of her sentimental education. He teaches her early on that, rather than an agent of divorce—the identity her mother and father made for her—she positively brings people together. He shows her that she is worthy of kindness, concern, and friendship, that her affection for a man can be requited, that she is good company, that there can be camaraderie, communication, and moments of equality—even intimacy—across the generation and gender channels (e.g., "he was liable in talking with her to take the tone of her also being a man of the world" [84]). Though he only gives her desultory, half-hearted education in art, music, and literature, he very effectively teaches her that she is desirable as she is, that she has, as he puts it "the fatal gift of beauty" (116), that he whom she adores finds her lovable ("I should be in fear if you were older" [106]), and that she deserves good treatment. Not least, he teaches her how to have fun and makes her feel what a good education ought somehow to include: the experience and possibilities of joy, rapture, and ecstasy.

He also teaches her practical lessons about sex. Through the information she gathers from Sir Claude—for instance, that even while talking seriously to Maisie, he can't help looking with desirous eyes at the venereal quality of a stranger ("she seemed . . . to see him . . . as he stood there and with an absent gaze—absent that is, from *her* affairs—followed the fine stride and shining limbs of a young fishwife who had just waded out of the sea" [184])—she begins to learn the power, if not the name, of sex. There is some mysterious force around that impels the adults she sees, drives them, but can't be spoken directly about—at least she doesn't yet know the way in which it could be expressed. But, in my pedagogical formula, let me now invoke French to stand for the verbal form of sexuality: Maisie might say, "When I was a child I spake as a child, but later it's French." At the very coast of France, where Sir Claude has brought her, she muses on her education: "As she was condemned to know more and more, how could it logically stop before she should know Most? It came to her . . . on the sands that she was distinctly on the road to know Everything . . . what in the world had she ever done but learn and learn and learn? She looked at the pink sky with a placid foreboding that she soon should have learnt All" (213). She, like any child, must grow up in a world battered by the two whirling hurricanes of sexual desire and economic drive. Sex and money, the proverbial staple of French literature, determine the conditions of her life, but not only can she not grasp them clearly—the narrative is a project toward the articulation of these things, from her point of view, among much else—the adults around her cannot speak of these matters except in a language of translation. When she cries *prenny*, she makes of their foreign language her self-expression.

But the world of *What Maisie Knew* is really a modern Sodom and Gomorrah, and even a good course in French and French literature by itself won't free us from its sexual corruption and its faithless, barren doom. We need sacred history, and what Maisie embodies, conveys, and teaches *is* a new sacred history. In erotic pedagogy, the student is always a teacher, and education is a mutual process. A key to the novel is the narrator's remark, "I am not sure that Maisie had not even a dim discernment of the queer law of her own that made her educate . . . those elders with whom she was concerned" (212). *French* brings Maisie to the articulation of desire that's necessary for selfhood and any sort of authentic freedom in the future, but Sir Claude is seen to learn a redeeming faith—that sense of the "sacred"—from the feeling that Maisie's love arouses in him. If the moral seed is to germinate, she must know her own desire, but he must learn the moral necessity of bracketing the pubescent sexual child off from the potential direct flow of erotic desire to and from the care-taking adult and teach her the painful lesson of erotic discipline. What Maisie and Sir Claude intuitively seem by the end to learn—and what their story teaches—is how little most people care about children, not because people are monsters, but because what they see in children is either a self-projection—a narcissistic vision—or a tool for self-gratification, or because they are so busy living out their own pilgrimages both back to and away from their own personal childhoods, nurseries and seedbeds of their desires, that the otherness and individuality of children get in their way.

James uses and revises sacred history from the novel's first page (" . . . the little girl . . . in a manner worthy of the judgement-seat of Solomon . . . was divided in two and the portions tossed impartially to the disputants" [35]) to the last, where Maisie appears as a refigured Lot's wife. Traditional sacred history, that old-time religion, often appears as tired, dessicated, dead—a matter of "silly superstition," like the Christian art that Sir Claude shows Maisie in the National Gallery, "stiff saints and angular angels, with ugly Madonna and uglier babies, stranger prayers and prostrations." The living religion becomes faith in the child. Poor Mrs. Wix, missionary for this religion, proselytizes Sir Claude: "Make her your duty—make her your life: she'll repay you a thousand-fold!" (101).

"That functionary," says James, "could not in this connexion have been more impressive, even at second hand, if she had been a prophetess with an open scroll or some ardent abbess speaking with the lips of the Church. She had clung day by day to their plastic associate [Sir Claude] . . . doing her simple utmost to convert him . . ." (163). France and the new sacred history meet in "the high gilt Virgin" of the Boulogne church, "the gold Virgin" that James juxtaposes with Maisie. It's another case of *Notre Dame* becoming *Notre Jeune Fille*. The gold Virgin of venal Roman Catholicism is inert idolatry, but the living virgin child with her mysterious knowledge, her quest to imagine what others know, her love for a father-figure and the dignity and will it brings her, her contagious sense of wonder, her catalytic moral effect—all that's the quickening seed of life preserved.

Sexual France and sacred history meet also in James's allusions to and revision of the Lot story, with which I conclude. Lot is one of the strangest, most equivocal, problematic, and compromised of Biblical myths, and one of the most haunting. Genesis 19 relates that after Lot, a good, well-meaning, but rather befuddled and weak man—a "plastic associate" of Jehovah, we could say—offered his daughters as sexual decoys to the dissolute Sodomites in order to protect Divinity's visiting angels, God spared him and his family, sending them out of the depraved city before obliterating it. Lot's curious wife (curious and wanton, say some Biblical commentators) looked back and was turned to a pillar of salt, but he and his two daughters escaped to a mountain cave. Here the young women, thinking they were the last people left on earth, conspired to get Lot drunk and sleep with him, so that they would "preserve seed of our father" (Genesis, 19:32)—preserve the seed of civilization, as it were—and have issue. The story of Lot, his wife and daughters—child-wives with a vengeance—fascinated novelists from Charlotte Brontë and Dickens, down through George Eliot, to Henry James and later James Joyce. It brought into focus influential nineteenth-century complexes, fantasies, conflicts, and tensions about sex, family, children, the patriarchy, paternal guilt and weakness, incest, gender roles, feminine opportunities, daughters' identification with fathers and their power, mother-daughter relationships, and the whole question of generational relationship.

The fissure in the Biblical Lot myth, its blatant contradiction, is that God blasts the cities of the plain for sexual corruption, but then human salvation for the survivors depends on Lot and his daughters, deserving escapees from a world damned by lust and tabooed fornication, breaking the incest laws in order to renew life. The Victorians, for their part, felt keenly the disjunction in the idea that sex is destructive but necessary for life, that it must be repressed and expressed, that libido, which can pollute and lay waste to home-and-family also can regenerate home-and-family.

Among the many key traces and reworkings of the Lot story I find in James's making of the novel, let me stress four: first, the words in the preface alluding to the preservation of vital seed "sowing on barren strands . . . the seed of the moral life" and those that, I read, allude to the poison atmosphere permeating Lot's dark cave: "at the cost of many conventions and proprieties, even decencies, really keep the torch of virtue alive in an air tending infinitely to smother it"; second, Maisie's imagined sight of the Lot's-wife-like destruction of Ida, her mother and Sir Claude's wife, presumably for sexual transgression: "there rose in her . . . a vision ominous, precocious, of what it might mean for her mother's fate . . . . There was literally an instant in which Maisie saw— saw madness and desolation, saw ruin and darkness and death" (*Maisie* 177); third, the fertile spirit of moral intoxication set loose in Sir Claude by Maisie in the final two chapters; and fourth, the figuring of Maisie as a reconception of Lot's wife on the last page:

She put out her hand to her stepfather. He took it and held it a moment, and their eyes met as the eyes of those who have done for each other what they can. "Good-bye," he repeated.
     "Good-bye." And Maisie followed Mrs Wix.
     They caught the steamer . . . . they gave up half the voyage to letting their emotion sink. It sank slowly and imperfectly . . . . Mrs. Wix had courage to revert. I didn't look back, did you?'
     "Yes. He wasn't there" said Maisie.
     "Not on the balcony?"
     . . . . "He wasn't there" she simply said again.
     Mrs Wix was also silent a while. "He went to *her*," she finally observed.
     "Oh I know" the child replied.
     Mrs. Wix gave a sidelong look. She still had room for wonder at what Maisie knew. (266)

Looking back, Maisie nevertheless leaves the modern land of sexual license. She subsumes and revises the fate of Lot's wife and redeems her.

The lesson she learns—in large measure from Sir Claude—is that to preserve the moral seed, she must reject the sterile older generation. She will no longer be used to further *their* erotic purposes; she must not lie to, for, or with her fathers or mothers any more. She reverses the myth. She will look back, but she will leave; she will not stay in the cave, in the new Sodom; she will not lie for her beloved stepfather and teacher. The wife redeemed becomes the child, the moralized seed—moralized remarkably, for the sake of civilization and its discontents, by the new Lot, Sir Claude. The point about the "lot" that Sir Claude didn't know—the revision of Lot—is that we might come to learn that preservation of the daughter's seed, besides "preservation of the seed of our fathers," might just be the main point of civilization and faith and the focus of wonder.

Father-lover and child-wife are sublimated into a faith and art of pregnant renunciation, sired and tutored by an author, Henry James: the novelist, as teacher-father-lover, takes Maisie Farange for his child-wife. The child gives him, with his theme, moral dignity, as she does Sir Claude. And, like Sir Claude, James give *her* dignity and importance. The moral seed of the artist James is preserved by the chaste intercourse of the child and the new Lot, and the child's seed of faith, hope, and charity is preserved by the intoxication and rapture of art.

Note

1. *What Maisie Knew*, edited with an introduction and notes by Paul Theroux; additional notes by Patricia Crick (London: Penguin, 1985), 253. All subsequent page references are to this editon.

ABBY H. P. WERLOCK

"With a Man There Is a Difference"

The Rejection of Female Mentoring in
Hemingway's *For Whom the Bell Tolls*

"Ayee . . . Ayee . . . Are all men like that?" asks Pilar at her first meeting
with Robert Jordan in Ernest Hemingway's *For Whom the Bell Tolls*.
When Jordan responds that he is, in essence, sexually attracted to Maria,
the nineteen-year-old victim of a gang rape by a group of Falangistes,
Pilar's reaction is: "Men. It is a shame to us women that we make them"
(32). Although here Pilar speaks only half-seriously, her comment on the
psychological division between the sexes signals a tension evident
throughout the novel. Ernest Hemingway was an heir not only to
Rudyard Kipling, but also, as Mark Spilka points out, to popular writings
such as Thomas Hughes's *Tom Brown's School Days*—a copy of which
was in Hemingway's library—with its precedent that "manliness is
achieved through separation from women" (Spilka 21, 71). Not surprisingly, therefore, in Hemingway's *For Whom the Bell Tolls* the voices and
values of men and women differ from each other, providing illuminating
examples of Carol Gilligan's findings in her socio-psychological study *In
A Different Voice,* which reframes qualities regarded as women's weak-
nesses and shows them to be distinctive strengths. Specifically, Gilligan
finds that, as they tell their stories, men and women speak in different
voices, revealing fundamentally different modes of thought. These differences, she suggests, are rooted in the male need for a separate identity:
"Since masculinity is defined through separation while femininity is
defined through attachment, male gender identity is threatened by intimacy while female gender identity is threatened by separation" (Gilligan
8). And indeed when Maria, speaking of her love for Jordan, asks "why
did you say that instead of what I meant?" he replies, "With a man there
is a difference" (263). In *For Whom the Bell Tolls* the tension between

the different voices and values of men and women is illustrated particularly through Hemingway's depiction of the ways in which his major characters articulate their experiences, and through the consequent interactions of the blond Spanish-speaking American man, Robert Jordan, and the two Spanish women, Pilar and Maria. The two women repeatedly attempt to educate the professor, but Jordan proves ultimately incapable of absorbing their lessons.

Initially, to American readers especially, Jordan appears to be the trustworthy compatriot who will guide us through the Civil War in Spain. He is, after all, the American professor fluent in its language, knowledgeable in its history and politics, cognizant of its geography, and sympathetic to its culture. In fact, the text seems to endorse the authority of a sympathetic male hero who may voice the author's own ideas. Because readers may like him and therefore wish to identify with his convictions, some time elapses before we realize that Jordan is the most tenuous of authorities: we learn that his one book, ten years in the making, was not a "success" because Jordan added very little new information about the country on which he is the supposed authority (248). Moreover, Jordan almost immediately breaks one of the cardinal rules for foreigners when he acknowledges his attraction to Maria, and he unconvincingly attempts to describe himself as "a bridge-blower now. Not a thinker" (17). But Jordan is wrong: he cannot "turn off" his thinking; he thinks in excruciating detail throughout forty-two chapters, not blowing up a bridge until the forty-third.[1] Since Hemingway concludes the first chapter on what is, in essence, a falsehood, the reader must question the persona of Robert Jordan, and examine Pilar's contentions at various points that Jordan "cannot see," "cannot hear," and is in fact boyish, like a "precocious child" (252, 250). In fact, I suggest that Hemingway subtly ensnares the reader with the text's seeming emphasis on the male code of bravery, heroism, dignified behavior, and self-respect[2]—and a highly sympathetic hero who embraces that code—only to employ repeated undercutting of such formulations by means of women's voices. The result, as Carol Smith argues, is that "the male code of sport and stoicism has its counterpart in women's willingness to love again," demonstrating courage in the aftermath of disillusionment and suffering (Smith 130–31). Hemingway depicts these voices in a contrapuntal manner not only through male and female dialogue, but through the rising volume of the conflicting voices sounding within Robert Jordan's head. The discouraging male voices compete with the potentially mentoring female voices.

Jordan, not an unsympathetic character by any means, is nevertheless a man whose personal problems are so entangled in his male identity that he is distinctly lacking in self-definition: he fights on the side of the communists, but does not accept their ideology; his American nationality is constantly confused by the Spaniards, who call him "Ingles"; and he is concerned about whether his male inheritance stems from his father, of whose suicide he is deeply ashamed, or from his grandfather, of whose bravery he is exceptionally proud. His confusion is clearly evident in the number of times he talks to and argues with himself. Like such nineteenth-century heroes as Natty Bumppo and Huck Finn, Jordan "lights out for the territories," in this case Spain, but his preoccupations continue to be American and highly personal, rooted as they are in American history and his own family story.

Thus Robert Jordan is, from the beginning, the foreigner, the outsider, the isolated individual, a deeply troubled man whose voices sound largely within his head. He never speaks his inner thoughts aloud, rarely speaks of his past, never shares his most significant stories. Although most of the other men—Anselmo, Joaquin, Primitivo, Agustin—have combined in their characters some of the compassion that women display through both words and deeds, Jordan is rigid in his separation of the more human emotional feelings from his dogged concentration on his work and, in Pilar's words, he is "a very cold boy" (91). The women, on the other hand, do give voice to their tales and, in so doing reveal the values that Gilligan finds predominant in women, those that substitute commitment and sympathy for male separation and individuation. As both victim and survivor, Maria comprehends suffering as Jordan cannot; like other Hemingway women, she knows, in Smith's words, "more of the pain of the loss of love than the heroes do," yet is still willing to "risk love again" (Smith 130). Generously—regardless of her personal sorrows—Maria encourages Joaquin to speak of his own losses in the war: "Mine are such a big bucket that yours falling in will never fill it" (139); and comforts Primitivo over his sorrow at El Sordo's death (324). Her survival technique lies in her refusal to be silent; here she educates Primitivo about the values of strength and compassion. Pilar, too, persists not only in making her voice heard, but in caring for other individuals, Maria in particular. Although Pilar, about fifty years old, has subsumed the most "feminine," i.e., subservient, aspects in herself, and adopted the more typically aggressive "male" attributes essential to her active participation in the fight against the Falangistes, she still manages to combine the traits of both bravery and human commitment. Even while actively participating in the attack on the train, she goads the men into helping her carry Maria: as Rafael, among others, recalls, all of them took turns with the task—"But what the old woman had to say to us to make us do it!" (28).

One of the clearest measurements of both the similarities and the differences among all those fighting for a common cause—the partisans fighting for Spain—is in their insistent use of the word "understand," arguably the most important word in the text. Variations of the word "understand" occur scores of times in the novel. Alike in their need to express themselves clearly, each character is simultaneously a unique individual. The characters are constantly compelled to question their listeners' comprehension of their statements, then explain themselves and frequently repeat their words in an effort to be understood. Comrade Golz enjoins Robert Jordan to "understand" the strategic importance of the bridge to Golz's battle plan—the word "understand" being repeated thirteen times during the four-page conversation in the opening chapter of the novel. Likewise, in an early scene that counterpoints Golz's opening instructions to Jordan, Pilar teaches the American to understand his obligation to Maria: "We will understand each other . . . Be very good and careful about the girl. The Maria. She has had a bad time. Understandest thou?" (32). Early in the novel Jordan is thus counseled by two strong leaders, Golz and Pilar, to comprehend two spheres of reality, one external and traditionally male, one internal and traditionally female.

To acknowledge the comic as well as the serious aspects of life is a sign of psychological health, as Jordan observes at the end of the first chapter: "All the best ones . . . were gay. It was much better to be gay and it was a sign of something too. It was like having immortality while you were still alive" (17). Jordan here undoubtedly echoes one of Hemingway's stated beliefs. But if to be "gay" means that one is fully integrated, if the mingling of seriousness and levity is our measure of Maria, Joaquin, Pilar, and El Sordo, then Jordan's high seriousness again marks him as an outsider, a foreigner. The intensely serious, committed Jordan is rarely humorous, and when he thinks he is "joking"—as when he causes Maria to blush and leave on their first meeting, or when he orders her to fetch his dry socks because his feet are wet with snow—the humor is not readily apparent and he has to explain that he is "joking" (32, 203). He does make a "funny" remark about men's *cojones,* but it elicits only men's laughter and is again inseparable from the male preoccupation with the physical differences between the sexes. But the most important slights are not presented as jokes. Indeed, most of the the sexual attacks, whether verbal or physical, are launched not in jest but in anger: Pablo accuses Pilar of having "brains between her thighs" (215) and she calls him a "horse exhausted maricon," a homosexual (216). During the atrocities of the *ayuntamiento,* Pilar hits a drunken man in the groin (125). In fact, a subtle punning seems to exist in the repeated use of the words *cojones,* meaning testicles, and *conejos,* meaning rabbit, which, as both Arturo Barea and Allan Josephs have demonstrated, is a well-known Spanish slang term for the female sexual organs (Barea 210, Josephs 212). Men are consistently measured according to their courage, inseparable from male sexuality, whereas women are measured according to traditional "feminine" traits. Certainly the most sexist pun in the text is Robert's nickname for Maria: "Rabbit." Josephs argues that this name exposes not Hemingway's limited understanding of Spanish but Jordan's, and thus "the butt of the accidental humor is the author's protagonist" (Josephs 213). Consequently, through this implicitly coded lesson in the Spanish language emerges an astonishing tension between Hemingway as instructor in feminism on the one hand, and the more obviously patronizing author on the other.

Yet Hemingway was, after all, a poet, and it is unlikely that either he or his Spanish-speaking protagonist could overlook the possibilities for wordplay in two such similar-looking—and suggestive—words as *conejos* and *cojones.*[3] I suggest that neither Hemingway nor his protagonist was ignorant of the sexual meaning of the word, unpublishable in English when Hemingway wrote the novel in 1939.[4] The repeated use of *"conejos"* and "rabbits" strongly implies that Hemingway was not only "chauvinistic and patronizing" to American readers in general (Josephs 217), but also that he was implicitly condescending and insulting to women in particular. Various critics, Joseph Waldmeir for one, have noted the implied insult to Gertrude Stein in Jordan's comment "a rose is a rose is an onion," and her likely basis for the portrait of Pilar, large and sandal-footed, aware of a submerged lesbian dimension to her character (Waldmeir 43–45). Moreover, Jordan's observation that "all the best ones were gay" seems a direct parody of Gertrude Stein's writing in such stories as "Miss Furr and Miss Skeene" (1922), featuring two women who "were regularly gay. They were gay every day."[5] Jordan, who most often thinks in English but is emphatically fluent in Spanish, calls Maria a rabbit when she first comes to his sleeping bag. Rabbits provide constant sources of comfort and nourishment, whether through cohabitation (Rafael kills a pair of copulating rabbits) or food (the characters are constantly eating cooked rabbit). The partisan Andres is from the village of Villaconejos, the village of rabbits, but he distances himself from the feminine suggestion of *conejos* and establishes his separate identity as a brave young man who runs with the bulls, even daring to bite their ears. His men friends, calling him the "bulldog of Villaconejos," slap him on the back and congratulate him: "That's what it is to have a pair of *cojones*! Year after year!" (365, 366). On the same evening that Andres carries Jordan's delayed message to Golz, Jordan, mistaking her for Maria, calls Pilar "Rabbit" when she awakens him to inform him of the theft of the explosives. For the remainder of the text he pointedly refers to Pilar as "woman," an impersonal if not actually condescending term he never once uses until this incident, which provokes his "rage" at her (360).

Yet Robert Jordan—even though he never openly jokes about the word rabbit—is, like most men who feel superior to women, insecure in his own manhood. A schoolboyishness inheres in his fantasies, as critics from Edmund Wilson to Mark Spilka have noted, preventing him from any "enrichment or emotional give and take" with the woman he loves (Spilka 250).[6] Despite his genuine feeling for her, he can never acknowledge her as a vibrant individual, for she is, in Spilka's words, "Jordan's film fantasy come true" (Spilka 248). He merges her image with those of "Garbo and Harlow" and—in his most obviously professorial role—instructs Maria on what length she will wear her hair. Her body is all "hills and valley[s]" (341); she is a soft animal (a rabbit, a kitten, a beaver, a marten) to be petted and stroked; and ultimately a girl-child who must be instructed and protected. Jordan, a product of his own cultural dictates of male bravery in the face of death—even a meaningless one—cannot help but condescend to the female victim of male violence. In loving Maria he dominates her, in protecting her he denies her individuality. Maria eschews the skirts so pointedly identified with femininity and, like Pilar, offers to combine battle tactics and love, seeing no need to separate them—as when she offers to hold the gun and love Jordan at the same time.[7] But Jordan displays a compulsive need to separate the two. The masculine is a separate part of his identity, and Jordan reacts angrily when it is threatened by intimations of the feminine. At Pablo's taunting suggestion that he wears skirts, he responds defensively that underneath their skirts men have "*cojones*" (206).[8] The concept of *cojones* is pivotal in this novel because, although for Robert Jordan and others *cojones* are a male metaphor for bravery, on another level they signify the male propensity for dominance and sometimes violence: it is, after all, men with *cojones* who rape Maria, the *conejo,* and it is Robert who awakens her for sex—even though she is in considerable pain—before he leaves to blow up the bridge.

In contrast to Jordan's seriousness and intensity, both Maria and Pilar enter the novel smiling. Pilar's nature is basically good-humored; only when, like Lady Macbeth, she "unsexes" herself for political reasons does she joke and curse in a masculine fashion, hurling epithets that rival those of the men. Maria laughs, even during her first meeting with Robert Jordan when he asks whether she is Pablo's "woman," literally finding his question a knee-slapper (24). Maria is at ease with most of the characters in the novel, knowing when to tell jokes and when to be serious. She jokes with the pompous Fernando (82), and with Joaquin, who has helped save her life by carrying her away from the train: "I have thanked him," she says to Pilar, "And I will carry him sometime. Allow us to joke. I do not have to cry, do I, because he carried me?" (133). Here Maria—not a male Hemingway hero—provides a clear lesson in behaving with grace under pressure. Indeed, the only joking that makes her uncomfortable is Robert Jordan's at the beginning of the novel. He later tells Pilar that he was "jok[ing] with her a little" (32), but in fact he has embarrassed Maria, and, despite his stated wish that she stay, she retreats into the cave whence she emerged.

Whereas at the opening of the novel we find both Maria and Pilar alone within the cave, all the men are outside, Anselmo and Jordan preoccupied with the bridge, Pablo preoccupied with his horses. If the bridge—voyeuristically guarded, scrutinized, and finally destroyed by the necessities of war—represents the outward commitments of the male view, and the horses the qualities that make a man feel more manly (268), then Maria—raped, humiliated, and imprisoned—represents the inner ravages of war and the deeds of brutal men, as, to a lesser extent, does Pilar, who has lost the great love of her life to a fatal illness precipitated by the repeated gorings of the bulls to whom Pablo is compared. Spilka notes the influence on Hemingway of the Captain Marryat novels, particularly *Snarleyrow,* in which a band of women occupy and successfully defend a cave against an assault; he suggests that the scene, in which both men and women wear female clothing, is the "youthful precedent for the guerilla cave dominated by Pilar" (Spilka 78). Notably, neither Maria nor Pilar is ever remotely implied to lack courage. Maria willingly partici-

pates in the partisans' activities and would prefer to die with Jordan at
the end of the novel. The stalwart Pilar remarks to Jordan, "I confess a
sadness to you, but do not think I lack resolution" (89). Within the cave
Pilar, decrying Pablo's manhood, opposes but ultimately advocates the
killing of Pablo; only Maria repeatedly says "No" in the vote to kill Pilar's
husband (220)—but her vote does not count. Nor does Pilar's heart seem
to be in the decision, for when Pablo returns after his defection, she
"generously" returns the title of leader to him (Spilka 247). Nor does she
selfishly hoard this knowledge: an excellent instructor, she tries to educate
Jordan in the history of the Civil War.

Both women, then, combine courage and compassion. The androgy-
nous Pilar, as mentioned, temporarily "masculinizes" herself so that she
may contribute to the cause: on the day the movement starts, separating
herself from the traditional feminine role, Pilar responds as a man to a
partisan's question "Will there be women?" "No," she answers, "There
are no women. We are not killing the women. Why should we kill the
women?" (105). Significantly, neither Pilar nor Maria has ever killed
anyone. Both of Pilar's stories reveal vividly the violence and death that
she sorrowfully abhors. Within Pilar are contained the components of all
life—love as well as brutality, human commitment as well as killing—and
she gives voice to her memories and her intuitive wisdom.

Her vivid tale about the slaughter of the Fascists recounts atrocities
almost too unspeakable to reveal. With almost agonizing irony, the drunk
she has just "hit hard where it hurt" frames her vision with the words,
"This, woman, you have no right to do," while Pilar watches

men flailing away with clubs and striking and pushing and heaving against people
with the white wooden pitchforks that now were red and with their tines broken,
and this was going on all over the room while Pablo sat in the big chair with his
shotgun on his knees, watching, and they were shouting and clubbing and
stabbing and men were screaming as horses scream in a fire.

As she sees the priest chopped with hooks and sickles, the drunk at her
side tells her again that she had no right to hit him, that she "could have
done [him] an injury" (125). Earlier Pilar has said she had already "felt
an actual sickness in all of me inside" (124) at what she has witnessed,
and her blow to the drunk in the *cojones* doubtless reflects her subconscious understanding of—and symbolic rejection of—the barbarity of the
men who perpetrate atrocities on each other. Pablo's disappointment with
the Spanish priest's undignified approach to death contrasts with Pilar's

haunting memory of the sobbing lament of Don Guillermo's widow for her murdered husband. In both this story and the next, Pilar provides lessons in knowledge and compassion, truths not found in Jordan's history books.

Pilar's second story recounts her matador lover Finito's lifelong involvement with violence and injury, culminating in his defeat and death, from which she could not save him. Pilar's silent thoughts at the end of her tale of Finito's death are significant: "neither bull force nor bull courage lasted, she knew now, and what did last? I last, she thought. Yes, I have lasted. But for what?" (190). The sensitive Pilar has already acknowledged "the feeling of the thwarting of all hope and promise. She knew this feeling from when she was a girl and she knew the things that caused it all through her life" (58). The implication of her lesson is that these sorrows are caused by men and the brutality they sometimes espouse, whether in the bull ring or in battle. Of significance here is Hemingway's decision to give Pilar, rather than a male character, the voice to criticize both war and bullfighting, as if, in Spilka's words, "only an ingested female persona—the tough mama inside a tough Papa—could speak to the inhumanity that men without the softening influence of women sometimes relish" (Spilka 253). Surely Pilar—the "most tough and resolute of all the comrades" (Beach, "Style," 83) whose "humanity is revealed in the sick disgust which assails her from time to time" (Baker, "Tragedy," 118), is one of the women about whom Roger Whitlow comments: they "offer a vision of life that is more humane and decent than that offered by the 'heroes' with whom they spend—and often waste—their lives" (Whitlow 113). Pilar embodies the gifts of the ideal teacher: she has not only learned her own lessons well, but she generously teaches them to others, using vivid illustrations.

Pilar, although a participant in the start of the movement and the blowing up of the train, also takes responsibility for Maria and forces the men to carry her. A "Demeter figure," according to Mimi Gladstein (68), Pilar, calling Maria "daughter," treats her with a fierce love reminiscent of that of the earth mother for her abducted daughter Persephone.[9] She fiercely guards Maria like a nun, a symbol of feminine goodness, the embodiment of Spain, even a substitute for the Virgin, to whom the partisans are not supposed to pray, but to whom nearly all of them do in fact address their prayers.[10] Although surprisingly few critics give her ordeal more than a sentence or two, Maria's is a moving and honest confrontation of the horrific facts of her past. Her story, bits and pieces of which are alluded to from the opening of the novel, is a horrible one of premeditated murder and brutal, multiple rape. The fullest version of the story is withheld until the last part of the novel when, still feeling the painful physical scars of the rape, she finally tells it to Jordan on their third night together because, as Pilar has said, not only does everyone need a listener, but also, the telling of it will rid Maria of the "black thing," the dark feelings that sometimes engulf her (350). As she tells her tale, Maria honors both her parents: her father, the mayor of her town, and her mother, a good Catholic. She saw them shot to death and hoped the murderers would shoot her, too, when she would say, "Viva la Republica y vivan mis padres." Yet most vividly remaining in the young woman's memory is the image of her loyal mother crying "Viva my husband who was mayor of this village," a phrase Maria repeats three times. However, the heroic death in which she would emulate her parents' courage and pay tribute to them did not transpire; instead, she says, there was "the doing of the things" (350)

The Falangistes tie Maria and the others together "in a long line of girls and women," and after identifying the seemingly nameless Maria as the "daughter of the mayor," they shave her head. In shock and horror she gazes into the mirror: whereas the men see only the female object, the political example to be humiliated and punished because of her father's beliefs, Maria simultaneously sees both "myself and them" (351). In Gilligan's terms, Maria, as a woman, sees herself in relation to others, even as they rob her of the outward sign of her femininity: "I cried and cried, but I could not look away from the horror that my face made with the mouth open and the braids tied in it and my head coming naked under the clippers" (352). Maria refers to the mirror as if "the horror" is happening to someone else; she sees the entire scene with all its participants and her own place in it. That her world suddenly teems with violent men is reflected again in the hysterical screaming of her friend Concepcion Garcia when she finally recognizes the shorn Maria. The sound of the female voice echoes the similar sound in Pilar's recounting of the massacre in the *ayuntamiento*. Just as Pilar's story contains the chorus-like weeping of Guillermo's widow, Maria's contains that of Concepcion. From the barber shop, her consciousness always punctuated by the screams of her young woman friend, Maria is shoved "across the square, and into the doorway, and up the stairs of the city hall and into the office of my father where they laid me onto the couch. And it was there that the bad things were done" (353). At this point Jordan, "as full of hate as any man could be," asks her to say no more. He has missed one of Pilar's lessons: "For what are we born if not to aid one another? And to listen and say nothing is a cold enough aid" (139). Maria agrees never to talk of it again. But then, although he repeatedly asks her not to talk of it, she describes her "crazy" behavior when Pilar rescued her from the train, and tells him she may be unable to bear children. Maria desires to be utterly truthful—as Jordan is not—and to demonstrate to him her own strength and heroic behavior. She always resisted: "Always I fought and always it took two of them or more to do me the harm" (350). Maria may be a "rabbit" to Jordan, but she is an admirable woman of exceptional strength and courage who earns our respect. She is potentially Jordan's mentor, but he repeatedly rejects her in this role.

Maria's story is important: as Pilar says, now that religion is gone, "for everyone there should be some one to whom one can speak frankly, for all the valor that one could have one becomes very alone" (89). When in an earlier scene Primitivo asks Jordan whether the letters from the Navarrese he has just shot contain anything "interesting," Jordan replies, "No, they are personal letters." The more compassionate Primitivo does not know that the letters are from the dead young man's "loving sister Concha" and the fiancée "completely hysterical with concern for his safety" (303). Here Jordan does listen to the voices of the female friends and relatives of the man he has just killed, seeing him, as Mark Spilka argues, as a human being now rather than a statistic, one more killing.[11] Reading these women's letters, Jordan, in distinction to his lack of interest and emotion in his murder of Kashkin (171), wavers in his beliefs: "All right, he said to himself. I'm sorry, if that does any good," and then asks, "How many is that you have killed?" (303). Again, the voices of women serve to make Jordan question his masculinist values, and he actually wonders, in a reference to the doomed El Sordo, "Wouldn't it be luxury to fight in a war some time where, when you were surrounded, you could surrender?" (306). But the potentially beneficial lessons of Pilar and Maria, reinforced by various other women's voices, produce only a minimal impact on Jordan, whose fate, already predicted by Pilar in the opening chapters, is inescapable. Now Jordan in effect dismisses the crime against Maria, telling himself "not to take it personally." Curiously, although Jordan is sympathetic, described as filled with hatred, that emotion is never convincingly illustrated or expressed. He dismisses her very carefully considered resolution to kill herself rather than suffer such abuse again (171). His thoughts at the end of her story are not of Maria and of the violent sexual abuse she endured, but of her mother, so unlike his own, whose dying words were "Viva my husband who is mayor of this town." The image of the loving wife, loyal even at the moment of death, contrasts with his thoughts of his mother, whose strength and superiority to his father have earned Jordan's hatred.

Perhaps because women are concerned with the personal, the relational, Jordan, despite his dim recognition of his own yearnings in that direction, is most often impatient, if not downright contemptuous, of their stories. Clearly, women are important to Jordan only as they relate to men. His mother is a "bully," Maria is a "rabbit," Pilar is merely "woman," and even Karkov's wife or wives (the number is vague) and mistress seem mildly pleasant to him: he likes the wife and the mistress he knows, and probably would like the other wives, too, for "Karkov had good taste in women" (232). Not surprisingly, Jordan's hearing of Maria's voice is selective in the extreme. After the earth "moves" for them the first time, Maria is joyously verbal in expressing her feelings: "In my happiness I would like to be on a good horse and ride fast with thee riding fast beside me and we would ride faster and faster, galloping, and never pass my happiness." He responds "absently"; only "half hearing" her words, he is already thinking of his "work" (161). This indifference persists; as he typically says later, "Soon you will be with Maria and you won't have to think" (340).

He is far more angry with Pilar and Pablo for the theft of the explosives than he is with the multiple rape of Maria. Indeed, when he learns that Pablo has stolen the explosives from the sleeping Pilar, he is so angry that he realizes he would have struck Maria had she awakened: "What an animal is a man in a rage," he thinks (370). He is likewise less inclined to listen to Pilar's stories of love and youth: Jordan stops her, saying, "You speak very well. But there are other things that interest me more than talk of beauty or lack of beauty . . . Where were you at the start of the movement?" (98). Jordan listens intently to Pilar's tale of the *ayuntamiento,* for it features Pilar in her most male role, telling stories that appeal to Jordan: violent tales of history and politics, bravery and cowardice. At the end he is so impressed with her ability to tell a vivid story that he asks to hear more (129). He would like to write that story—not the personal one of Pilar, or of Maria, or of Joaquin, or of the Navarrese.

Whereas Maria and Pilar, using their voices through their storytelling, can control and master their traumatic experiences, Robert Jordan can only imagine storytelling in his head and through the possibility of writing it sometime in the future. Pilar's tale of slaughter, like her earlier story of Valencia, makes him think of writing, a way of controlling his own response. Writing about the war, he muses later, will help him circumscribe the experience that seems so confusing: "But my guess is you will get rid of all that by writing about it," he says to himself. "Once you write it down it is all gone. It will be a good book if you can write it" (165). But he will never write it. His only previous book was unsuccessful (248), and the writing that currently seems to gratify him is the operation orders: "He was thinking clearly and well on these and what he wrote pleased him" (226).

Part of his problem is that, unlike Maria and Pilar (and Joaquin and even Pablo, each of whom tell bits of their stories), Jordan does not tell his stories. Instead he listens to his own voices. He is an island, cut off from his mother and father, whom he despises for different reasons. Whereas both Pilar and Maria have survived disappointment or abuse to reconnect with others, Jordan remains rigid and reticent, refusing to tell what is on his mind—that which might help him come to terms with his problems and his identity. When Maria asks about his father, he tells her half-truths and then changes the subject, never sharing with her his profoundly disturbing preoccupation with his father's suicide. When Maria directly asks whether they will all die, he lies, euphemistically "going to Madrid," the locus of republican fantasies. Jordan remains the outsider, the foreigner. He is stiffly and formally referred to throughout the novel as "Robert Jordan," who sleeps outside the cave away from the others. Although he promises to "take up the study of women" when the war is over, he fails to listen as both Pilar and Maria try to make him "see," "understand," trying in effect to instruct him in the more humane and emotional aspects of life.[12]

Robert Jordan either fails to hear the voices of the women, or chooses not to listen. He should, of course, have listened, for Pilar "sees" things that he cannot see and speaks in a voice that he cannot hear. Cassandra-like, Pilar not only foresees Jordan's death, but has such mystical powers that she seems omniscient in matters of sex, as when she goads Jordan and Maria into admitting that the earth "moved" for them. At least one critic sees Pilar as "a shaman" responsible for initiating Jordan "into a spiritual or mystical relationship" (Wylder 148). She smiles at Jordan, telling him that after this experience he will have trouble regaining his dignity. Even as Jordan—infuriated, as always, with her ability to see, smell, or hear truths and qualities that he cannot—struggles to ignore her, she looks at the sky and predicts that it will snow even though the month is May. It snows. (176).

Thus Jordan seems to be making progress when various characters say they are "teaching the professor"; he learns, for example, that there are two "centers" to the world in which he finds himself: the masculine bridge, a feat of masculine engineering and connection, to be blown up and destroyed with masculine ingenuity; and the feminine Maria and Pilar, associated with unmechanical, natural and spiritual phenomena. His progress in learning is aborted, however, mainly because the loud clashing voices within his own head compete for his attention. In the end he "understands" what to do with the bridge, but he never fully comprehends Maria or the alternative she offers to separation and death. He doggedly adheres to the male "virtues" that virtually imprison him and seal his fate. Even when he comes closest to having the attack aborted, his fear of being labeled a coward intrudes and overrides his more intelligent impulse: when he writes his letter to Golz, it is not only too late, but he tries "to put it so the attack would be cancelled, absolutely, yet convince them he wasn't trying to have it called off because of any fears he might have about the danger of his own mission" (333).

Robert Jordan says he fights for Spain, as indeed he does, but in his head he battles his own very American and very personal past. These preoccupations are intensely and fatally masculine. Indeed, from the middle of the novel to the end, the third-person narration is interrupted with increasing insistence by the conflicting voices in Robert Jordan's head, arguing between the virtues of the male code of heroism, duty, and bravery, and the more feminine code of personal relationships and commitment to living. Although one part of him is drawn to the more traditional feminine values, the other part of Jordan repudiates them, causing his anger at Pilar who, as already noted, sees truths that he represses (all the other men, even Pablo, believe in Pilar's ability to see the future [251–52]). Jordan's resistance to the more feminine values of intuition and human connection continues, despite his dimly growing perception of the way he values these Spaniards.

As the voices within Jordan increase in intensity, drowning out the voices of his Spanish friends, particularly those of Maria and Pilar, it becomes clear that his inner conflicts are rooted in his obsession with the images of his grandfather and other Civil War heroes. The near stream-of-consciousness begins as Jordan divines El Sordo's predicament through an implied reference to General George C. Custer: "We are surrounded.

That was the great panic cry of this war" (306), and intensifies with the appearance of Lt. Paco Berrendo and the severed heads of Sordo and his band. In Jordan's mind the Spanish Civil War fuses with the American Civil War and the Indian wars in which his grandfather had fought. These male mentors compete for his attention: eight times in the novel he recalls memories of American Indians or notes Indian characteristics in the Spaniards.[13] As Spilka notes, the Indian images are prompted by the scalps or heads that Lt. Berrendo has taken (Spilka 256). In several references to General Custer, Jordan is imagistically associated with his blond looks, as he is to his blond "doubles" the fascist Captain Mora and the communist Kashkin, both of whose attitudes lead to their suicides or suicide-like deaths.[14] In Jordan's recollection of the Anheuser-Busch lithograph of Custer surrounded by the Sioux, he thinks that the doomed general would never have led his men to disaster had Jordan's grandfather been there (337). Again he reaches out to the male models he has reverenced: Jordan wishes he could learn more from his grandfather, and he would like to tell Golz about him. His thinking is pleasant when it concerns his grandfather, but turns sour when memories of his father intrude. The scene ends with his comforting knowledge that he will blow up the bridge—"But you are going to have to blow that bridge, he suddenly knew absolutely" (340)—just as earlier he wanted "absolutely" to call off the attack. Notably, Jordan unrepentingly "breaks the rules" about leaving women alone (24) and acting superior to the Spaniards (248), yet he will not defy the orders to blow up the bridge.

By the time he nears his final arguments with himself, Jordan's two voices are actually characterized as "schizophrenic": "I was ashamed of you, there for a while. Only I was you. There wasn't any me to judge you. We were all in bad shape. You and me and both of us. Come on now. Quit thinking like a schizophrenic. One at a time now. You're all right again now" (394). The "I" tells the "you" that he must blow up the bridge and resist thinking of Maria. Here Jordan is similar to the men in Gilligan's study, for whom "the male 'I' is defined in separation, although the men speak of having 'real contacts' and 'deep emotions' or otherwise wishing for them" (Gilligan 161). Although ten pages earlier he says he has learned from Maria, and one page earlier that he has learned that "himself, with another, could be everything" (393), Jordan has merely intellectualized the lesson, not internalized it. In Spilka's words, Jordan's is an "interesting mind," but one that "systematically dodges complex ideas, on the one hand, and emotional depths on the other—a mind that prefers to externalize scenes and actions rather than probe inner feelings or express them freely" (Spilka 255). As he says goodbye to Maria just before he blows up the bridge, she is displaced by his recollection of the embarrassingly tearful farewell when, as he first went away to school, his father saw him to the train (405). This scene, of course, has been well documented as a fictional version of Hemingway's own embarrassment at a similar moment with his father. Incapable of accepting displays of human emotion, Jordan is clearly imprisoned in a male past that insistently takes precedence over his newly acquired feelings of love and loyalty.

This male heritage is repeatedly presented in images of guns and ammunition and explosives. For a time Robert can separate from his relationship with Maria the guns that obsess him, literally putting them aside while they make love. But a significant transitional scene occurs as he lies on the pine needles just before blowing up the bridge. Whereas a few hours before he had lain next to Maria and run "the tip of his tongue along her cheek and onto the lobe of her ear and along the lovely convolutions" (378), now he "put the [submachine gun] muzzle to his lips and blew through the barrel, the metal tasting greasy and oily as his tongue touched the edge of the bore" (410). The image of love is replaced by an image of death. But in the next scene they are actually conflated: after he blows up the bridge, he holds Maria "tight, tight, with the automatic rifle leaning against his side, the flash-cone pressing against his ribs," and her "small, round and tight" breasts against his chest (456). And again, Pilar has predicted correctly: the earth was destined to move three times for him: but only twice with Maria, the third time as a prelude to death: "he saw a small fountain of earth rise with a plume of gray smoke. Sweeish-crack-boom! It came again, the swishing like the noise of a rocket and there was another up-pulsing of dirt and smoke farther up the hillside" (459). As "the earth spouted the little black and gray geyser ahead of him" (459), and "the dirt fountained up the hillside," the enemy gun fires "with the rocket whish and the cracking, dirt-spouting boom," shooting his horse out from under him (460).

By the end of the novel, he is alone with the submachine gun of Kashkin. The mortality of his horse—one of those which make men like Pablo larger than life (268)—leaves him completely vulnerable. He forces Maria to leave him, despite her initial protest that he does not "understand." Jordan's own understanding is indeed different, and his orders impose silence on her. Three times the narrator repeats "She said nothing," and then

Maria speaks decisively: "No" she says. But Jordan overrides her decisive feminine protest, treating Maria as a child who can be cajoled into doing as he asks. The scene is impressively complex. On the one hand, Jordan is clearly abusive and demeaning in his treatment of Maria, yet on the other, he is also exercising his power to preserve her life, sensibly and rationally denying her wish to die with him rather than be separated. Yet a peculiar selfishness inheres in Jordan as well, for he needs to be alone to listen to his voices, and to die without the cowardice he so fears. Thus he simultaneously degrades and saves Maria, and fails even to say goodbye to Pilar, essentially, in Delbert Wylder's words, "excluding her" (Wylder 160). With their departure continues the real drama going on in his head—an entirely male one. Incapable of listening to any but his own confused voices, again "I" speaks to "you," for the last time, one voice asking "who are you talking to?" the other saying "Grandfather, I guess. No. Nobody." One voice urges him to kill himself: "Go on and do it now"; the other saying "*No, you have to wait*" (469, 470). Once Jordan dismisses Maria's authority, he himself regresses into the role of student.

Robert's definition of himself seems inextricably bound up with his ability to pass the test of bravery, to emulate the heroic deaths of Fernando and El Sordo, for whom "living was a horse between your legs and a carbine under one leg and a hill and a valley and a stream with trees along it." At the end, bereft of the "hills and valleys" of Maria, his horse shot from between his legs, Robert is left with his male inheritance, the submachine gun. His last thoughts are not of Maria, but of his grandfather, who fought bravely in both the Civil War and the Indian wars that followed. Like him, Robert aims his sights on the scalper—the collector of heads—Lt. Berrendo. Both male ancestors' roles lead ultimately to death and away from Pilar, Maria, and their life-affirming values. One of his final thoughts is to acknowledge that he was "bitched when Golz gave those orders." But the responsibility is his, too. The unfortunate Jordan was in fact doomed when he decided "absolutely" to obey them.

Roger Whitlow points out that "in response to Maria's most noble of human ethics (espoused by Socrates, by Jesus, and by the distinct minority of decent and loving men and women throughout the centuries)," Jordan fails to offer "love and selflessness" in exchange: "Despite his professions of love and talk of marriage and Missoula, he offers instead a uselessly demolished bridge, a handful of dead Fascists, and a substantially larger number of dead friends. . . . " (Whitlow 39). Certainly Robert Jordan is a complex man, torn by his desire to live up to a code that is at odds with the more feminine values to which he has become increasingly attracted. Like Hemingway himself, Robert Jordan cannot resolve the split between a masculine code whose validity he must assert more and more insistently, and the feminine one, which, at the end, he refuses even to acknowledge. Hemingway's awareness of this tension is, I believe, clearly demarcated in his use of the conflicting male and female voices throughout the text. Perhaps Hemingway mourns Jordan's—and his own—ability to learn from women. Mark Spilka's observation about Hemingway and his mother serves equally as a fine insight on Robert Jordan, Pilar, and Maria: ironically,

In his own shortsighted denial of his mother's influence, he continued to deny also those emotional resources—fearless friendliness with women, manly courage in domestic relations—which might have strengthened his own relations with women, enriched and expanded his art, and preserved his life and sanity in old age. (Spilka 64)

Likewise could Robert Jordan have enjoyed and learned from the women in his life, written more and better books, and lived a much longer life. Although Hemingway would go on to explore these voices and values in greater depth, particularly in his final work *The Garden of Eden,* he, like Robert Jordan, would ultimately be unsuccessful in resolving the masculine and feminine impulses that so preoccupied him, and ended in emotional defeat and the suicide with whose dark attraction he had dwelt so long.

Notes

1. I am indebted to Susan Shillinglaw, San Jose State University, for this insight. A number of the ideas in this essay—particularly the textual relevance of the concepts of "understanding" and "joking"—derive from our extensive collaboration on a paper, "Neither Bull Force Nor Bull Courage Lasted: Feminine Subversion in *For Whom the Bell Tolls,*" presented jointly at the Fourth International Hemingway Conference, Boston, July 7–11, 1990.

2. For a more complete discussion of the Hemingway "code," see Rovit, 107–110.

3. I am indebted to Alice Hall Petry, Rhode Island School of Design, for this insight during a conversation in August, 1990.

4. According to Lynn 487, Hemingway also had to substitute sensations of thickening and swelling of the throat "for what happens to [Jordan's] member when he strokes Maria's hair." See also Meyers 326.

5. Gertrude Stein, "Miss Furr and Miss Skeene," in *Selected Writings of Gertrude Stein.* "They were quite regularly gay there, Helen Furr and Georgine Skeene, they were regularly gay there where they were gay. They were very

regularly gay." Cf: Robert Jordan's thoughts, "All the best ones, when you thought it over, were gay. It was much better to be gay and it was a sign of something too. . . There were not many of them left though. No, there were not many of the gay ones left" (17). This is the only time in the text that he uses the word "gay." Notably, in 1933 Gertrude Stein called Hemingway a coward in *The Autobiography of Alice B. Toklas* (Meyers 250). Given that much of this novel focuses on Jordan's preoccupation with cowardice, it is not unlikely that Hemingway is paying back Stein—she called him a coward, he mocked her "gay-ness."

6. Wilson, in *The New Republic* and *The Wound and the Bow,* quoted in Lynn 485, Meyers 111.

7. For discussions of this propensity, see, for example, Spilka 251.

8. Mark Spilka, discussing the occurrences of scenes in which men are dressed as women in both Marryat's and Twain's novels, suggests that the scenes contain "the male ethos, which, by insisting on that division, probably betrays an inordinate fear of female powers" (Spilka 81).

9. For more detailed discussions of Pilar's and Maria's mythic dimensions, see, for example, Wylder 152; Garcia 151; Smith 136; Adair, "Debt," 11.

10. For discussions of Maria's symbolic qualities, see, for example, Garcia 167; Backman 250; Rovit 142–46; Baker, "Tragedy," 127; Wylder 138; Beach 242; Carpenter 198.

11. Conversation with Mark Spilka, August 1990.

12. For insights on the role of wives, mothers, and daughters as "sources of instruction" see Spilka 21.

13. These references are to the partisans from Pilar to Fernando: see, for example, 141, 198, 200, 260, 298, 336, 360.

14. According to William Adair, "Oedipus," 2, the novel is in a sense "bracketed by suicides": Kashkin's—Jordan's double—and Jordan's father.

Works Cited

Adair, William. "Hemingway's Debt to *Seven Pillars of Wisdom* in *For Whom the Bell Tolls.*" *Notes on Contemporary Literature* 17:3 (May 1987):11–12.

———. "*For Whom the Bell Tolls*: Oedipus in Spain." *Notes on Contemporary Literature* 12:2 (March 1982):2.

Backman, Melvin. "Hemingway: The Matador and the Crucified." In *Hemingway and His Critics: An International Anthology,* edited by Carlos Baker, 245–58. New York: Hill and Wang, 1961.

Baker, Carlos. *Ernest Hemingway: A Life Story.* New York: Scribner's, 1969.

———. "The Spanish Tragedy." In *Ernest Hemingway: Critiques of Four Major Novels,* edited by Carlos Baker, 108–30. New York: Scribner's, 1962.

Barea, Arturo. "Not Spain but Hemingway." In *Hemingway and His Critics: An International Anthology,* edited by Carlos Baker, 202–12. New York: Hill and Wang, 1961.

Beach, Joseph Warren. "How Do You Like It Now, Gentlemen?" In *Hemingway and His Critics: An International Anthology,* edited by Carlos Baker, 227–44. New York: Hill and Wang, 1961.

———. "Style in *For Whom the Bell Tolls.*" In *Ernest Hemingway: Critiques of Four Major Novels,* edited by Carlos Baker, 82–6. New York: Scribner's, 1962.

Carpenter, F. I. "Hemingway Achieves the Fifth Dimension." In *Hemingway and*

His Critics: An International Anthology, edited by Carlos Baker, 192–201. New York: Hill and Wang, 1961.

Garcia, Wilma. *Mothers and Others: Myths of the Female in the Works of Melville, Twain and Hemingway*. New York: Peter Lang, 1984.

Gilligan, Carol. *In A Different Voice*. Cambridge: Harvard University Press, 1982.

Gladstein, Mimi Reisel. *The Indestructible Woman in the Novels of Faulkner, Hemingway and Steinbeck*. Ann Arbor: UMI Research Press, 1986.

Hemingway, Ernest. *For Whom the Bell Tolls*. New York: Scribner's, 1968.

Josephs, F. Allen. "Hemingway's Poor Spanish: Chauvinism and Loss of Credibility in *For Whom the Bell Tolls*." In *Hemingway: A Revaluation*, edited by Donald R. Noble, 205–223. Troy, N.Y.: The Whitston Publishing Company, 1983.

Lynn, Kenneth S. *Hemingway*. New York: Simon & Schuster, 1987.

Meyers, Jeffrey. *Hemingway: A Biography*. New York: Harper & Row, 1985.

Nagel, James, ed. *Ernest Hemingway: The Writer in Context*. Madison: University of Wisconsin Press, 1984.

Reynolds, Michael. *The Young Hemingway*. New York: Basil Blackwood, 1986.

Rovit, Earl. *Ernest Hemingway*. New York: Twayne, 1963.

Smith, Carol H. "Women and the Loss of Eden in Hemingway's Mythology." In *Ernest Hemingway: The Writer in Context*, edited by James Nagel, 129–144. Madison: University of Wisconsin Press, 1984.

Spilka, Mark. *Hemingway's Quarrel With Androgyny*. Lincoln: University of Nebraska Press, 1990.

Stein, Gertrude. *Collected Works*. New York: Random House, 1964.

Waldmeir, Joseph. "Chapter Numbering and Meaning in *For Whom the Bell Tolls*." *The Hemingway Review* VIII:2 (Spring 1989):43–45.

Whitlow, Roger. *Cassandra's Daughters: The Women in Hemingway*. Westport, Conn.: Greenwood Press, 1984.

Wylder, Delbert E. *Hemingway's Heroes*. Albuquerque: University of New Mexico Press, 1969.

DRANDA TRIMBLE

Making Love to the Gods
Four Women and Their Affairs with Education

No one has a right to judge anyone who falls in love with, or wants to make love to, the gods. In various mythologies, gods take on human form until mere mortals understand the mysteries they symbolize. For many women, and for some men as well, our professors are transitory gods. We see the knowledge we receive in their classrooms as gifts and as the answers to our prayers. Sometimes we offer ourselves and our emotions as the tithes and sacrifices we must pay for their mystery of learning. We barter with our own gifts and sacrifices. If the gods will answer our prayers and impart their knowledge, we will repay them in kind as much as possible.

Women of all ages sometimes find themselves in love with their teachers, whether the teacher is male or female. More often than not, the teacher is male once we enter college. In the fall of 1986, when I began my second year of graduate school, I had just turned twenty-nine. My office-mate Barbara was forty and was beginning her first semester of graduate work. Across the hall from us were Katherine and Joanne, new graduate students in their mid-thirties. That autumn, and for the next year or so, we were surrounded by men who were handing out the knowledge, learning, and experience that we had come looking for. It was an unbeatable seduction scene.

When Brenda and I talked about why she was in graduate school she told me about her neighbors in her well-to-do subdivision and said, "I was tired of shopping. The only thing left to shop for were trees to replant." Brenda had begun graduate school at the same time the wealthy suburbanites in her neighborhood realized they could replant nearly full-grown trees in their treeless yards.

Brenda's husband was a self-made man who made a fortune in plastics (more specifically, urine sample cups). Katherine, a mother of two preschoolers, worked as an adjunct professor and took a few fiction writing classes while she watched her husband advance his legal practice. She talked of going to the University of Vermont for an intensive semester in the MFA program. Down the corridor, Joanne worked as an adjunct, a research assistant, and took an occasional class in criticism. She was always there any time any professor needed her; her husband was a minister.

I was there because of my obsession with education. I had quit high school to marry as a teen-ager, and for the ten-year period between 1978 and 1988 I went to college. I was wife, mother, student, instructor, and mistress to a different subject every semester. Like most of my women friends in graduate school, I made love to academics as long as there was a willing male professor in need. We did this to the detriment and exclusion of our families and former friends. Like teenagers in love with love we were continually starry-eyed, and as soon as we had had our fill of one man we would move to the next. It was as easy as registering for classes every semester.

In our small southern university, we only knew of "feminist thought" as a type of literary criticism that we touched on briefly. Ironically enough, this class was taught by a professor whose second wife was a young woman who had been his graduate student. Ironic, perhaps, but not odd, considering we only had one female professor and one female full-time instructor in the English department.

The group of us that gathered together in those two years were there because we worshiped academics. We loved the thought of becoming women of letters. We loved literature, we loved writing, and to varying degrees, from the physical to the metaphysical, we all screwed or were screwed by academics. Our particular group may have been more susceptible than some because we were all southern women, women who by birthright are raised to be politely subservient. We were all married with children. My husband was also a graduate student in the history department, so I had a third partner in my affair. His being in school with me disguised my rendezvous with professors and lecturers.

My friends and I were like the replanted trees in the yards of Brenda's subdivision. We tore ourselves from the woods—home life and/or K-12 teaching—and replanted ourselves in the university experience. Maybe it is where we belonged in the first place. Maybe we reappeared there by circumstance: our public school teaching demanded an advanced degree; divorce or domestic discontent drove us to do more with ourselves, and school was what we remembered as fulfilling, or at least was a place where we were singled out for affection or recognition. To some extent the university experience was sacred to us. We were learning, not just trying to advance our lives or careers.

As older female students, we were, for the first time in a long time, interacting with people who had wonderful thoughts, brilliant ideas. Most of the time those people were male. What we didn't realize was that often we were the creators of those ideas. In the movie *Moonstruck*, Olympia Dukakis's character listens patiently to the male professor talk about why he dates his younger female students: they think he is full of ideas, new thoughts. He is the god of knowledge and future. When they realize he has clay feet they throw a drink in his face and leave him. Olympia chides him: "What you don't know about women . . . " Her character knows all too well that until the professor understands the growth of the women he teaches, he will continue to get drinks thrown in his face. More importantly, he needs to understand his role as mentor or creator, who brings his student to an understanding that all human beings have godlike possibilities.

My friends and I were even more susceptible to the enchantment of ideas from the mouths of our professors. Not only were the ideas they offered important; if not for them, we would have wasted away in our safe private worlds of home, K-12 teaching, or the succession of jobs that never quite became careers.

Brenda, my office-mate, lasted one semester before she found her first professor. He was interested in the philosophy of Wendell Berry. Berry's philosophy concerned environmental conservation, the gentleman farmer providing for himself, his family, and the extended family of his community. Professor David extended this philosophy to free love and communal living, even though he was married to a woman who taught business management at a private business school. David was Pan-like in his looks and ideas. The first time I met his wife I was surprised by her contrast to Brenda. David's wife was austere by comparison: tailored, with tight hair. Brenda, even at forty, was blonde, vivacious, Reeboks, and strawberries. She was the perfect foil for the horny, goat-hooved little man.

Brenda was attracted to David because he represented all the things she had given up when she married. Brenda had missed the '60s. She finished her undergraduate work at a small Mississippi college and taught elementary school while her husband built his business. Like many women of our age and background, she had spent her younger years being responsible to her family, not responsive to herself. David gave her Wendell Berry, pot-smoking, love-making in a trailer in the woods, and praise when she wrote about the writer he was interested in.

David responded to many women. I did not tell Brenda about the class I took with him as a returning undergraduate where his personal interest in me disturbed me, and where I later saw him transfer his interest to a young blonde. The class was a graduate seminar in the English romantic poets. I dropped it. I wasn't interested in the Romantics at that stage of my career, and I certainly wasn't interested in David. He was balding and thin, and a shabby dresser. Nothing about him stimulated me, either intellectually or physically. Three years later he and Wendell Berry had seduced my best friend, Brenda.

Brenda was the mother of two teenage boys, the wife of a successful businessman, and a brilliant and sympathetic writing instructor; these were her priorities. Professor David was as much a contrast to her husband as she was to his wife. The ideas he espoused represented freedom to her: freedom to live a life separate from her home and responsibilities, freedom to think her own thoughts after the affair—and her marriage—were over.

Joanne and Katherine experienced similar dramas. Katherine was across the hall from me for one semester. She was married, with a three-year-old son and a husband struggling to build his new legal practice. Joanne, too, was married, with two children in elementary school and a husband who was a Baptist minister without a church. He was employed at a local tire plant. Both women worked as adjuncts and took occasional classes toward their Masters degrees in English.

Katherine wrote short stories. Her creative writing instructor was still waiting to receive a full-time appointment. Katherine fell in love with her instructor's writing style, and found in him a cause to fight for. But the instructor was not on good terms with the established faculty in the department, and there was no chance that he would get the position. Unfortunately, Katherine had yet to understand academic politics. With a little prodding from the instructor she wrote letters of support for him, and had a long argument with the chairman of the department over the issue. During that period, there were many closed-door discussions between Katherine and her instructor. She didn't consider for one moment that her defense and support of him would cost her both comfort and position in the department, and officially it didn't. But, like any good wife, Katherine would not stay where her spouse was not wanted. And in a sense, he was a spouse: to consider the male professors as just lovers is not fair to either party. As graduate students we often spent more time with our advisers than we did with our actual husbands. Some of us ran personal errands for our professors, and dinner together was common. After all, we did the same things for the men at home. Katherine left the department.

Joanne was in love with the professor who had married one of his graduate students. He was one of those men who simply love all women. At parties he danced with us all, and gave us knowing glances and touches. Generally, if one recognizes these men for what they are, then the danger is averted. Unfortunately, Joanne did not know the game. At thirty-five she was a remarkably intelligent young woman, but as blind emotionally as she was physically without the large, heavy-rimmed glasses she wore.

We didn't like Joanne very much. We often prodded her into debates in classes where we knew we excelled. Usually those debates took place in the criticism classes where her favorite professor presided. Our mistrust of her was based on her readiness to agree with his every interpretation of the critics we studied. But we did not see our situation as akin to hers; our professors responded to us, and agreed with us.

As far as any of us knew, Joanne's relationship with her professor never became sexual, and I think that is what we really held against her. She couldn't get her man. Later, after I had left the university, I found out she had divorced her husband because she thought she loved the professor. Subsequently, the professor took a position at another university and Joanne did not go with him. Did he ever know that she was in love with him? Probably. Was it his fault? That's debatable. He did not do anything that directly led Joanne to fall in love with him, or at least convince herself that she had. On the other hand, his general behavior toward the women under his instruction needed considerable change. He was a flirt. And when the opportunity was safe, he went farther than flirting. He would probably argue that since he did not go to bed with Joanne and made no declaration of lasting affection, he could not be blamed, and Joanne would undoubtedly agree. Both, however, would fail to take into account the vulnerability of a woman finding herself in love with her career, but uncertain of her ability to succeed. Fortunately, after Joanne realized how easily she could get over her feelings for the professor, she and her husband began seeing each other again, and talking of ways for the family to be together and for Joanne to seriously pursue her career in academics.

What I saw in my friends I didn't acknowledge in myself until I had one of those eye-opening discussions with a friend during a particularly low time in my life. A little bit of wine and a sympathetic listener brought my own academic history into focus. I was aware that I had always loved school. I remember sitting at the kitchen table the day after school closed at the end of the first grade. My class photograph in front of me and a box of Kleenex at my side, I cried my heart out over the fact that school was over. At six years old, the three-month summer break seemed a lifetime. I still remember that grief because I have felt it all my academic life. I am the classic example of a woman in love with knowledge—and the authority and attention it brings.

Perhaps the greatest pain and awareness of my affair with academics comes today when I read my own poetry. At fourteen I began writing poetry to express my infatuation with a student teacher at my parochial high school. My writing impressed him, or seduced him, or maybe just fascinated him. Whatever his feelings were, mine were clear. I wanted this young man's attention, and words worked. I made a twenty-one-year-old boy into one of my fleeting gods. Ten years later, when he and I met again, the attraction I had for him was gone. He was neither a teacher nor a god; he worked in public relations. We are still friends, and during the past twelve years of our off-again, on-again friendship, I've often felt myself to be the nurturer and creator. Our roles reversed for a while, and I didn't like my new position. The outings with him were not comfortable until we realized we were equals.

When as a young mother I began my undergraduate studies at a local community college, I fell head over heels into an infatuation with my first male composition instructor. I hung on his every word. He was at least twenty-five years older than I was and slightly balding, with a habit of coloring the little bit of hair he had. It didn't matter. He also read poetry, mine, and introduced me to Joyce, and Lawrence, and all of those wonderful writers in introduction to literature books. I offered him my poetry and he gave me the attention I sought. In return, I excelled in the class. He truly was and is a brilliant and kind man. He handled my infatuation well, except for a moment late in our relationship when once again the reversal came and he thought he was in love with me. I was a symbol of comfort for him while he was going through a particularly tough time with his daughter. Of course by then I had found another god to worship.

Unfortunately, the friendship didn't hold up through time. Whether we just lost touch, or he felt he had done his job, I'll never know. But with tenderness, humor, and just a slight bit of embarrassment, I still remember how much I thought I cared about him.

When I entered graduate school at twenty-eight, I entered free from attachment to any professor in the English department. For the first semester I fumbled around without any real direction until I decided to pursue my interest in poetry. Once I had committed to creative writing, all of my old obsessiveness came back. My first serious poem I recognize today as a key to my mind-set at the time:

Women in Love with Literature

So this is what happens
to women in love with literature.
I sit for hours
my ears keyed to silence.
So used to the hush
I hear ashes

fall from my cigarette,
tea bags diffuse into warm water.
I feel the pages' fog
creep into my body.
I taste it.

Strapped in my chair
I read and devour
the carnival of words.

Outside in the sun
a young man without a shirt
caresses his car,
rubbing away the dust.

I sit in my chair
fifteen feet from the front door,
fourteen feet from the back door
and offer silence to the young body

while I dream of books.
So many books,
that now their plots have replaced memories
of men reading,

poetry on the grass,

the crush of my lawn skirt
under their touch.
They brought me lavender gardenias

> to wear on my wrist.
> I don't remember their names
> only that we read Byron,
> and when I closed my eyes
> I kissed the fleshy lips of my poet.
>
> In my near dark room,
> I wait for a man to walk out of the shadows.
> I wait for my bridegroom
> like a nun who has been promised Christ.

With this poem I began a series that centered around a woman named Ethel who had a degree in English from Brown University, but who lived as a recluse. I actually knew such a woman. I am angry now to realize that, subconsciously, I saw Ethel as a model for what happens to women who seriously pursue knowledge. Worse, I am angry with myself for believing that men only had direct access to the life of knowledge, as "Women in Love with Literature" suggests.

In my third semester as a graduate student my poetry was developing with decidedly religious overtones. Initially, my work brought in Greek mythology. There is nothing astounding about such symbols in poetry, and at the time the words felt good, as if they poured from my soul. All I have to do now is look at the titles of what were once my favorite pieces to know what my subconscious knew at the time: "The Girl Who Wanted a Centaur for a Lover," "Instead of Praying," and "Prayer."

In the "Centaur" poem I wanted to make love to Chiron, who, legend declares, taught some of the great male heroes. In "Instead of Praying" I wanted to sacrifice myself to this new religion of knowledge and force the gods to notice me for my own knowledge. In "Prayer" I came back to some sort of Judeo-Christian reality, and like Simone Weil, wanted to sacrifice my sexual passion for the passion of Jesus Christ and God. I took on Christ as a lover in the supreme match of teacher and student.

At that time, religion and God seemed like safe topics. Now, however, I have to question who this god was, for me. In the poem he is knowledge, and male, and always existing. In my mind he was knowledge, and knowledge was the male to my female. I screamed at this god to acknowledge that "we were lovers." Knowing that my college career was coming to an end, I wrote "Prayer" the semester I graduated. It was my prayer. At this point there were no professors to fall in love with, no one to impress, nothing but success in finally attaining my Masters' degree, and nowhere to go.

After receiving my degree I did some teaching as an adjunct at my old university and at a local community college. With a wonderful ironic twist I became a "goddess" to a couple of young men, who wrote to me in their journals and wore too much aftershave when they came to my class. At first their affections were humorous to me. Then I realized the seriousness of their feelings (at least to them), and finally I realized the responsibility of my actions. My goal was to make them understand that everything I had to give to them I would give freely. There was nothing I expected in return, except that they learn.

Even with my own teaching experience I did not realize how often I had put male professors in such a precarious position, or how often they had willingly sat on the summit. Both the worshiped and the admirer have to be willing to play their parts.

When I look back at the poem "Women in Love with Literature," with its adoration of males and their knowledge, I know that that is where I was—and possibly still am, to some degree—and where, even today, my friend Brenda has ended. As mature women, older women, we entered school for reasons other than those of our younger sisters. Our goals were to get what we didn't get the first time around, which was quite simply all the knowledge and learning our minds could hold. This left us with a two-fold problem: knowledge, at least in our minds, was still a gift for which we had to trade ourselves and our emotions; and once we had access to knowledge we found there was even more, and that we couldn't keep up the barter system we had used in the past. The sexual and emotional currency, we discovered, was counterfeit. The exchange had to be legitimized by the genuine need and love of knowledge, uncorrupted by the need to worship at the alter of a god, however willing or unwilling he might be.

MONTANA KATZ

Truth or Consequences

Mamet's *Oleanna* in the Real World

David Mamet's play *Oleanna* hit the stage in the aftermath of the confirmation hearings of Clarence Thomas in 1992–93. With so much coverage during and after the hearings about sexual harassment, the theater audience was hungry for material that would challenge their thinking about this issue. Considering the lively and often heated debate that flowed on the streets and in the press after the play's opening night, *Oleanna* apparently satisfied that need. Much of the focus at the hearings was on the *truth*, both determining the truth and the consequences thereof. In that case, it was the truth teller, Anita Hill, who suffered the consequences. In *Oleanna* the situation is reversed, and it is the (falsely) accused man who endures life-changing and dire consequences.

The setting for opening a dialogue about the subject of sexual harassment in *Oleanna* is a college campus. This is an interesting choice for at least two reasons. First, instances of sexual harassment between professor and student can more often occur than in other contexts behind completely closed doors. Second, the ivory tower has remained a stronghold against the illumination and eradication of gender bias generally, and of sexual harassment and rape specifically, as compared to other social contexts in contemporary culture.

In the play it is John, an Education professor, who is accused by a student, Carol, first of sexual harassment and later of rape, and who is harshly punished for these alleged crimes. This is in spite of the fact, as the audience is made patently aware, that the charges are not only unfounded, but were made by Carol under the influence of, and as a means to a sinister end on behalf of, an unnamed campus political organization.

In a culture in which the emphasis is on punishment for rather than the prevention of crimes, the issue of sexual harassment becomes a heated debate over its very existence, rather than an exploration of what it is.

Because these two concepts, truth and consequences, loom so large in discussions of sexual harassment, and because they are the building blocks of *Oleanna,* this essay will take a close look at the role they play in distracting our attention from what is actually at stake concerning sexual harassment; namely, an articulation of what its dynamics are and how to arrest them.

Curiously, the audience walking out of the play on the night I attended *Oleanna* seemed exhilarated, both women and men. What accounts for this response? *Oleanna* falls into a tradition in theater of works that highlight and confirm society's fears and anxieties. In the case of *Oleanna,* the most salient are the male fantasy of unjust accusation and the fear of powerlessness vis-à-vis female sexuality.

At the dawn of Western patriarchy we had *The Orestia,* which at the time confirmed current anxieties surrounding the fledgling concepts of male right and dominance. In the stark words of Richard Lattimore in his introduction to *The Orestia*:

The Furies are older than Apollo and Athene, and, being older, they are childish and barbarous; . . . they are female and represent the woman's claim to act . . . in a Greek world they stand for the childhood of the race before it won Hellenic culture . . . Apollo stands for everything which the Furies are not: Hellenism, civilization, intellect, and enlightenment. He is male and young. The commonwealth of the gods—and therefore the universe—is in a convulsion of growth; the young Olympians are fighting down their own barbaric past. (*Aeschylus 1: Oresteia*)

Now, at the dusk of Western patriarchy, we have *Oleanna* weakly attempting to prop up trends that have one foot in the grave.

JOHN: Now, look, granted. I have an interest. In the status quo. All right? Everyone does . . . . I want to tell you something. I'm a teacher. I am a teacher. Eh? It's my *name* on the door, and *I* teach the class, and that's what I do. I've got a book with my name on it. And my son will *see* that *book* someday. And I have a respon . . . No, I'm sorry I have a *responsibility* . . . to *myself,* to my *son,* to my *profession* . . .

You're *dangerous,* you're *wrong* and it's my *job* . . . to say no to you. (*Oleana* 56, 76)

Judging by the audience response during my viewing of the movie version of *Oleanna,* it was an effective tool for eliciting and confirming our collective tension over the facts of sexual harassment. Toward the end of the film several men spontaneously called out that John should "get that cunt," and that he should *kill* her. There was enough applause at the end when John beats Carol for me to feel unsafe, not to mention depressed.

When the curtain closed on the first of three acts of *Oleanna* I had the distinct impression that the stage had been set for a second act in which Carol would become the object of sexual harassment by John. Instead, the curtain opened on a scene in which John was already accused by Carol of having committed sexual harassment.

Thus, by the time that the play is less than half through, it is well established that the actual subject matter is not what it purports to be, namely, professor-student interaction and sexual harassment. Rather, it is about the male fear and fantasy of even delineating the very concept of sexual harassment. It is a theatrical exemplification of what has occurred through the past decade to obscure the potential for discussion of the issue.

In Act I, the audience is presented with the timid and self-conscious Carol, an undergraduate whose background did not afford her many cultural and class advantages of use in an academic setting. In contrast, the professor, John, seems to have fulfilled the expectations of his middle-class upbringing to become a professor on the brink of receiving tenure, purchasing a substantial home, and who has created a family of his own. The entire act takes place in John's office, where Carol has come for help with the subject matter of the course she is taking from him. She makes it clear that she feels deficient and stupid, that there is much that she does not understand and perhaps cannot understand.

John's responses are sympathetic, if patronizing and pompous. He genuinely attempts to help Carol understand his lectures and to relieve her anxiety. The strategies that he employs are benign, yet to the audience they are clearly ill-advised, considering that Carol demonstrates disturbed behavior while in his office. John suggests that he will let her start the course over as a private tutorial and that she will get an A. At the conclusion of the act he puts his arm around her shoulder when Carol is overcome with anxiety to the point of hysteria. The gesture is clearly orchestrated as a reflexive human response, completely devoid of sexual content.

Act II opens with Carol in John's office again, some time later. It rapidly becomes clear that Carol has filed charges of sexual harassment against John among other claims, in response to which he is justifiably bewildered. He has called Carol to his office to attempt to resolve the matter efficiently and privately. Carol is now a more defined character. Where her clothing and comportment in the first act were vague and ambiguous, her demeanor is now more clearly directed and her clothes more shaped. This trend culminates in the third act, in which Carol's clothing is tailored and fitted and she has clearly identified herself as a political activist and member of an organization. Her speech is sharp, articulate, and determined. For example:

Act I:

CAROL: Nobody *tells* me anything. And I *sit* there . . . in the *corner.* In the *back.* And everybody's talking about "this" all the time. And "concepts," and "precepts" and, and, and, and, and, WHAT IN THE WORLD ARE YOU TALKING ABOUT? And I read your book. And they said, "Fine, go in that class." Because you talked about responsibility to the young. I DON'T KNOW WHAT IT MEANS AND I'M FAILING . . . (14)

Act II:

CAROL: You see. I don't think that I need your help. I don't think I need anything you have (49)

Act III:

CAROL: Now. The thing which you find so cruel is the selfsame process of selection I, and my group, go through *every day of our lives.* In admittance to school. In our tests, in our class rankings . . . Is it unfair? I can't tell you. But, if it is fair. Or even if it is "unfortunate but necessary" for us, then, by God, so must it be for you. *(Pause)* You write of your "responsibility to the young." Treat us with respect, and that will *show* you your responsibility. You write that education is just hazing . . . (69)

In Act II, Carol's charges against John include the complaint that John embraced her and that he attempted to trade an A in the course for her attention because he likes her. Throughout the act, John clumsily tries to resolve the matter. In frustration over not being able to converse with the one-dimensional, maniacal Carol, John restrains her tepidly and briefly from leaving. Carol cries for help.

In the third and final act, the tenure committee has found John guilty of Carol's charges and has not only denied him tenure, but has suspended him as well. As a result, John will lose his new house and the deposit he put down for it. Carol has returned to his office for the third time. John tries to apologize, to make amends. Carol suggests that she will recant if John agrees to censor a list of books drawn up by her group. John is shocked and indignant and tells Carol to leave. John is at this point informed by telephone that Carol has filed an additional charge of rape against John resulting from their last meeting. Further, broaching the last sphere of John's life, Carol instructs John not to call his wife "baby," which she heard him do over the telephone. At the conclusion of the play, John beats Carol, smashing her with a wooden chair.

Mamet's combination of sexual harassment and rape is not arbitrary. Difficult as it is to recollect, our current attitude about sexual harassment is much like the attitude of yesteryear toward rape. No one could conceive of how a wife could say her husband raped her, for example. It was impossible, by definition. It was also legislated as legally impossible. In the early days of our society's comings to terms with rape, the concept of "crying rape" came into being with full force. The idea seemed to be that if we acknowledged marital rape as criminal, the floodgates of false accusation would rip open. Never mind that bringing a charge of rape was a humiliating, exhausting experience in which the accusing woman had to subject herself to multiple physical examinations which were insensitive at best and often brutal; to interrogation and character scrutiny and, often, character assassination; and to protracted legal battles. All for the pleasure of seeing the rapist go free most of the time, or get by with the equivalent of a slap on the wrist. Why would anyone subject herself to such torture unless the charge were not only true but she felt she could not live in safety without so doing?

So it is now with sexual harassment, and, often, sex discrimination as well. Predictably, the question looming larger than life over everyone's heads is, *what about false accusation?* Underlying this query is fear, and the fear serves the function of distracting us from the true issues that cry out for clarity. David Mamet has contributed to this trend by creating *Oleanna*, which is principally focused on the male fear of false accusation, of "crying rape" about sexual harassment, so to speak. Carol and John's story is a pure fabrication by Mamet, literally and figuratively. Nevertheless, it embodies much of our collective angst about the subject of sexual harassment.

The male fear of unjust accusation runs deep in our culture and serves several functions. Above all, it shifts the focus of the discussion in a manner that inverts and obscures the true balance of control of harassing behavior. The college campus is a strange, upside-down sort of place with regard to sexual harassment. It is a place in which male professors, some of whom actively perpetrate harassing behavior, walk about in supposed fear of unjust accusation, and the female students, almost all of whom are victims of harassment in one form or another, walk around fearless. They appear almost oblivious to the fact of sexual harassment, while, concurrently, they bear the full force of its consequences.

Sexual harassment is about *dominance,* not sex. Most people know this, if only on an intuitive, unverbalized level. The kind of dominance involved in sexual harassment is not the same sort one comes across in, for example, chess. It does not take much skill; it is arbitrary. One merely has to have been born male to have the privilege of exercising it.

Much of men's fear of unjust accusation is actually fear of being dominated in just this seemingly arbitrary fashion, and, moreover, being dominated in the worst possible way: being overcome by someone on the lowest end of the pecking order, a woman. This fear obliterates the fact that, veridical or not, there is *content* attached to a complaint of sexual harassment; it is not arbitrary, as Mamet suggests that it is in *Oleanna.* It may seem arbitrary to many because, in dismissing the very idea of sexual harassment, the concept has been left either undefined or defined in such a way as to be ludicrous (as in statements of the following sort: "Now I can't ask a woman to lunch without her turning around and claiming I harassed her").

Like John, like most men accused of sexual harassment, they slough off the claim as utter nonsense. Engaging in *biased,* let alone criminal, behavior does not square very well with most male professors' liberal view of themselves. By definition, as it were, they could not do such a thing. It's not unusual for the incredulous professor to ostracize the student effectively in any case, nor is it unusual for a professor to consult the university counsel about the matter to cover his bases.

At the same time that a claim of sexual harassment is rolling off their backs, professor ring out as loudly as possible about the dire consequences (of having done nothing, according to their accounts, remember). They have it both ways. They didn't do anything out of the ordinary (of course, part of the problem is that they are in a sense correct: sexual harassment remains within the ordinary for now), women are just too sensitive and trigger-happy. And yet, the man's world will cave in.

JOHN: I was hurt. When I received the report. Of the tenure committee. I was shocked . . . They will meet, and hear your complaint—which you have the right to make; and they will dismiss it. They will *dismiss* your complaint; and, in the intervening period, I will lose my house. I will not be able to close on my house. I will lose my *deposit,* and the home I'd picked out for my wife and son will go by the boards. (44–45)

Raising the stakes of a complaint of sexual harassment is an effective tool. It casts doubts on the possible contents of an accusation, while at the same time making it psychologically more difficult to bring such a claim. Never mind that in the real world, the current power structure is such that there are virtually no actual consequences to harassing behavior on campus unless the behavior is severe, sustained, and extreme, preferably directed at more than one student, all of whom are willing to come forward. Even among the handful of professors who have actually been asked to leave their posts (and these were cases of extreme abuse), some have been quickly snapped up by another university.

The fear also serves the function of obliterating the fact that a claim of sexual harassment is not about female dominance over the accused man, but rather that the reverse has (allegedly) occurred. In this way, the responsibility of the accused, or even of the potentially accused man who fantasizes about this fear, evaporates. Sexual harassment is transformed from a certain kind of (prevalent) male behavior toward women, to female dominance (yet again) over men. And thus, it is (yet again) the woman who looks like the guilty party. Consider how guilty Anita Hill was made to look for causing all that trouble.

Not only are the real consequences of the professor's harassing behavior minuscule and fleeting, but most female students who have experienced sexual harassment from a professor never bring a claim at all, even to their friends, and even to themselves in the privacy of their own minds. On the contrary, our collective social attitude toward sexual harassment is still so early in its development that instances of this kind of harassment are rarely recognized as such. Most often, a student who is bearing even continuous sexual harassment from a professor will feel confused and seek an explanation based on her own behavior.

The questions running through her mind, if any, will be about how *she* has caused the situation and what it says about her. She will typically go through another round in the series of a female's drop in self-confidence and will alter her self-concept accordingly. In short, she will internalize and personalize the *professor's* behavior and attitude. She will incorporate the fantasy into her mental framework. Generally, this is not conscious, deliberate thought on the student's part, but tacit. It is one of the many results of our culture's acceptance of pervasive gender bias. It is a purposeful result, however. It allows the issue to remain on an individual basis, it helps to pit woman against woman, and thus is part of the guarantee of women's sustained silence.

This being the case, what of this larger-than-life fear of accusation? It is of a piece with our almost steadfast refusal to come to terms with campus sexual harassment in a meaningful way. It shifts the debate away from prevention and remediation, back to a stereotypical and typically ambivalent view of women as the irrational and vengeful prime movers. *Oleanna* uses this theme with full force in the third act, in which Carol has grown tougher still and exacts the maximum penalties from John for his make-believe crimes, about which Carol has entrenched conviction.

In addition to the theme of false accusation there are at least two more that Mamet explores, and in so doing he puts his finger directly on the pulse of our distractive obsessions. One such theme is the male fantasy of fragility in the face of female sexuality. The 1995 Hollywood movie *Disclosure* epitomized this theme in its focus on the big, bad, powerful (and incompetent) professional woman. In *Oleanna*, the fragility is professional, but often in our thinking it can be personal weakness as well. This is an old theme that runs through Western culture, but it is cast in a new light with regard to sexual harassment. Now, not only can men tremble in terror of the force of female sexuality, but it will turn around to bite them for a second time in the name of sexual harassment. They are twice powerless; first to resist the temptation of female sexuality, and second to avoid falling into its snare through sexual harassment legislation, which they do not comprehend and feel continuously muddled by.

John is the embodiment of the male fantasy of fragility in the face of female sexuality. Or, more precisely, in the face of the woman's *exploitation* of her (powerful, dominating) sexuality. This is the fantasy, at any rate, that women use sex to crush men, to consume them, to render them powerless. In John's case, he is crushed professionally. And so he physically beats Carol.

CAROL: You think I am a frightened, repressed, confused, I don't know, abandoned young thing of some doubtful sexuality who wants power and revenge. *(pause) Don't* you? *(pause)*

JOHN: Yes. I do.

      . . .

JOHN: You vicious little bitch. You think you can come in here with your political correctness and destroy my life?

> *(he knocks her to the floor)*
> After how I treated you . . . ? You should be . . . Rape you . . . ? Are you kidding me . . . ?
> *(He picks up a chair, raises it above his head, and advances on her.)*
> I wouldn't touch you with a ten-foot pole. You little *cunt* . . . (68, 79)

What is the function of this fantasy in regard to campus sexual harassment? Yet again, it serves as a time-worn tool to turn the tables of attention and blame toward women, toward those who are the actual victims of sexual harassment. In this picture, the man is freed from responsibility. He is merely reacting to a powerful and dangerous force. He projects his own quest for dominance onto the woman, based on some archaic, deep-seated, and *convenient* mystification of her anatomy.

At the same time, the effect of the fantasy is almost an inversion of itself: women are reduced to their sexuality and defined in terms of it. Carol is a cunt who seeks power and revenge. Men, the fantasy concludes, have only one recourse open: to view women as sexual objects and to treat them accordingly. In the case of punishment, rape is then the logical choice, as the violent undercurrent to John's reference to a ten-foot pole attests.

Women, too, have learned to incorporate a fear of the power of their own sexuality into their conceptual framework. Evidence for this can be found everywhere, even down to the pervasive, and almost exclusively female, posture-deforming fashion of sitting with legs crossed at the thigh, closing the unspeakable chasm of temptation. If a woman sat in class with legs spread as her male peers do, she would be courting abuse, she would be *enticing* it. Just as wearing a tight shirt or walking with a wiggle asks for rape (how much time have teenage girls *wasted*, trying to learn to walk straight with not a hint of horizontal hip movement, feeling this could help ensure safety?).

Women, along with men, have formed and believed Western culture's portraits of female and male. As far as sexual harassment on campus goes, this is another piece of the female student's internalization of the social model. She will implicitly consume virtually whole the idea that much of her identity is wrapped up in her sexuality. That, therefore, it is that part of her that is being responded to by others. By the professors, who are actually there to teach her. And so again we are thrown upon the notion that the nexus of power rests with women. Because women are defined by their sex and sexuality, men are compelled to behave in a certain predictable and justified fashion toward them.

A final theme in the play (passing over a jab at political correctness) is that women, particularly strident feminists, bring attacks (of sexual harassment, of violence) upon themselves. They provoke it by their aggressive pursuit. This is certainly Carol's fate by the end of *Oleanna*. In trying to define and circumscribe gender issues and bias, women so aggravate their audience as to incite the behavior they seek to describe and eradicate. If only they would stop making everyone angry, there wouldn't be a problem.

Until there is some enhanced awareness of the depth of sexual harassment, we can have little understanding of prevention. In this regard, *Oleanna* is a reactionary distraction from reality. The fact is that *Oleanna* paints a picture entirely false to human reality. Its subtext speaks directly to our worst and most retrograde feelings about women and about sexual harassment. In the actual world of campus life, over half its population live with real sexual harassment every day. For them, the choice of the moment is not so much truth *or* consequences as it is truth and consequences, or, silence and consequences.

Works Cited

Aeschylus. *The Oresteia*. Translated Richard Lattimore. Chicago: University of Chicago Press 1953.
Mamet, David. *Oleanna*. New York: Vintage, 1993.

MYRA GOLDBERG

But I Thought He Liked My Paper

I wrote some of the stories in *Whistling* when I was in my early thirties. This was the early '70s, as it turned out. Decades do not feel like decades until afterward; in other words, there were no '70s until the '80s came along. Sexual harrassment was not an issue then, nor were studies that showed that adolescent girls had low self esteem, identity problems, and difficulty taking themselves and their work seriously. It was the beginning, more or less, of the women's movement, and as a writer I had a number of strictly literary agendas and one more or less political one. I would assume, I decided, that women were strong, independent, and intelligent, instead of writing stories about heroines who yearned to become these things in the style of those times.

As it turned out, my heroines, intelligent and strong, were often, at crucial moments, blurry or confused in a way that belied their intelligence. Not in every story, but in the four out of the five stories that involved some affair between female students and male professors.

Twenty years later, when I look at these stories, which came out recently, collected with some later cousins, I see a relation between the following in my young women: affair with professor, guilt, renunciation, the inability to carry through on what's personally important, and confusion, that disease of young women. Instead of getting angry and pointing to what they know to be the case, given the power and fearfulness of what they are facing, they retire into some version of "I don't know, you know? Well, anyway. Whatever."

First off, though, I was surprised that I had written that much about the subject. I now think it came up not because I had had an affair with a professor, but because the relatively modest incidents in which I'd been involved had such profound implications that my fiction-writing self explored the implications of these things, as if they had actually happened.

Some Historical Recollections

In my own college life I attracted mentors, all male, because all my professors were male then. There was one particularly nice man who was, I saw one day in a flash of insight as he wrote something on the board about the clash in George Eliot between the actual and the ideal, not all that smart. This shook me terrifically, because I had been brought up to revere professors and men, and the guilt I felt as a result made it especially difficult to distinguish between my mentor's interest in my scholarly progress and his interest in my being. (He made puns on my name, saw me as mysterious, he said, and showed up in my bedroom one morning, when I had failed to return some papers he needed and had left the apartment door unlocked.) Since I was also guilty about the unmarked papers, I could hardly remonstrate that he should not have come uninvited into my house. Moreover, he was so innocent of his own vibes, so apparently married, and so earnestly solicitous about my graduate work, that I think my assessment at the time was correct: he had a mild crush on me, at least partly because he *did* like my mind, and it was up to me, at twenty-one, as it had been at fourteen when my eye doctor kissed me, to handle my confusion as best I could (assuming that he, the grown man, could not handle his.) I should add, however, that I rejected this man's offer of help in my career, something I could have used, and I think many other young women probably do the same, opting out of ambiguously uncomfortable but professionally desirable situations.

The next time I ventured into academia the professor was not a young man, like my first mentor, but an old one, for whose wisdom, intelligence, and knowledge I had the utmost respect. I read him a paper on the differences between psychology and literature in their depictions of character, a paper that was probably, as he said then, original and full of observations this man had never heard before. Still, he'd added, leaning forward, the portrait, to me, of a Talmudic scholar turned secular, that he'd missed a lot of what I'd read, because he had to admit he'd found my face so fascinating.

I have never had a moment that so clearly defined something I had found puzzling in my life: surely, like all other people, let alone women, I wanted love. And here was this wise old man, on some leval offering it to me. And yet, the paper that I was so proud of which he had found so original, had slipped by him, upstaged by a face I happened to have inherited. I left the office and bought a children's book I'd remembered entitled *The Bear That Wasn't*, about a bear who wanders into a factory and gets told despite his protestations that he's not a bear, but a silly man who needs a shave and wears a fur coat. But I am a bear, he keeps saying. Shortly after, I wrote a story about the incident, left the psychology program, and became a fiction writer.

Before we turn to these fictions, though, it seems important to say that these stories from *Whistling* are deliberate, not incidental or accidental. But they are deliberate in an aesthetic rather than an ideational or ideological way, attempts to create wholes, rather than propositions. Thus it is interesting for me to unravel these wholes a little and see what some of the threads are. In other words, it's not that authors don't know what they are writing, it's that they have been paying attention to something quite different as they write and it takes an opportunity like this one to look again.

Hierachy, Art, Rage: "Country Music"

In "Country Music," a young woman, who lives on the Upper West Side of Manhattan and works at the Museum of Natural History painting dioramas for the stuffed wild animal exhibits, feels that she's lost the key to something. That key has something to do with some soul records she misplaced. When she looks back, she realizes that the loss of these records took place around the time she broke up with the professor she'd been having an affair with. She finds a memory:

Her graphics teacher takes her hand, examines it, places it, palm up, on the table. He strokes his Buffalo Bill mustache. His children need him, he says. His son especially.

The woman studies her hand. Ordinarily, she'd be glad to discuss her lover's son, who's wild and wants to be a cop or a country music singer. She likes taking sane responsible positions, the kind her father used to take when she stood barefoot in the hall, listening to her parents discuss her younger brother. Now, instead of saying, "He needs limits," or "You've made too much of him," she listens to her lover say, "I've got to go home. There's no way around it." She doesn't say "What do you mean 'home' although last weekend, in New Hampshire, they decided to live together in his studio after she graduates. The deep red blanket she's bought in Filene's for his cot rises before her eyes. She closes them. The color fades. When she opens them again, she's congratulating him on doing the right thing. His children need him, she says. His son especially. He's startled. "I thought you cared for me." She shrugs, walks to the wardrobe, takes her sheepskin jacket out. He begins shouting. It's not his fault. Life is cheap. Art is expensive. "What in God's name are you talking about?" she cries. He doesn't know exactly. He waves at the carved oak wardrobe to indicate that his wife, his children, the woman, his work, have been tumbling inside his head all week like clothes in a dryer. "I'm a serious person," he says. "I should be working seriously."

The woman, who's a serious person too, stares at his face. While she's been looking forward to working in the studio beside him, he's been waiting for her to leave, so he can work. She snaps her sheepskin jacket shut, pulls on her embroidered mittens. "It has nothing to do with you," he says. "I know," she says. "You don't have to say it."

On her way downstairs, she counts steps to keep from crying. Then she dashes across the street and begins arguing about the value of the work he's sent her away to do. He's played out. Pathetic. The truth of what she's thinking strikes her like a slap. She covers her mouth with her hand, peers through the iron Common railing at the black wintry tree inside. Its branches are slender, unbearably frail. It's not his work that's clever but pointless, she sees. It's hers. She feels relieved, begins walking again. By the time she reaches her apartment, a seven-mile walk, she's feeling proud. She's forgiven her lover, faced her limitations. She'll move from Boston when she graduates, live alone, get a job. She spends the evening writing job letters: three museums, a nursery school in the slums of Seattle and "would you please send me an application blank for your master's in social work program?" As a child, she refused to go to nursery school. Museums depress her. Her mother is a social worker. Her crayons, her newsprint pad, her etching knife get packed into a carton marked ART SUPPLIES. The world, she tells the pony-tailed woman, is full of clever people. She's decided to be useful. She doesn't say anything to the blonde man, who'd want to debate her decision, until she hears from the Museum of Natural History. Then she hands him the letter. "Isn't it wonderful?" she says.

It turns out that she's left this soul music, two James Brown 45s that a black kid gave her, at this graphic teacher's studio. She has also left her artistic career and her rage there, and later on, in the park, left her assessment of her teacher's work and her own, and taken up, to replace it, renunciation. She has decided to be useful (good) instead of skillful, expressive, or ambitious.

In other words, her sense of the needs of her soul is compromised by the love affair. Her treatment as secondary in relation to the teacher's real life (his wife and son) is mimicked by her treatment of herself, her desires, as secondary. What's important in these passages (and this story) is that the mixture of love, work, power, authority, and the ability to make judgments are all compromised by each other, and she is left with renunciation and a rage that eventually affects someone else in the social landscape.

"I'm not going to live here anymore," she thinks, as she is awakened from a dream by the noise of a street kid who is trying to climb through her window. Then she moves to the window, barely recognizing the kid, whom she knows, and slams the window shut. The boy falls to the sidewalk.

What's important later in the story is that the fact that this rage has killed the little boy has almost no effect on the woman, who simply moves a few blocks a way to another neighborhood, where she and the blonde friend and her work get together. The story, in other words, sees a hierarchy of social worth in which one person's power displaces and affects the next person down. A ritual exorcism of "badness" through the murder of this black kid allows what has been sundered by the white man to come together.

Girls, Friendship, Difference and Abandonment: "Sylvia and Wendy"

In "Sylvia and Wendy," the pattern is different. Two freshman college roommates become best friends, but their friendship is based on the arty city mouse's (Wendy's) role as initiator into sophistication for the country mouse (Sylvia):

She [Sylvia] learned to talk again. Listening, at first to Wendy. The light from the window was "like Vermeer." Katherine, across the hall, was "horsey, asexual." Sylvia's sweatshirt had "the texture of my grandmother's upper arm."

Sylvia had a friend. She had a best friend. Someone to characterize: "You seem impulsive, but you're cautious, in fact." Someone to trade things with (her sweatshirt for Wendy's flesh-colored nightgown; the B minus on her poem— "Your prosody is rigid; your diction abstract"—for the C on Wendy's economics paper, "You're writing, it seems, from some stream of consciousness." Someone to sit beside at breakfast when Katherine began the story of her trip to the housing office to complain about her roommate. And when Katherine reached the part where the dean assured her "a variety of criteria" had been used to match them, Sylvia leaned forward as Wendy asked, "What criteria do you think she was talking about?"

"Do you smoke?" said Sylvia. "Do you listen to folk music?"

Wendy laughed. Sylvia laughed. Katherine laughed.

"Katherine hates life," said Wendy afterwards.

How could Katherine, with her loud laugh and her Russian crossword puzzles, hate life? reflected Sylvia on the library steps. Wendy must see depths. She saw only surfaces.

Sylvia is afraid to assert her difference from Wendy, whom she is in love and like and awe and admiration with. Each incident in which Wendy appears less than honest or even glamorous is explained away by Sylvia, until finally Sylvia finds a cause worthy of risking abandonment for. Wendy is having an affair with her painting teacher, and Sylvia goes back to her room struck by the secret that this best friend has been keeping from her. They act out their positions in a skit, something they've been doing all semester.

"But I didn't have to tell you," said Wendy. "Besides, you were always asleep when I got in."
Sylvia nodded.
"Also there's his wife. She was a student here once. His student, actually. She calls every time I'm in his office. He was afraid she'd find out."
"I feel sorry for her," said Sylvia.
Wendy stared.
"Well, I do." Sylvia's eyes filled up. She looked down to find a fist. "Lenny." The fist by her ear became a telephone receiver. "Would you please come home? The washing machine is broken."
"Look Jane," Wendy's feet went up on the desk. "Can't you wash the clothes by hand or something?"
"Diapers, Lenny?"
"You're trying!"—Wendy's feet came down—"to make me feel bad."
Sylvia closed her eyes. She pressed her fist so hard against her lips, she felt her teeth.
It was true.
She opened her eyes, prepared to nod.
The room was empty.

The assertion of female solidarity causes Wendy, the beloved, to flee. The fear of abandonment has been there since the beginning, as have the differences, but it's only the affair, and Sylvia's identification with the other woman and her child, that makes her feel strong enough to assert what she knows even if it breaks the friendship.

"If there were a verb 'to believe falsely' it would have no significant first person indicative." Sylvia underlined the sentence, then carried Wittgenstein from the snack bar, where she'd been reading every night, looking up, periodically, for Wendy.
She took the bus to Cambridge. "We were in the snack bar," she told Jake. "And I got into an argument with her boyfriend, her man friend, whatever you call someone who's middle-aged and married. Only it wasn't exactly an argument. And she never said she had a boyfriend." She got off his bed. "Not that she was required to. Then afterwards. In our room." She shook her head. "I wouldn't have looked at what she was doing the way she did. She didn't want to be around me."

Sylvia accepts Wendy's affair and Wendy's abandonment of her for viewing the affair in a "moralistic" way, (i.e., from the perspective of the wife, instead of the husband or the student). The morality Sylvia is expressing is, in the context of this story and this school, old fashioned, female, familial, rather than collegial. (Many college girls feel they are, for a time, participants in a gender-neutral patriarchy.) Sylvia is not confused about what has happened, but she is confirmed in her assumption that to uphold a female-centered point of view is not only square but grounds for ending the friendship. (To *judge* a friend, if you remember, from college days, is to betray them in some way.) Still, she accepts both her own views and their consequences.

Wendy's affair gets her a studio. She also takes on, with the affair, a male view of relationships.

"I loved you," Sylvia tells her former friend in the last scene, when they see each other again.

"We had fun," said Wendy, "Didn't we."

I Paint What I See: Emily

Emily came from a town in Massachusetts. But not from one of those Massachusetts towns that make us think: New England. For Emily wasn't from big-city Boston or watery Marblehead or Salem where there were witches. Nor from one of those college towns, whose maples flaming each October by a white-steepled church make people from soot filled cities nostalgic for other origins. No, Emily's town was a manufacturing town with its maples flaming beside other traditional regional sights: a polluted river with an Indian name, an empty shoe factory with its windows smashed, tenements with wooden balconies on High Street.

Emily has a brutal alcoholic father and several generations of women who take to their beds for years on end behind her. Her father raises her to be competent and beats her when she gives him trouble.

So at seventeen, Emily traveled to a college near New York City for girls who were so spirited and rich, it had no rules at all. And she painted huge explosive abstract expressionist canvases and welded sculptures made of broken fenders and stolen traffic signs.

Every evening she left the campus with a painter in overalls, who had marijuana in the pocket of his fringed doeskin jacket, blonde curls to his narrow shoulders and an apartment full of his canvases on Sixth Street and Avenue C.

Emily saw this man standing flat against the cyclone fence around the empty lot by his apartment. Looking like the hero of those French movies that were so popular in her college that semester. "The last angel before destruction arrives," she told her roommate, whose father owned a hotel in Last Vegas and who went home without explanation in the middle of the semester. And when this angel took Emily to live with him, she felt safe beneath his wing from something—the painting teacher she'd slept with on the floor of his office and the paintings she might have done, that would have shattered this man and everyone else she cared for.

Again, the familiar connection between fear of expressing oneself and the affair with the powerful figure, who by Freudian standards is probably a father. (But father in the cultural sense, one might add. One who carries correct thought and observation around with him, and whom one can offend by thinking or saying or painting the wrong thing. Especially if it refers to him.)

The sentence about the affair in the text is written as if the affair were incidental, which is the way young women often perceive these things, denying the power of the experience over them, as they deny that of the men.

Still, in these stories at least, life decisions are made in reaction to these incidental affairs.

Later the teacher shows up again:

Her painting teacher from college, now an extremely famous man, had come to see her show. "I expect great things of you," he'd said, then invited her to his apartment for a drink, which she refused. For several weeks after that she'd sat in her apartment with moldy dishes in the sink, worrying that she'd ruined her career by not offering to sleep with him and fearful that she'd have disappointed some long line of women if she had. Meanwhile, her paintings, she felt, would enrage some line of men, looking blankly or critically at what she'd hung up.

This is the same dilemma as in "Sylvia and Wendy," but this time it is not between women but within one. Sleeping with powerful men is reputed to be a way of getting ahead in the art world, and not sleeping with them is a way of getting dropped. Painting what you see about your life and its dilemmas is another way to get into trouble.

A story called *Whistling* serves as a contrast to the binds these other young women are in. A professor and a woman have an affair. She is not his student, and although we don't know her age or profession, Louie and Laura seem to be evenly matched. What's not equal is that Louie has a wife and a kid, although he is separated from them, and Laura is single.

Laura tells Louie a story about her friend Pru, to highlight the problems and the solutions to their romance. The story she tells is comic, as is their own story, and although they do not end up together, life is embraced rather than renounced at the end.

This comic attitude and tone becomes possible because we are in the world of Hepburn and Tracy, or Portia and Anthony; in short, among equals. When the romance breaks down, it is because Louie uses his wife and child as an excuse to get quit of Laura, and even then she has some weapons: she leaves him, flees to the mountains, and then tells a story that reflects his behavior back to him.

There is nothing, in other words, confusing or dangerous to her about the affair, his behavior, her future, what she thinks of him, or what she says to him.

A Freudian might say that what is confusing to these other young women is that the professors are stand-ins for their fathers. Some feminists might say that these women have been harassed, subject to victimization in the name of love. A man, or professor of desire, might see these young women as willing and beautiful participants in a good time. A young woman writer, who happened to be me, knew somehow that romance has to do with equals, and that serious power inequalities in relationships leave at least one side with serious consequences, a problem seeing themselves clearly, because it feels too dangerous to name what has happened to them. What has happened to them is in part a betrayal; someone who promised to look after their souls looked after their bodies instead, and therefore refused them what most young men get, which is a time and a place to be free of their bodies and their sexuality and to live for their ambitions and their minds.

What is confusing here is that the invitation to step over boundaries that civilization has declared important is extended by the very men who are presenting and representing that civilization. In other words, these young women are being invited to join this civilization and to transgress its rules all at the same time, and the more seriously they take the chance to join up, the more serious are the consequences of the failures of romance for them.

What I would say now is that there is no true "I" that is separate from the verb "to believe falsely," no romance or relationship that is separate from our positions in a social network. The illicit is like the licit, only more so. And the feelings we feel, the thoughts we are capable of thinking or not thinking, the stance we take toward our own victimization, are inexplicably tied to what is being thought or not thought, said or not said, by the powerful people around us.

Finally, I asked my current college students for stories of their own, and although I got many indications that they had stories, I was told only one story at any length, something that had happened in high school instead of the college I teach in now. It is not about an affair, but about a teacher/lecher, but I'm including it because the the attitude toward the man is so different from what went before. (Which may have to do with a change in the times, or high school versus college, or the man himself and my student.)

Sometimes I Just Felt Sorry for Him: Anita

Well, the teachers name is S———, and he has like a reputation of hitting on his female students, this was a public high school, so it wasn't like anyone—no one went in there blind, unless they were new, he taught English, I was in the advanced class, he is the most horrible teacher ever, so bad, he would get us to teach his standard classes, a loser, like middle aged, late forties, not married, the administration totally knew, people in my class complained three times, they weren't willing to do anything about it, because all his students get high scores on the national AP English tests, obviously he was a bad teacher, but we had the background already, so he never did things that were very, he was pretty smart, he was kind of into mind tricks, in class, if he thought things were getting out of hand, he would put his foot down, like snap at someone and be overly mean, he would just like stand too close to me and like other girls too, and be too familiar and friendly, he like invited me over to his house, and I was like I don't think so, it made me totally repulsed by him, if I had any particle of respect for him, it was lost, I could see how he had to use power over these young kids, we went to the administration together, for the girls in the advanced class, he would have more respect for, the girls in his standard classes, he made them feel so dumb.

Every time we went to the administration they said they would do something about it, I remember once the principle asked me what she should do, I said fire him, everyone knows you know it's going on, everyone knows you think it's okay because you let him stay, I think that they did talk to him, because for awhile he got a little more subdued, I told them they could use my name, so I think I noticed changes in his attitude, then it culminated between me and him, because I had this publication, called the Zine, and I kind of slandered him, and he saw it, and said who is doing this thing . . . he pulls me out of the classroom the next day to this little storage area and I was like scared and he said I have seen your publication, and I can't believe you said that about me, and I said, I am not going to pretend that I didn't say that, I have no respect for you and I think the way you act is totally inappropriate and then he had the nerve to tell me that he wanted a written apology in the next one and in the next one I got three girls to write things about why they didn't like him.

I didn't feel intimidated but some of my friends did. When I was in the room alone with him, I was scared, because anything could have happened with the door closed and no witnesses. But there were definitely other students who couldn't stand to go to class, because they'd feel so uncomfortable, one of my friends, who was loud and obnoxious, he would touch her on her head, and yell at her, when everybody would be like talking . . .

He had that poetry reading voice, stand up, put his foot on the chair and go like that, in this little rhythm, that was the worst, (some rocking motion, with genitals stuck out) sometime I really hated him and sometimes I was just sorry for him.

Most of the boys didn't hate him, they just didn't notice the things he did, he was pretty much an asshole to everyone. I'm trying to think of an adjective aside from bad. Slimy.

Times have changed. Everyone, except the boys, now knows the story.

Contributors

REGINA BARRECA, Professor of English and Feminist Theory at the University of Connecticut, is editor of *The Penguin Book of Women's Humor* and author of *Sweet Revenge: The Wicked Delights of Getting Even,* as well as *Perfect Husbands (and Other Fairy Tales): Demystifying Marriage, Men, and Romance; They Used to Call Me Snow White, But I Drifted: Women's Strategic Use of Humor;* and *Untamed and Unabashed: Essays on Women and Humor in British Literature.*

MARY ANN CAWS is Distinguished Professor of English, French, and Comparative Literature at the CUNY Graduate Center. A past president of the MLA, she writes on the interchange between art and literature (*The Eye in the Text, The Art of Interference*); and on poetry (*The Poetry of Dada and Surrealism*), which she also translates and edits. Most recently, she is the author of *Robert Motherwell: What Art Holds* and *The Surrealist Book: An Erotics of Encounter,* and editor of *The Surrealist Painters & Poets* (all forthcoming).

VANESSA D. DICKERSON is Associate Professor of English at Rhodes College. She has published articles on Victorian women and on contemporary African-American women writers. She is editor of *Keeping the Victorian House;* her book *Victorian Ghosts in the Noontide* will be published in November 1996. Currently, she is working on a study of the Black Victorian.

JOHN GLAVIN is Associate Professor of English at Georgetown University and is a widely performed playwright. He is the author of "Muriel Spark's Knowing Fiction" and articles on Oscar Wilde and theater criticism.

MYRA GOLDBERG teaches fiction writing at Sarah Lawrence College. She is the author of *Rosalind: A Family Romance* and *Whistling.* She lives in New York City with her daughter, Anna.

GERHARD JOSEPH, Professor of English at Lehman College and the Graduate School of the City University of New York, has written two books on Tennyson and articles on other nineteenth-century subjects. He is completing a study on plagiarism and copywriting in the nineteenth century entitled *The Guilty Art of the Copy.*

MONTANA KATZ serves on the advisory board for the Barnard College Center for Research on Women, and is the editor of the series "Gender In Crisis" for

Jason Aronson publishers. She is co-author of the award-winning book *Get Smart: What You Should Know But Won't Learn in Class About Sexual Harassment and Sex Discrimination*, and author of *The Gender Bias Prevention Book: Helping Girls and Women Have Satisfying Lives and Careers*.

JAMES KINCAID is Aerol Arnold Professor of English at the University of Southern California. He is the author of *Child-Loving: The Erotic Child and Victorian Culture, Annoying the Victorians*, and the forthcoming *Manufacturing Virtue: The Culture of Child Molesting*, along with earlier books on Dickens, Tennyson, and Trollope; several collections of essays; and articles on Victorian literature and literary and cultural theory.

DEBORAH DENENHOLZ MORSE is Associate Professor of English at the College of William and Mary, where she teaches Victorian literature. She is the author of *Woman in Trollope's Palliser Novels*, as well as articles on Anthony Trollope, Elizabeth Gaskell, Kay Boyle, Mona Simpson, A. S. Byatt, and Maxine Hong Kingston. She is currently writing a book on history and female identity in Elizabeth Gaskell's fiction, and an autobiographical novel entitled *"Water, Wealth, Contentment, Health": A Modesto Childhood*.

ROBERT POLHEMUS is Howard H. and Jesse T. Watkins University Professor of English at Stanford. He is the author of *Comic Faith: The Great Tradition from Austen to Joyce* and *Erotic Faith: Being in Love from Jane Austen to D.H. Lawrence*.

REBECCA A. POPE is co-author, with Susan Leonardi, of *The Diva's Mouth: Body, Voice, Prima Donna Politics*. She is also the author of many essays ranging in topic from Wordsworth to mystery fiction to AIDS. She lives and teaches in the Washington, D.C. area.

DRANDA TRIMBLE is an independent scholar whose work includes several short stories, poems, and essays. She lives in Connecticut.

ABBY H. P. WERLOCK, Associate Professor of English at St. Olaf College, is the co-author of *Tillie Olsen* and has written articles on Chandler, Cooper, Hemingway, Steinbeck, Tolstoy, Wharton, and mother daughter myths. She is also editor of the forthcoming *British Women Writing Fiction* and *A Reader's Companion to the American Short Story*.